PSYCHOLOGY OF EMOTIONS, MOTIVATIONS AND ACTIONS

TRAIT ANXIETY

PSYCHOLOGY OF EMOTIONS, MOTIVATIONS AND ACTIONS

Additional books in this series can be found on Nova's website under the Series tab.

Additional E-books in this series can be found on Nova's website under the E-books tab.

PSYCHOLOGY OF EMOTIONS, MOTIVATIONS AND ACTIONS

TRAIT ANXIETY

ANNA S. MORALES
EDITOR

Nova Science Publishers, Inc.
New York

For permission to use material from this book please contact us:
Telephone 631-231-7269; Fax 631-231-8175
Web Site: http://www.novapublishers.com

Library of Congress Cataloging-in-Publication Data

Trait anxiety / editor, Anna S. Morales.
p. cm.
Includes index.
ISBN 978-1-61324-551-4 (hardcover)
1. Anxiety. I. Morales, Anna S.
BF575.A6T73 2011
152.4'6--dc22

2011014570

Published by Nova Science Publishers, Inc. † New York

CONTENTS

PREFACE

Trait anxiety refers to the level of proneness of individuals to experience anxiety. High trait anxiety individuals perceive events as more threatening and are more likely to respond with increased state anxiety. In this book, the authors present topical research in the study of trait anxiety. Topics discussed include understanding maternal anxiety in health primiparous women; trait anxiety and dental anxiety; the cognitive theories of social anxiety; sociodemographic factors and anxiety of infertile women and state/trait anxiety, aviation and the frontal lobe.

Chapter 1 – Event-related potentials (ERPs), which are based on electroencephalogram (EEG) technique, refer to any kind of stereotyped electrophysiological responses to internal or external stimuli. For researchers and clinicians, the ERP method serves as a non-invasive tool to measure brain activity during cognitive processing. This chapter reviews the author's ERP research on the relationship between levels of trait anxiety and a variety of cognitive functions (including attention, memory, & decision-making). In these studies, even though the behavioral measures might not reveal significant difference between high trait anxiety (HTA) and low trait anxiety (LTA) individuals, the ERP components were consistently sensitive to different level of trait anxiety (i.e., the P1 in cue-target attention task; the feedback-related negativity in decision-making task). Overall, the author's results indicate that the HTA participants showed a tendency to overreact to broadly "negative" information (including threatening stimulus, incorrect feedback, and outcome that indicating monetary loss). This finding extends the traditional viewpoint that trait anxiety is characterized by reactions to threat-related stimuli, and might be benefit to both clinical and nonclinical studies. For human beings, the influence of emotion on the author's physiological states, as well as on cognitive abilities, are very easy to be recognized in daily lifes. Fear, for example, causes sexual dysfunction, insomnia, ulcers, and gives us dry mouth and jitters at the very moment when author have greatest need be calm and brave. It it worth noting that, however, "no emotion is useful or not except in relation to a particular situation". In other words, the impact of emotion could be very helpful or even critical in specific situations. Recently, it has been pointed out that emotioanl process is essential in sensory coding and high-level cognitive activities, and that it might be unnecessary to distinguish between emotional and cognitive function. Among different kinds of emotions, the authors of this chapter are most interested in the impact of anxiety on cognition. Anxiety is an emotional state accompanied by expectations of negative outcomes and concerns about the severity of those outcomes. The perception of threat and danger are central for evoking anxiety. The influence of anxiety on cognitive processes, such as attention, working memory, behavioral control, and decision making, has been proven by many studies. There are two major aspects in anxiety: state anxiety, a *transient* level of arousal associated with reactions to adverse situation; and trait anxiety, an individual *dispositional* level of anxiety that is not reactive to external stimuli. Compared to transient emotion, emotion dispositions are: (a) reflected in relatively stable differences in underlying neurochemical systems, (b) heritable, and (c) stable across the life course. Accordingly, most of the author's studies introduced below are focus on trait anxiety, but the relationship between state anxiety and cognitive function is also of interest.

Chapter 2 – Although anxiety is the most common phenomenon among women during the transition to motherhood, equivocal results have been reported in studies both on the relationships between situational (state) and dispositional (trait) anxiety, on effects of maternal anxiety, and on treatment evaluation. The purpose of this chapter is to present a new way of examining and understanding maternal anxiety in healthy primiparous women from the idea that "inter-individual differences cannot be understood without reference to intra-individual differences". Changes in anxiety were explored from intra-individual differences in terms of gap (discrepancy) between state anxiety at different time points and between dispositional and situational anxiety. In others words, take a fresh look at measures of anxiety to see things differently. A sample of 77 participants were administered the French version of the Spielberger State-Trait Anxiety Inventory Form Y (STAI-Y) during the eighth month of pregnancy (A-trait and A-state) and the first and third month after birth (A-state). The main result has related to the women characterized by an extreme trait-anxiety score. Those with the highest (vs. lowest) dispositional anxiety had state-anxiety scores significantly lower (vs. higher) than their A-

Trait. These findings indicate a self-regulation of anxiety and even a normalization of mood variation during the perinatal period. Findings in this chapter show an alternative at the common assumption that individuals high in trait anxiety are expected to respond to new/stressful situations with elevated state anxiety. Here, it is as though women were adapting to the new situation – becoming a mother- by adjusting their level of anxiety through a reversal process. Studies in animals, cognitive psychology of affective disorders, and part of Apter's theory, provide evidence to support my interpretative hypothesis, and an explanation for the function of perinatal anxiety. Several implications can be considered. Lack of knowledge about this normalization could explain the heterogeneity of the results reported in the literature and why there is little evidence of improved outcomes for mothers within professional intervention groups. Women's groups with a high level of anxiety may be heterogeneous, i.e. composed of women who experience normalization of their anxiety and of women who suffer from occasional anxiety disorders.

Chapter 3 – The continual advances in dental treatment in recent years have not affected the fact that considerable numbers of patients undergo psychological discomfort, in the form of anxiety syndrome, in relation to such treatment. Dental anxiety may lead to negative effects on dental and also in general health or physical recovery after treatment, especially after surgical interventions. The possibility of successful treatment is reduced by insufficient knowledge, among dental clinicians, about dental anxiety, its presentation and evaluation, and the characteristics of the patients. Theories that link trait anxiety (the tendency for anxious people to perceive situations as potentially threatening) to dental anxiety suggest that identification of trait anxiety may be useful for predicting dental anxiety predisposition in patients. A prior awareness of the patient's predisposition to dental anxiety may thus be of value to the dentist, enabling him or her to take appropriate preventative and/or therapeutic measures. In accordance with this, in some situations it may be useful for the dentist to evaluate trait anxiety before interventions of this type, although bearing in mind that trait anxiety is only a partial predictor in the multifactorial etiology of dental anxiety. This chapter provides a theoretical introduction in which the conceptualization, etiology and manifestations of dental anxiety are considered, and some of the self-report measures most commonly used in this area are described. The results of different studies in which trait anxiety and different measures of dental anxiety have been explored in relation to surgical removal of the lower third molar, are then discussed. The effect of anxiety on both the duration of the intervention and the post-operative recovery of patients is also discussed. Finally, the relationship between trait anxiety and different aspects of dental anxiety is considered.

Chapter 4 – The behavioral and electrophysiological correlates of attentional bias to physical threat words were investigated in healthy participants with high and low Anxiety Sensitivity using a word dot-probe task while recording high-density brain electrical activity. Behaviorally, both groups displayed a small advantage in response time to targets in the location of a previous emotional word cue, independent of its emotional valence. The event-related electrical response to threat-neutral word cue pairs showed enhanced occipital P1 amplitudes in the high relative to the low AS group. In contrast, low AS participants displayed greater P1 amplitude to positive-neutral word cue pairs compared to threat-neutral ones. Selective threat-related modulations also affected a later occipital P2, in response to the cued words, in the high AS group. More importantly, the event-related response to targets following the emotional word cue pairs showed modulations as a function of trait-anxiety, spatial location, and emotion. In the high AS group, an occipital N1 wave was *increased* in response to probe targets in the same location as previous presented threat versus positive words. In contrast, in the low AS group, occipital N1 amplitudes were *decreased* in response to probe targets following threat word cues relative to neutral word cues, independent of validity. In addition, over parietal scalp, N1 amplitude to threat invalid trials was *increased* relative to threat valid trials. Voltage of the later P3b wave also varied as a function of AS group, spatial location, and emotion. In the high AS group, P3b was *attenuated* for probe targets in the same location as previously presented threat words than to probe targets in the same location as positive words. In the low AS group, P3b to probes were reduced following positive relative to threat word cues, independent of validity. The present results in the dot-probe task are interpreted within a model in which early hypervigilance to threat in high trait anxiety leads to early enhancement of occipitally distributed sensory components (P1 to the threat pairs, N1 to following probe targets) and later attenuation of conscious top-down processing of threat stimuli (as indexed by the P3b). In contrast, low trait anxiety is accompanied by early attenuation of occipitally distributed sensory components (P1 to the threat cue pairs, N1 to following targets).

Chapter 5 – A persistent fear of social or performance situations in which embarrassment may occur is the essential feature for social anxiety. Cognitive theories of social anxiety emphasize the role of negative self-appraisals and the anticipation of negative consequences for oneself. Nevertheless, other cognitive constructs have a significant role in the maintenance of social anxiety; specifically, the tendency to see oneself as overly responsible for other people's discomfort and the distress arising from concerns of being negatively judged by others. The interest in the assessment of these fears in patients with social anxiety is increasing, but research is also required to determine their impact in the development of social anxiety in non-clinical samples and the extent to which gender differences may arise in a specific cultural setting.

Chapter 6 – Infertility is defined as the lack of conception after 12 months of unprotected intercourse and is perceived as a problem in all cultures and societies. It is estimated that between 16 and 26% of European women trying to have children face infertility. From recent studies, it appears that a common reaction during fertility treatment is anxiety, while after an unsuccessful IVF, feelings of sadness, depression and anger may appear. A range of psychosocial variables (personality traits, coping strategies, social support) may influence infertile women's anxiety and stress during infertility treatment. The objective of the present chapter was to review studies describing specifically the impact of sociodemographic factors on anxiety experienced by infertile women undergoing fertility treatment. The sociodemographic background information includes variables concerning age, educational level, annual income and occupational social position. Sociodemographic factors are known to influence a wide range of issues, opinions, beliefs and feelings. According to Waser and Isenberg, reproductive suppression should vary according to the economic and social resources available to the individual because, humans as a species are social, and these resources are fundamental tools in the defence against stressful life events. Individuals with more resources have stronger defences and are better able to withstand the effects of stress than those with fewer resources. Therefore, it is expected and hypothesized that sociodemographic factors may influence levels of anxiety and stress during fertility treatment and that women of lower educational level, lower income and lower social class will experience a higher level of anxiety because they lack environmental 'buffers' against psychosocial stress. A systematic search of the psychological and medical electronic databases (Medline, PsycINFO, CINAHL, EMBASE and Scopus) was performed. Finally, thirteen studies that were relevant to the objective of the review chapter were included. The majority of the included studies failed to find a significant association between female age and levels of anxiety during fertility treatment. The majority of the included studies found that educational level and annual income level are statistically associated with levels of anxiety during fertility treatment. Nevertheless, the association between occupational social class and levels of anxiety is not significant.

Thus, this chapter suggests that certain sociodemographic factors might make particular infertile individuals more vulnerable to anxiety. Low educational level and low income could be considered as risk factors for increased anxiety in infertile individuals undergoing infertility treatment. By assessing these factors, medical professionals who work in infertility clinics, may be able to identify individuals who are at greater risk of adjustment difficulties. Health care professionals should provide counselling which is tailored to the educational and social needs of the women.

Chapter 7 – Thirty-four students with extensive aviation experience (A+) and 35 students without such experience (A-) completed tests designed to tap into the impact of frontal lobe function and State/Trait anxiety performance. Experienced Aviation students showed worsening executive function performance (motivation/drive, organization) with increases in State, but not Trait, anxiety. ($rs > -.34$, $ps < .05$). Inexperienced aviation students showed the exact opposite; worsening executive function (motivation/drive, organization) with increases in Trait, but not State, anxiety ($rs = -.41$, $ps < .05$). Implications for the impact of anxiety in an applied setting will be discussed.

Chapter 8 – The stop-signal paradigm (SSP) is an experimental method that allows research into brain mechanisms of executive control. In the SSP, subjects either react to a target stimulus or withdraw a reaction when a stop-signal appears after target. In this chapter author investigate neurophysiologic mechanisms underlying regulation of motor responses in healthy subjects given different trait anxiety (TA) levels. SSP experiment with simultaneous EEG recording was performed on 21 subjects. Event-related spectral perturbations were analyzed in order to study brain oscillatory activity in different frequency bands. The data were partitioned into four experimental conditions: successful reaction (Go), successful withdraw (Stop), missed reaction (unsuccessful Go), and failure to stop (unsuccessful Stop). In the Go condition, power increase in delta and theta bands (1-7 Hz) was observed between 150-1000 ms after the target onset. Beta (15-25 Hz) desynchronize-tion (power decrease) appeared before button-press (200-700 ms), while posterior alpha and central mu (7-14 Hz) desynchronization were revealed in 200-1200 ms, i.e. both before and after button-press. Successful reaction invited beta “rebound” (power increase, 1000-1600 ms). In the Stop condition additional low-frequency (1-7 Hz) power increase appeared 200-800 ms after the stop-signal onset. The low-frequency synchronization had maximal amplitude in the occipital-parietal region in Go condition, while in the Stop condition, the two maxima were observed – early in the posterior and late in the frontal area, implying co-occurrence of two different processes – activation of sensory areas, and active inhibition of prepared motor activity. Both types of mistakes were associated with prolonged low-frequency power increase (200-1200 ms). Several components of EEG reactions depended on the TA level. Post-movement desynchronization in alpha and beta bands was significantly stronger in subjects with higher TA, while beta "rebound" had higher amplitude and shorter latency in subjects with lower anxiety. The amplitude of delta (1-4 Hz) synchronization was positively related with TA level in all experimental conditions. Author have interpreted these results basing on attentional control theory. Author hypothesize that subjects with high TA exert more attention to experimental task, which is reflected by higher amplitudes of alpha and beta desynchronization. On the contrary, subjects with low TA are less predisposed to elevated attentional control, and instead, they are more inclined to relax after a successfully completed task. The latter feature is mirrored in shorter latency and higher amplitude of "beta rebound" after successful performance of the trial in subjects with lower TA.

In: Trait Anxiety
Editor: Anna S. Morales
ISBN 978-1-61324-551-4

Chapter 1

THE IMPACT OF TRAIT ANXIETY TO COGNITIVE FUNCTION IN ERP STUDIES

Yue-jia Luo[1,2,3], Ruolei Gu[1], Yu-xia Huang[1], Xuebing Li[2], Xinying Li[2] and Xiyao Xie[1]

[1]National Key Laboratory of Cognitive Neuroscience and Learning, Beijing Normal University, Beijing 100875, China

[2]Key Laboratory of Mental Health, Chinese Academy of Sciences, Beijing 100101, China

[3]Academy of Psychology and Behavior, Tianjin Normal University, Tianjin 300074, China

ABSTRACT

Event-related potentials (ERPs), which are based on electroencephalogram (EEG) technique, refer to any kind of stereotyped electrophysiological responses to internal or external stimuli. For researchers and clinicians, the ERP method serves as a non-invasive tool to measure brain activity during cognitive processing. This chapter reviews our ERP research on the relationship between levels of trait anxiety and a variety of cognitive functions (including attention, memory, & decision-making). In these studies, even though the behavioral measures might not reveal significant difference between high trait anxiety (HTA) and low trait anxiety (LTA) individuals, the ERP components were consistently sensitive to different level of trait anxiety (i.e., the P1 in cue-target attention task; the feedback-related negativity in decision-making task). Overall, our results indicate that the HTA participants showed a tendency to overreact to broadly "negative" information (including threatening stimulus, incorrect feedback, and outcome that indicating monetary loss). This finding extends the traditional viewpoint that trait anxiety is characterized by reactions to threat-related stimuli, and might be benefit to both clinical and nonclinical studies.

For human beings, the influence of emotion on our physiological states, as well as on cognitive abilities, are very easy to be recognized in daily lifes. Fear, for example, causes sexual dysfunction, insomnia, ulcers, and gives us dry mouth and jitters at the very moment when we have greatest need be calm and brave (Loewenstein, Weber, Hsee, & Welch, 2001). It it worth noting that, however, "no emotion is useful or not except in relation to a particular situation"(Nesse, 2006). In other words, the impact of emotion could be very helpful or even critical in specific situations. Recently, it has been pointed out that emotioanl process is essential in sensory coding and high-level cognitive activities, and that it might be unnecessary to distinguish between emotional and cognitive function (Pessoa, 2008; Quartz, 2009).

Among different kinds of emotions, the authors of this chapter are most interested in the impact of anxiety on cognition. Anxiety is an emotional state accompanied by expectations of negative outcomes and concerns about the severity of those outcomes (Eisenberg, Baron, & Seligman, 1998). The perception of threat and danger are central for evoking anxiety (Mitte, 2007). The influence of anxiety on cognitive processes, such as attention, working memory, behavioral control, and decision making, has been proven by many studies (Paulus, Feinstein, Simmons, & Stein, 2004).

There are two major aspects in anxiety: state anxiety, a *transient* level of arousal associated with reactions to adverse situation; and trait anxiety, an individual *dispositional* level of anxiety that is not reactive to external stimuli (Bekker, Legare, Stacey, O'Connor, & Lemyre, 2003). Compared to transient emotion, emotion dispositions are: (a) reflected in relatively stable differences in underlying neurochemical systems, (b) heritable, and (c) stable across the life course (Lerner & Keltner, 2000). Accordingly, most of our studies introduced below are focus on trait anxiety, but the relationship between state anxiety and cognitive function is also of interest.

1. Anxiety and Attention

High anxious people have distinctive characteristics with respect to the cognitive functions. For example, they are more sensitive to the threatening information in the environments, i.e., they show up an attentional bias to threats relative to the low anxious individuals (Bar-Haim, Lamy, & Glickman, 2005).

The attentional bias is well-known in the field of emotion studies. Considerable evidences have revealed that people tend to pay attention to emotionally negative or threatening events preferentially and even automatically. When people were required to respond to the emotional properties of the stimuli, the threatening stimuli often facilitated the task more than pleasant and neutral stimuli. Meanwhile, if the threatening stimuli become disturbing information to the current task, they will also impair the task more heavily than other stimuli. The attentional bias may be followed by an evaluative bias and a reaction readiness bias (Huang & Luo, 2006). In contrast to the quick and automatic process involved in the *attentional bias*, a deliberative and controlled process may be the underlying mechanism of the *evaluation bias*. In this stage, information is represented and analyzed more carefully, with more factors considered and more experiences referenced. The negative or threatening events usually recruit more psychological and physiological resources on evaluation, presumably because of its importance and urgence for survival and daily life. Threatening events also elicit higher action readiness than do pleasant and neutral events. This response bias ensures organisms to take action as soon as possible to deal with dangerous situations.

It is noteworthy that a recent meta-analysis (Bar-Haim, Lamy, Pergamin, Bakermans-Kranenburg, & van IJzendoorn, 2007) reported that the threat-related attentional bias was not observed in nonanxious individuals though the bias is evident across different types of anxious populations (individuals with different clinical disorders, high-anxious nonclinical individuals, anxious children and adults). Although the methodological reasons may contribute to the negative result, it is reasonable to hypothesize that the attentional bias is more robust in the anxious populations. Moreover, the nonanxious people may show an opposite pattern to the attentional bias, i.e., an avoidance of threat-related stimuli.

Our ERP study has evidenced the proposition above. We screened 210 college students with the State-Trait Anxiety Inventory (Shek, 1993; Spielberger, Gorsuch, Lushene, Vagg, & Jacobs, 1983) and got 15 high and 15 low trait-anxious participants respectively. They were instructed to respond to targets in a cue-target task. The location of the target was cued by a threatening or neutral picture from the International Affective Picture System (Lang, Bradley, & Cuthbert, 2008). The target was two dots both horizontally or vertically arranged, and was presented beneath the location of the cue picture. In the valid trials, the reaction time of the high anxious individuals was found faster in the threatening condition than in the neutral condition. In invalid trials, the reaction time following threatening and nonthreatening pictures were nearly the same. While in the low anxious group the cue-type effect was not significant. An ERP component, P1, was evoked by the targets. The P1 component started in the hemisphere contralateral to the visual field of the target at around 90 ms after the target onset, reaching its peak at 120–130 ms, and then spread to the ipsilateral hemisphere with a peak at 150–160 ms. In the high anxious group, amplitudes of contralateral P1 for valid threatening trials were significantly larger than that for valid non-threatening trials. No P1 amplitude difference was observed following the two types of pictures on invalid trials. However, an inverse result was found in the low anxious individuals. They showed larger P1 amplitudes when completing invalid threatening trials, while there was no difference found on valid threatening versus neutral condition.

In ERP studies with the cue-target paradigm, the occipitoparietal P1 elicited by the target is thought to be modulated by the visual attentional resources. P1 amplitudes will be enhanced if more attention is distributed on the target or the location of target. The generator of P1 has been located in extrastriate cortical structures (Heinze et al., 1994; Martinez, Anllo-Vento, Buxton, Wong, & Hillyard, 1998). A sensory gain control mechanism may enhance the neural activity in the visual extrastriate cortex, facilitating the visual processing of attended locations. Behaviorally, response to the attended target will be speeded up by enhanced sensory processes.

Similar with our study, another study (Pourtois, Grandjean, Sander, & Vuilleumier, 2004) investigated the visual components evoked by targets following emotional face pairs. As the researchers expected, the lateral occipital P1 was larger when the target replaced a fearful face than when it replaced a neutral face. They deduced that the threat-related information is able to influence subsequent visual inputs.

Our study also found that the P1 component was modulated by the threatening information contained in the pictorial cues. This modulation occurred as early as 90 ms poststimulus and was observed in the contralateral hemisphere. More interestingly, a group difference was clearly revealed in the study. In the high anxious group, the amplitude of P1 was enhanced by valid threatening cues relative to valid nonthreatening cues, reflecting vigilance to the location of threat. In the low anxious group, however, the P1 amplitude tended to be enhanced on threatening invalid trials, reflecting avoidance from the location of threat. Clearly, the high and low anxious individuals deal with the threatening information in quite different way. The behavioral results also showed a threat-related attentional bias in anxious individuals that the threatening cues quickened the target detection in the high anxious group. It was in line with the ERP findings. They suggest that the biased behavioral performance caused by threat-related cues may arise from biased sensory processing.

Although lots of studies including ours above seem to suggest that high trait anxious people tend to attend to threats, while low trait anxious people will avoid them, there are still findings revealing that things are not always the case. For example, in Mogg et al.'s (2000) study, both highly and mildly threatening stimuli were used. Along with the increase of the threat value, the vigilance to threat increased, but the avoidance decreased. Mathews & Mackintosh (1998), as well as Mogg & Bradley (1998) proposed a model to interpret this phenomenon. They presumed that, when the threat value of stimuli is high enough or participants are under stress, they will display a pattern of attentional vigilance instead of avoidance.

To explore this issue further, we used some high threatening stimuli in our study. Pictures were selected from IAPS and were reassessed with respect to their threat value. A 9-point scale was used to evaluate the extent of threat taking '0' as not threatening at all and '8' as extremely threatening. Finally, 32 high threatening pictures (bloody scenes or corpses with a mean threat value of 6.9) and 32 neutral pictures (domestic scenes with a mean threat value of 0.5) were included in the study. We screened 213 veterans in the Armed Police of Beijing with the State-Trait Anxiety Inventory (Shek, 1993; Spielberger et al., 1983) and recruited 15 high trait-anxious and 17 low trait-anxious participants in our study. They reported no past or current mental disorders or past traumatic experiences. A visual spatial cue-target paradigm was used to detect the attentional bias of the high and low anxious people with the threatening and neutral pictures as cues. Two blue frames were presented on either side of the central fixation cross. The picture cue was presented in the upper half of one frame for 450 ms. Then a target was presented in the lower half of either the same frame or the other frame until the participant responded. There were 75% valid trials in which cue and target presented in the same frame, and 25% invalid trials with cue and target presented in separate frames. Half of the picture cues were threatening and the other half were nonthreatening. The experiment consisted of three blocks and the latter two blocks repeated the first one in all the respects of experimental design.

Analyses of the reaction time showed that responses of both high and low trait-anxious participants were slowed by the threatening cues, i.e., both of them took a similar behavioral pattern when encountering high threatening events. This result is comparable with the finding of Wilson & MacLeod (2003) who took high threatening faces as stimuli in their study. Thus, consistent studies with different type of stimuli and experimental paradigms validate the models of Mathews & Mackintosh (1998) and Mogg & Bradley (1998). It is suggested that threat-related attentional bias is a ubiquitous phenomenon, not confined only to clinically anxious and highly anxious populations.

In our study, responses following threatening cues were significantly slower than that after neutral cues, regardless of the cue validity and anxiety level. This is probably due to the general slowing effect of the extremely threatening cues. Yiend & Mathews (2001) suggested that high threatening pictures initiated task-irrelevant processing. Perhaps threat depletes the working memory resources that the task demands, as suggested by Eysenck and colleagues (Eysenck, 1979; Eysenck & Calvo, 1992). In a recent study, visualspatial working memory was impaired under threat of shock (Lavric, Rippon, & Gray, 2003). Furthermore, the more anxiety participants reported and the higher the mean heart rate, the more impaired their spatial working memory performance. In our study, 75% cues were valid, so the cue location must be temporarily stored in the working memory. Thus, when the working memory was impaired by the threatening picture, the reaction speed should be slowed down. Another explanation is that, in this study, targets appeared just below the location of the cue. Even on valid trials, the locations of the target and the cue were not identical. Thus, it required participants to disengage their attention from cued location on all trials (Fox, Russo, Bowles, & Dutton, 2001), which should be more difficult for threat cues relative to neutral cues (Fox, 2002; Yiend & Mathews, 2001).

Another interesting finding is that the high anxious participants responded slower to the targets than the low anxious individuals across all conditions. Perhaps the executive function of high trait-anxious people was more impaired by threat than low trait-anxious people. Trait anxiety and threat might influence the general executive function through an unknown mechanism.

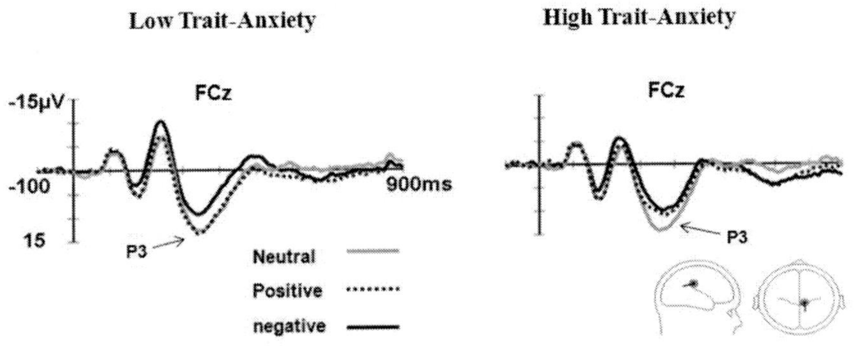

Figure 1. High trait-anxiety individuals have an over-inhibition tendency of the emotional information indexed by the variations of P3 amplitude.

In addition, there was a significant interaction of trait anxiety by block. Low anxious people performed consistently throughout all the blocks. However, high anxious people showed obviously slowed responses in the first block and became faster and faster on subsequent blocks. This phenomenon may be attributed to 'habituation' (Breiter et al., 1996). As the threatening pictures were repeated, high anxious participants could conquer the general slowing effect of threat and improved their reaction speed gradually. In contrast, the attentional biases toward threatening cues existed throughout the whole experiment and showed no habituation effect.

From studies above, we can see high anxious people show an attentional bias to the threatening information when it is the current target or relevant to the current task. One may ask how anxious people will do if the threatening stimuli are not related to the current task but act as disturbing information.

According to Mogg et al.'s (Mogg & Bradley, 1998; Mogg, Bradley, Williams, & Mathews, 1993) alertness-avoidance theory, when anxious people process emotional distracting stimuli, they will become alert as a first response and subsequently evade the stimuli. They focus excessively on threatening stimuli, which induces anxiety and subsequently, exhibit avoidance behavior, which decreases the possibility of adapting to and objectively appraising the threat-related stimuli. McNaughton & Gray (2000) addressed the cause of anxiety disorder with respect to the inhibition function. They proposed that people have a behavior activation system (BAS) and a behavior inhibition system (BIS). The systems interact with each other. Anxiety is associated with excessive activation of BIS. Newman et al. (1997) proposed that there is another nonspecific arousal system (NAS), which is modulated by both BAS and BIS. The enhancement of NAS accelerates priming of attention and inhibition; concurrently, it shortens the appraisal of the information from BAS and BIS. He also points out that unusual activation of BIS is positively correlated with anxiety.

Previously, some studies have investigated the executive inhibition function of anxious individuals. Relative to normal subjects, anxious individuals have more difficulties in suppressing the disturbances in emotional information (Mogg & Bradley, 1998; Mogg et al., 1993). Even if the stimuli are presented under subliminal condition, the results are similar to that obtained under supraliminal condition. For another example, Morita and colleagues (2001) used the auditory oddball paradigm with emotional faces as interference stimuli. They found that amplitudes of P300 under happy conditions are smaller than those under the sad or neutral conditions, which is regarded as the manifestation of attention inhibition by the happy faces. Cabeza & Nyberg (1997) suggested that executive inhibition controls information processing and corresponding responses. It activates the interference control function of the anterior cingulate cortex and the motion control function associated with the lateral orbitofrontal cortex.

To explore further the neural mechanism of inhibition function of anxiety people, we conducted an ERP study with emotional (pleasant, unpleasant and neutral) pictures as novel distracting information in an oddball task. The standard and target stimuli were geometric figures. Participants were instructed to discriminate the size differences between the standard and target stimuli. In order to complete the discrimination task, they had to inhibit the interference of emotional stimuli. This paradigm is supposed to be able to probe inhibition mechanisms of emotional interferences (Yamasaki, LaBar, & McCarthy, 2002) and can be widely used in studies on attention and emotion. A total of 210 undergraduate students were screened with the State-Trait Anxiety Inventory (STAI) (Shek, 1993; Spielberger et al., 1983). 14 high and 14 low trait-anxious students participated in our ERP study.

Their mean response speed to the targets and the accuracies showed no difference between the high and low anxiety group. We compared the ERP data induced by unpleasant and pleasant pictures, with the neutral condition as the control group. We were mainly concerned about the P3 component that is related to the inhibition process. It was found that the P3 component (Figure 1) peaked at central-posterior scalp area. In the high trait-anxiety as well as low trait-anxiety group, P3 amplitudes induced by unpleasant pictures were smaller than those induced by neutral pictures. This implies that they inhibit the influences from unpleasant stimuli. In the low trait-anxiety group, P3 amplitudes showed no significant difference between the positive and the neutral conditions. P3 amplitudes induced by pleasant pictures in the high trait-anxiety group were smaller than those induced by neutral pictures. It indicates that high anxious individuals adopt the same inhibition strategy toward pleasant and unpleasant pictures and have a trend of excessive inhibition.

Some researchers suggested that inhibition studies should focus on endogenic components, such as N2-P3-P4 (Ilan & Polich, 1999). The P3 component is considered as the index of inhibition to task-irrelevant information. Falkenstein et al. Falkenstein, Hohnsbein, & Hoormann (1999) proposed that P3 marks the completion of the entire inhibition process. Moser et al. (2006) found that LPP amplitudes were significantly decreased when subjects were required to actively inhibit the influence of unpleasant pictures. Fallgatter et al. (2002) also suggested that P3 may associate with high-load inhibition.

From an evolutionary perspective, unpleasant stimuli usually associate with urgent situations. They may result in serious outcomes to survival if they cannot be dealt with in a proper and timely manner. Hence, the brain possesses a certain extent of vigilance toward this kind of information to ensure that they are processed preferentially. If they are irrelavant to the current task, i.e., they are interference stimuli, they would become the major target of inhibition. Our study used an improved oddball paradigm, in which subjects would involuntarily pay attention to novel stimuli that interfered with the discrimination of standard and target stimuli. Participants have to actively inhibit the interference in order to successfully complete the discrimination tasks. This anti-interference effort manifested as significantly decreased P3 amplitudes of both high and low anxious individuals under the unpleasant condition compared with that under the neutral condition. The difference between the two groups of participants was that they showed different degrees of inhibition to pleasant stimuli. Relative to the neutral condition, P3 amplitudes elicited by pleasant pictures were decreased in high anxious individuals, while there was no such difference among the low anxious individuals. The contrast indicates that low anxious individuals selectively inhibit emotional stimuli and do not make much effort to inhibit the influences of pleasant stimuli since this kind of information is not as intrusive as the unpleasant stimuli. Nevertheless, high anxious individuals appear to feel that pleasant stimuli are very disturbing too, which makes them treat the two types of information comparably such that they manifest an over-inhibition tendency. Behavior inhibition model postulated by McNaughton & Gray

(2000) suggests that BAS would be activated when one perceives some reward or beneficial information, while BIS would be activated when one meets some conflict stimuli (including non-reward stimuli, punishment stimuli, and novel stimuli irrelevant to the present tasks). The activation of BIS would increase the response inhibition and also enhance the attentional vigilance. The current study evidenced the abnormal activation of BIS in high trait-anxious individuals.

In our study, the inhibition function localized by dipole source analysis revealed that most of the P3 variations are attributed to the activation of the right cingulate cortex (Figure 1). This is in line with the results of a few previous studies. For instance, one ERP study (Liotti, Woldorff, Perez, & Mayberg, 2000) investigated the time course of the Stroop task and found that interference stimuli first activated the ACC, then the left temporoparietal cortex. Another fMRI study involving the Stroop task also reported the activation of ACC (Swick & Jovanovic, 2002). Fuster's study (1997) of patients with brain injuries also revealed that the cingulate gyrus plays an important role in attention concentration and interference inhibition. In conclusion, the cingulate gyrus may be the brain area where the BIS system executes the conflict supervision and response inhibition function.

Besides the trait-anxiety, we have also explored other kind of anxiety, such as the social anxiety disorder (SAD). Social anxiety affects 3–5% of the general population. Its fundamental characteristic is severe anxiety in social situations, with excessive concern that others may evaluate the sufferer's behavior negatively (American Psychiatric Association, 1994). Socially anxious individuals are particularly concerned with situations humiliating or embarrassing themselves when under the scrutiny of others, so they tend to avoid social or performance situation for their intense anxiety and distress in social interactions.

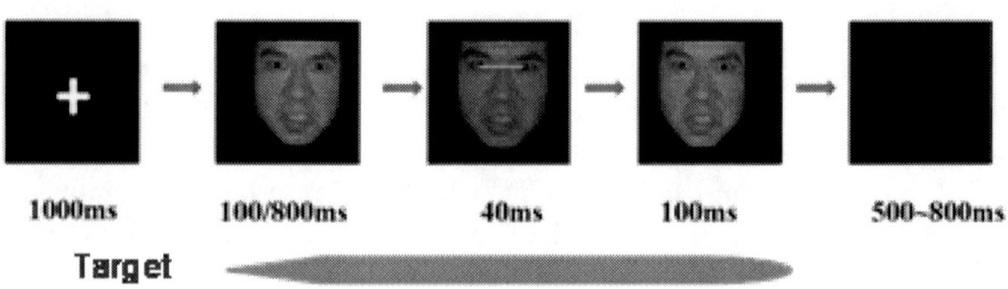

Figure 2. A modified version of the attention-shifting paradigm, used in our experiment.

Different theoretical models try to elucidate the emotional processing alterations in SAD. Clark & Wells (1995), for instance, suggest that people with SAD confronted with the feared situations tend to direct attention toward themselves, disregarding emotional information available in the environment. Conversely, other cognitive models state that people with SAD allocate greater attentional resources to threatening information (Mathews & Mackintosh, 1998; Mogg & Bradley, 1998). Recently a new cognitive models of anxiety, propose that SAD individuals are characterized by early hypervigilance to facial expressions immediately followed by the avoidance of such stimuli, subsequently recognized as threatening (Garner, Baldwin, Bradley, & Mogg, 2006). The hypervigilance/avoidance model merges critical features of the former models, and might be the most satisfactory theoretical model which could explain the results from multiple researches.

The eye region plays a fundamental role in social and non-verbal communication. It is noteworthy that eye contact can be of positive as well as negative social value: staring can be interpreted as a sign of anger and hostility, but also be taken as a sign of friendliness, romantic attraction, or general interest (Abele, 1986; Kleinke, 1986). Threatening information from the eyes can be a sign of disapproval and rejection, and might therefore function as an anxiety-provoking cue in people for whom approval is especially important. Clinical observation suggests that social anxious individuals are sensitive to eye region, and might show avoidance of eye contact in social communication. Several studies have investigated the eyes processing in social anxiety, but there are inconsistencies in findings from these studies (Albert et al., 2009; Horley, Williams, Gonsalvez, & Gordon, 2004; Wieser, Muhlberger, & Pauli, 2007). So there is still no consistent evidences on emotional eyes processing in social anxiety to support any cognitive model mentioned above.

We conducted two experiments to investigate directly how high-socially anxious individuals (HSA) process emotional eyes compared to low-socially anxious individuals (LSA), as well as the cognitive and neural mechanism under the emotional eye processing in HSA.

Experiment one is a behavioral study. Two hundred and fifty undergraduate students filled in the Chinese version of the Brief Fear of Negative Evaluation Scale (BFNE), the Social Interaction Anxiety Scale (SIAS), the Social Phobia Scale (SPS), and the Social Avoidance and Distress Scale (SAD). Seventy-eight individuals (39 females) selected from the Chinese Facial Affective Picture System (CFAPS): 26 happy, 26 neutral and 26 angry faces. The highest and lowest-scoring 20% were referred to as HSA and LSA. A modified version of the attention-shifting paradigm (Figure 2) was used in which faces with happy, neutral or angry expression were presented at two exposure duration: 100ms and 800ms. Participants had to fixate on the face cue and then discriminate a target direction that appeared randomly on the upper, middle, or lower part of the face, corresponding to the eyes, nose and mouth region of the face.

The results showed that in the 100-ms condition (Figure 3), HSA were slower to respond to targets which appeared on the upper part regardless of the emotion expressed by the face cue, while no region differences emerged in LSA. In the 800-ms condition (Figure 4), HSA still showed longer reaction times (RTs) to upper targets, but which just happened when the expression of the face cue was neutral or happy. In contrast, LSA just showed longer RTs to upper targets when the expression of the face cue was angry in 800-ms condition.

According to the results, there might be an increased attentional dwelling on the eye region in HSA at early stage of face processing, while an avoidance of eye region at the late stage of face processing, which partly support the vigilance-avoidance hypothesis in social phobia: an automatic hypervigilance for salient features (such as the eyes) that tap into evaluative fears may direct subsequent focal attention away from these features.

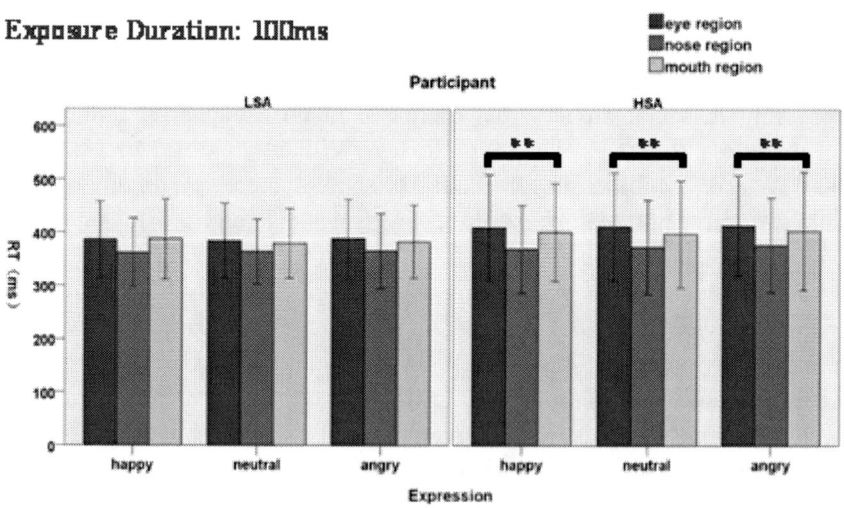

Figure 3. The participants' reaction time in the 100-ms condition of the attention-shifting task.

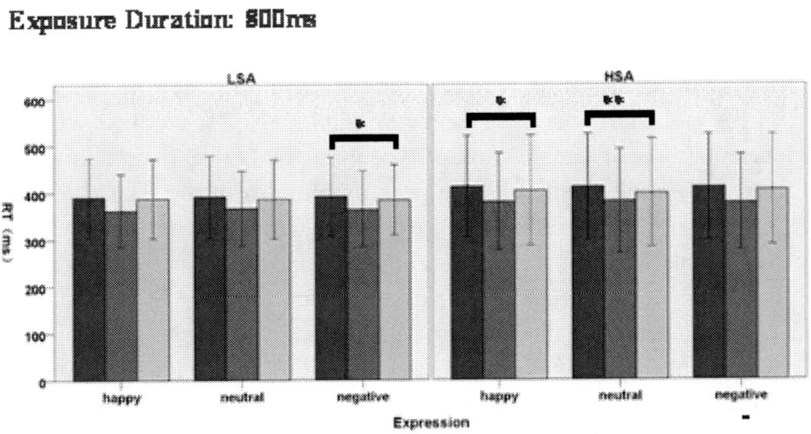

Figure 4. The participants' reaction time in the 800-ms condition of the attention-shifting task.

On the basis of experiment one, an ERP experiment was conducted to investigate time course as well as cognitive and neural mechanism of emotional eye processing in HSA. According to the hypervigilance/avoidance hypothesis, vigilance to threatening stimulus might be presented as easier orientation and increased engagement at early stage of attention process, and avoidance might be presented as easier inhibition and increased disengagement at late stage of attention process.

Modified Go/NoGo paradigm (Figure 5) demonstrating recognition and inhabitation clearly (Aron et al., 2007; Dillon & Pizzagalli, 2007) could help revealing the deep mechanism of emotional eyes processing in HSA. The primary task adapted from previous ERP reports (Chiu, Holmes, & Pizzagalli, 2008), used emotional eyes (Negative/Positive) as "Go" (target) and neutral eyes as "NoGo" (distractor). Participants viewed a series of individually presented eyes, 67% of which belonged to a "target" or "Go" valence category and 33% of which belonged to a "distractor" or "NoGo" valence category. Participants were asked to respond with a key press to eyes of the target valence and to withhold responses to all other eyes. The following three experimental blocks were presented: (1) positive targets, neutral and negative distractors; (2) negative targets, neutral and positive distractors; (3) neutral targets, negative and positive distractors. Each block consisted of 90 eyes, 67% of which were as target and 33% were as distractor. 45 grayscale pictures of angry, happy and neutral facial expressions were selected from the Chinese Facial Affective Picture System (Huang and Luo, 2004). All pictures were clipped to create images which showed the eye region only (including eyebrows). These images of eye region were valance and arousal matched through assessment. Using the same procedure and standard in the experiment 1, 19 LSA and 21 HSA were screened. Individual ERP averages were derived for correct trials of each stimulus type (Go, NoGo) and emotional valence (Negative, Neutral, Positive). The peak amplitudes of the P1 (100 to 150 ms window), the N2 component (200 to 350 ms window) and the P3 component (350 to 700 ms window) at fronto-central scalp locations were analyzed.

Percentages of correct responses and reaction times of people with high and low social anxiety in each experimental condition are shown in Table 1. All participants were quicker to respond to both Positive and Negative relative to Neutral Go eyes, exhibited greater accuracy for Go trials than for NoGo trials, and least accuracy for Positive NoGo eyes. Comparing to LSA, HSA showed less accuracy for Positive Go eyes and slower to respond to both Positive and Negative eyes. What's more all participants also exhibited high sensitivity (d') to Negative eyes, and only HSA exhibited low sensitivity to Positive eyes.

Figure 6 shows event-related brain potentials to emotional eyes over fronto-central cortical sites in Go and NoGo trials. For all participants, negative eyes elicited smallest N2 amplitudes in both Go and NoGo trials. And NoGo stimuli evoked larger P3 amplitudes than Go stimuli in all three effective salience, which was more significant when the eyes were Negative. Only HSA exhibited enhanced NoGo P3 magnitude to Negative relative to both Positive and Neutral stimuli, and had larger NoGo P3 amplitudes than LSA when the eyes were Negative and Positive. What's more, LSA had larger Go P1 than HSA over right lateral occipital-temporal scalp (EGI sites 58, 64, 65, 90, 95 and 96) when the eyes were Positive.

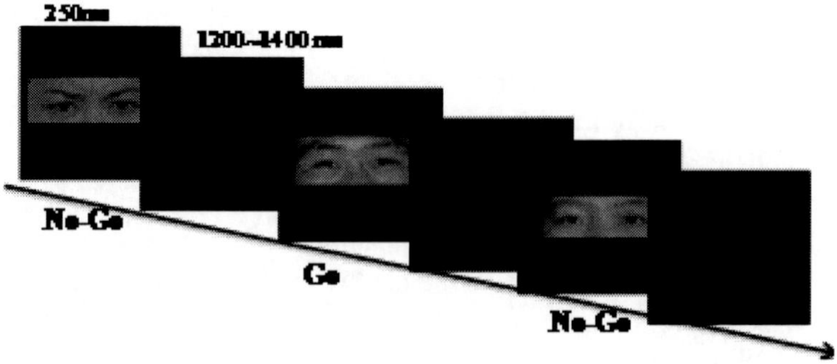

Figure 5. A modified version of the Go/NoGo paradigm, used in our experiment.

Table 1. Accuracy (ACC) and reaction times (RTs) in different experimental conditions in Experiment 2'

	ACC		RTs	
	M±*SD*		*M*±*SD*	
	LSA	HSA	LSA	HSA
Go				
Negative	0.98±0.02	0.96±0.05	347.54±106.53	424.05±111.25
Neutral	0.96±0.04	0.93±0.06	385.28±119.63	451.53±107.75
Positive	0.97±0.04	0.93±0.06	356.14±101.71	428.81±107.90
NoGo				
Negative	0.93±0.06	0.92±0.06		
Neutral	0.94±0.07	0.95±0.04		
Positive	0.91±0.05	0.89±0.07		

These data show that emotional eyes elicit faster behavioral and neural responses than neutral eyes, especially the negative eyes. And withholding a prepared response to positive eyes was more difficult than negative and neutral eyes, which suggests positive emotions facilitate approach-related behaviors and continued action (Cacioppo, Gardner, & Berntson, 1999; Lane et al., 1997). Comparing to LSA, HSA exhibited higher sensitive to negative eyes, and lower sensitive to positive eyes. More specifically, HSA exhibited greater inhibition to both negative and positive eyes, but the inhibition to negative eyes was more effective than the inhibition to positive eyes according to the behavioral results. These findings suggest HSA has more effective inhibition to negative eyes at the late stage of attention process, which partly supports the hypervigilance/avoidance hypothesis.

In addition, there was a preliminary study which asked participants to evaluate emotional eyes to ensure the materials used in the ERP experiment were reliable and effective. 27 HSA and 26 LSA assessed pleasantness, threatening and arousal of the 36 eyes regions. The results showed that HSA led to increased ratings. HSA rated angry and neutral eyes as more threatening, angry eyes as more arousal and happy eyes as more pleasantness. That means people with high social anxiety might evaluate threatening eyes as more negative, arousing, or unpleasant, and at the same time they evaluate positive eyes as more pleasant, than people with low social anxiety, which was consistent with previous studies (Dimberg & Thunberg, 2007; Goldin, Manber-Ball, Werner, Heimberg, & Gross, 2009; Straube, Kolassa, Glauer, Mentzel, & Miltner, 2004).

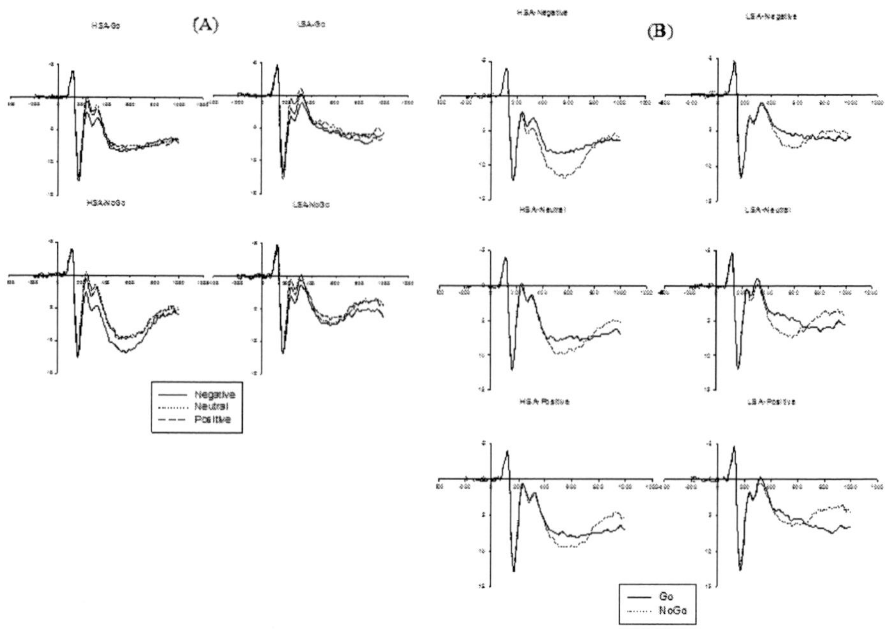

Figure 6. The mean amplitudes in response to emotional eyes in Go and NoGo trials, at fronto-central cortical areas.

In conclusion, in the present research we characterize the cognitive and neural difference of emotional eyes processing between HSA and LSA. Specifically, we find that eyes region provides sufficient diagnostic information for ERP and behavioral discrimination among angry, happy and neutral facial expressions, and people with high social anxiety are sensitive to the emotional attributes of eyes which lead to increased ratings. The present results suggest that the mode of emotional eyes processing in HSA, which partly give support for the hypervigilance/avoidance hypothesis. HSA are sensitive to eye region at early stage of processing, and also show avoidance of eyes at the late stage of face processing. Together these findings point to that deviant processing ways of emotional eyes might be related with the pathogenesis of social anxiety. More research needed to further investigate the neural systems underlying eyes processing in social anxiety, which may aid in diagnosis, intervention and prevention.

2. Anxiety and Working Memory

Processing efficiency theory suggests that the effects of anxiety on cognitive performance may be mediated by their effects on working memory (WM) and here have been considerable evidences supporting their hypothesis (for a review, see Eysenck & Calvo, 1992). It is easy to explain that anxious individuals may care more about anxiety responses unrelated to the current task (i.e. compulsive thought, negative cognition), which would distract attention and consume the limited WM resource. As a result, response accuracy reduces or response time (RT) prolongs — low efficiency of cognition. WM refers to a system used for the temporary storage and manipulation of information that is deemed necessary for a range of more complex cognitive activities. Baddeley (1992) hypothesized that WM is composed of three major components that work independently of one another: (i) a verbal WM system for tackling verbal information in the phonological loop; (ii) a visuospatial WM system for processing non-verbal information in the visuospatial sketchpad; and (iii) a central executive that determines the information that is made available for conscious processing by exerting control over voluntary action. Eysenck and Calvo (2002) proposed that the major effects of anxiety (e.g., worry) are exerted on the modality-free central executive, which initiates a chain reaction on the verbal and spatial components of WM and ultimately disrupts both systems (Eysenck & Calvo, 1992; Eysenck, Derakshan, Santos, & Calvo, 2007). However, in contrast to the general effect of anxiety on the central executive, some clinical studies have shown that people with anxiety or depression disorders have specific deficits in verbal or visuospatial memory, which implies that the two WM systems are disrupted unequally by negative effects. For example, obsessive-compulsive disorder (OCD) appears to be associated with deficits in visual or visuospatial memory, but not with verbal WM (Tallis, 1997). Depression disorders are linked to a specific deficit in the performance of spatial tasks, but have no significantly different effect on verbal performance compared with controls (Quraishi & Frangou, 2002; Weiland-Fiedler et al., 2004). In addition, a high trait anxiety results in worse performance in verbal WM than in spatial WM, with the opposite being the case for low trait anxiety (Ikeda, Iwanaga, & Seiwa, 1996).

Although the aforementioned research relies mainly on studies of mental disorders, more recent evidence obtained from healthy people is also consistent with the possibility that the effects of negative emotion on verbal WM may not be the same as those on visuospatial WM (Gray, 2001; Lavric et al., 2003; Lavric, Shackman, Sarinopoulos, Sarinopoulos, & Davidson, 2000; Shackman et al., 2006). For example, Lavric and colleagues (2003) employed threat-of-shock to induce anticipated anxiety in college students, and found that threat-evoked anxiety selectively impaired the performance of spatial n-back tasks but not verbal n-back tasks. They proposed that threat-evoked anxiety mood and spatial WM rely on a common visuospatial attention mechanism. Because negative affect commonly draws visuospatial attention (e.g., attention to threat), which is also essential to spatial WM (Awh, Anllo-Vento, & Hillyard, 2000; Awh & Jonides, 2001; Postle, Awh, Jonides, Smith, & D'Esposito, 2004), there is an attentional resource competition between negative affect and spatial WM. In contrast, this competition is less pronounced when it comes to verbal WM due to its primary dependence on phonological processes (Buchsbaum, Olsen, Koch, & Berman, 2005). Thus, visuospatial attention may overlap both negative emotion and spatial WM, which may result in induced selective impairment of spatial WM.

Besides the attention resource competition, previous research also revealed a possible explanation based on hemispheric asymmetry view that emotional states modulate cognitive functions via separate cerebral hemisphere (Gray, 2001; Gray, Braver, & Raichle, 2002; Shackman et al., 2006; Simon-Thomas, Role, & Knight, 2005). Based on neuroimaging evidences that there exist two separate and independent anatomical systems with the left cerebral hemisphere specialized for processing positive or approach-related emotions and the right hemisphere specialized for processing negative or withdrawal-related emotions (Drevets et al., 1997; Wheeler, Davidson, & Tomarken, 1993), cognitive functions could be either interfered (because of neural resource competition) or facilitated (because of increased arousal) by an emotional state of the same hemispheric dominance (Drevets et al., 1997; Gray et al., 2002; Heller & Nitschke, 1997; W. Sato, Kochiyama, Yoshikawa, & Matsumura, 2001). According to Baddely's cognitive model, WM at least has two type subsystems, verbal and spatial networks. The former requires active maintenance of verbal information that depends more on left prefrontal cortex (PFC) (Broca's area, supplementary motor and premotor areas), and the latter depends on right PFC (premotor areas) for maintaining spatial information depending more (Smith & Jonides, 1998, 1999; Smith, Jonides, & Koeppe, 1996). As both spatial WM and negative emotion have right hemisphere dominance, spatial WM is likely to interact with negative affections than with verbal WM and vice versa.

There are few studies for testing the underlying mechanism of this possible selective interaction between emotion and working memory. The aim of the current series of studies was to test the key prediction that negative emotional state can selectively affect spatial working memory and the possible hypothesis of neural mechanism.

Participants in all experiments were right-handed China Agricultural University undergraduates, age range 18-27. All were right-handed with normal or corrected-to-normal vision and had no prior neurological/psychiatric history. They gave informed consent and were paid for their participation. None participated more than once.

The key aspect of the first study was for each participant to watch emotional picture intended to induce an emotional state during the period of performing verbal and spatial WM tasks. Pictures were interspersed into the ongoing tasks to meet the requirements of ERP superposition principle. In order to ensure that the induced emotion was stable during a period of time, each experiment was divided into two sessions. In one session only the aversive pictures were presented, and in the other only neutral pictures were presented. There was a twenty minutes interval between the two sessions to avoid emotional interference. Each session included both verbal task blocks and spatial task blocks that were pseudorandom in each session.

Eighty-four digitized color pictures were selected from the International Affective Picture System (Lang et al., 2008): 42 were classified as aversive pictures (e.g., mutilations, pointing guns) and 42 were classified as neutral pictures (e.g., landscapes, household appliances). According to IAPS scoring, aversive pictures were more negative in valence than neutral ones (2.15 ± 0.43 vs. 5.00 ± 0.35; $t(41) = -36.534$, $p < 0.001$), and were more exciting in arousal than the latter (6.34 ± 0.62 vs. 3.24 ± 0.59; $t(41) = 23.324$, $p < 0.001$). When presented, all pictures occupied between 3 to 4.5° of visual angle on either side of the visual midline. Each target stimulus was drawn from a set of 12 capital letters from the Latin alphabet. During presentation, the letters on a given trial would appear at 1 of 12 positions, each of which was on 1 of 6 equidistant radii of an imaginary circular array 2 or 6 cm from the screen's center.

Prior to the beginning of the experiment, participants were given a Positive and Negative Affect Schedule (PANAS), consisting of 10 positive affects (interested, excited, strong, enthusiastic, proud, alert, inspired, determined, attentive, and active) and 10 negative affects (distressed, upset, guilty, scared, hostile, irritable, ashamed, nervous, jittery, and afraid) (Watson, Clark, & Tellegen, 1988). Participants were asked to rate items on a scale from1 to 5 (1 = very slightly or not at all, 5 = extremely), based on the strength of emotion they were feeling at that moment. After each session of the experiment, participants filled out another PANAS scale.

The electroencephalogram (EEG) was recorded from 64 scalp sites using Ag/AgCl electrodes mounted in an elastic cap according to the modified expanded 10–20 system (NeuroScan Inc.). Continuous data were recorded relative to linked mastoids with a forehead ground. Vertical electrooculogram (EOG) recording electrodes were positioned above and below the left eye, and horizontal EOG recording electrodes were positioned at the outer canthi of both eyes. All electrode impedances were kept below 5 kΩ. The EEG and EOG were sampled at a digitization rate of 500 Hz and were bandpass filtered 0.05-100 Hz (Experiment 1) and DC-100 Hz (Experiment 2). Reaction times and accuracy were also recorded.

The EEG data was offline analyzed by Scan 4.3 software (NeuroScan Inc.). Ocular artifacts were identified and corrected with an eye-movement correction algorithm. EEG and EOG were digitally filtered with a 16Hz lowpass filter. Trials with various artifacts were rejected with a criterion of ± 100 μV. The ERPs were averaged for trials with correct responses. The data were baseline corrected by subtracting from each sample the average activity of that channel during the baseline period. Repeated-measures analyses of variance (ANOVA) were conducted on each ERP component with different factors and Greenhouse-Geisser correction was used when the data violated the assumption of sphericity.

Experiment 1 tested the key prediction that spatial and verbal controlled processing would be influenced selectively by negative emotion. In classical ERP studies with the n-back paradigm, frontal late positive component (LPC) and parietal P300 elicited by memory items were regarded as working memory-specific ERP components. Their amplitudes were directly related to working memory load in both spatial and verbal working memory tasks (Gevins, Cutillo, & Smith, 1995; Gevins et al., 1996; Kusak, Grune, Hagendorf, & Metz, 2000). Given that negative emotion selectively impairs spatial, but not verbal, working memory, we predicted that the frontal LPC and parietal P300 should be modulated by a negative emotional state only in spatial working memory tasks.

Fifteen volunteers (7 females) performed spatial and verbal 2-back tasks. All trials began with a picture, which remained on the screen for 1000 ms, followed by a short interval (varied randomly from 200 to 400 ms). Then a capital letter, serving as target stimulus, was presented for 300 ms. Participants were asked to decide whether the letter was the same or different from that displayed two trials previously (hence, 2-back task). The stimulus sets of verbal and spatial working memory tasks were equivalent, but different instructions were given to the participants before the beginning of each task. In the verbal task, participants were instructed to remember the name of the letter and ignore its location. In the spatial task, the location of the letter was to be remembered (see Figure 7). Half of them were told to press the "v" key with their left index finger for the same stimuli and the "m" key with their right index finger for the different stimuli. The same and different stimuli were in equal proportions. For the other participants, the assignment of the response hand was reversed. If no response was made, the next trial would begin after 1500 ms. Participants were informed that the pictures had nothing to do with their tasks, but they were requested to look at the pictures when they were presented. As general method mentioned, the experiment was divided into two sessions. Each session was composed of one verbal task and one spatial task. Each task contained 4 blocks and each block had 37 trials, resulting in 148 trials in each experimental condition (verbal-negative, spatial-negative, verbal-neutral, and spatial-neutral). All trials in each block were automatically generated and fully randomized by the E-prime program.

The ERP waveforms were epoched into periods of 1200 ms, from 200 ms prior to the onset of target stimuli to 1000 ms post-target stimuli. The following 24 sites were chosen for statistical analysis: FPz, Fz, FCz, AF3, AF4, F1, F2, F5, F6, FC3, FC4, FT7 and FT8 (13 sites for anterior); Pz, POz, Oz, P1, P2, P5, P6, PO3, PO4, TP7 and TP8 (11 sites for posterior). The slow wave component may have separable anterior and posterior subcomponents. Thus the anterior LPC and posterior LPC (we labeled it as P300 in this study) were measured separately in 300-600 and 280-430 ms time window, respectively. Three factors were conducted on ERP components: emotional state (negative/neural), task type (spatial/verbal) and electrode site.

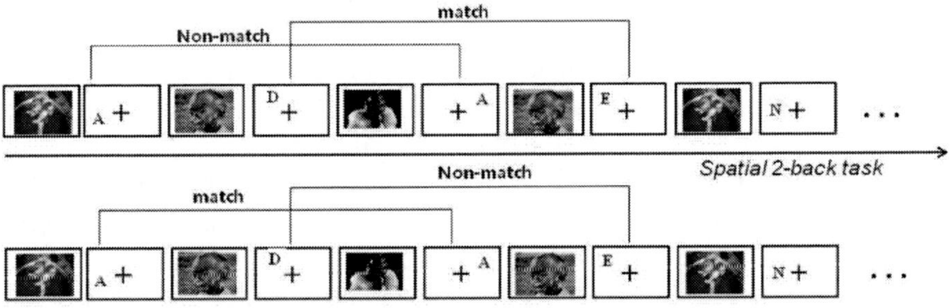

Figure 7. The sequence of events within a single trial of the spatial (upper panel) and the verbal 2-back task (lower panel) in Experiment 1.

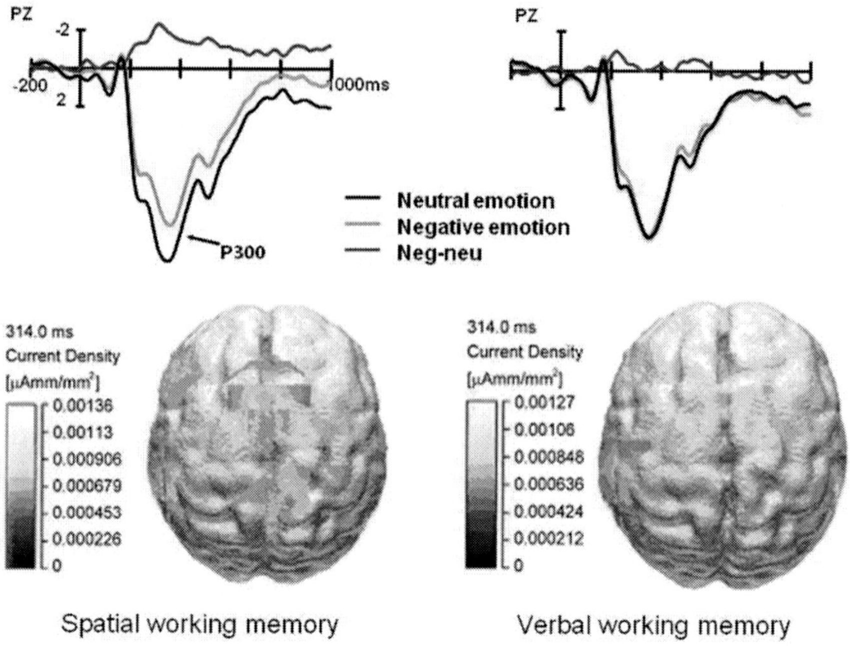

Figure 8. Grand average ERPs in the spatial and verbal tasks, as well as the results of source analsism, in Experiment 1.

Source analysis was performed on the negative emotion minus neutral emotion difference wave, using Curry V4.5 software (Neurosoft, Inc.). After the grand-averaged ERPs were obtained, the standard MRI head image supplied by Curry software and the fiducial landmarks (the left and right preauricular points and the nasion) identified on it were fed into Curry. A computer algorithm was automatically performed in Curry to calculate the best-fit sphere encompassed by the array of electrode sites and to determine their spherical coordinates. The spherical coordinates for each recording site were used for the ERP current density analysis. In the present study, we tentatively reconstructed the distributed sources over the time range of 280-430 ms of difference waves in a three-shell head model using the Low Resolution Electromagnetic Tomography method (LORETA).

Based on the self-report changes in emotion, the pictures induced the expected emotional states. Paired t tests between baseline and post-session PANAS scores were conducted on positive and negative PANAS sub-schedules in all subjects. After the aversive experimental session, the negative PANAS scores increased ($t(14) = 3.66$, $p = 0.03$) and positive PANAS scores decreased significantly ($t(14) = -3.63$, $p = 0.03$). On the other hand, there were no overt changes in sub-schedule scores after the neutral experimental session.

ERP data analysis revealed significant main effects of emotional state ($F(1, 14) = 30.16$, $p = 0.0001$) and task type ($F(1, 14) = 7.3$, $p = 0.02$) on anterior LPC amplitudes. More importantly, there was an overt task type × emotional state interaction ($F(1, 14) = 25.6$, $p = 0.0001$). Further analysis showed that the LPC of negative emotion was smaller than that of neutral emotion in both spatial tasks ($F(1, 14) = 44.7$, $p = 0.0001$) and verbal tasks ($F(1, 14) = 7.2$, $p = 0.018$), and spatial tasks elicited larger LPC than verbal tasks did only in neural emotion ($F(1, 14) = 18.7$, $p = 0.001$).

P300 amplitudes revealed a task type × emotional state interaction ($F(1, 14) = 20.15$, $p = 0.001$). Further analysis showed that in the spatial task, P300 amplitudes in the negative emotion condition were smaller than those in the neutral emotion condition ($F(1, 14) = 16.34$, $p = 0.001$). In contrast, in the verbal task, P300 amplitudes of negative and neutral emotion conditions were nearly the same ($F(1, 14) = 0.009$, $p = 0.93$). In addition, there was a main effect of electrode site ($F(10, 140) = 26.69$, $p < 0.001$). Further analysis indicated that the largest amplitude was recorded on Pz electrode. No significant emotional state and task type main effects were found.

The ERP source analysis was carried out on the grand-averaged difference wave between the negative emotion and neutral emotion to locate its neural generator. The reconstructed results overlaid onto the cortex of standard brain model showed strong current density in the frontal-parietal and temporal cortex in spatial tasks. In verbal tasks, only temporal cortex was activated in the current density mapping (see Figure 8).

The ERP results confirmed our prediction of differential influences of negative emotion on ERP correlates of spatial and verbal working memory. On the one hand, the degree of frontal LPC affected by negative emotion was different in the two types of tasks. On the other hand, the negative emotion selectively decreased parietal P300 of spatial tasks. These results can be interpreted in terms of the reliance of negative emotion and spatial working memory on a common visuospatial attention mechanism. Firstly, the induced negative emotion in the present study may automatically draw partial attentional resources away from tasks themselves and the attentional resources taken up by negative emotion could be no longer available for other cognitive processes (Ellis & Ashbrook, 1987; Huang & Luo, 2006; X. Y. Li et al., 2005; Murphy et al., 1999). Secondly, the attentional resources are distinctly demanded in spatial working memory, but not necessarily demanded in verbal working memory. As suggested by previous studies, the rehearsal of locations in spatial working memory tasks is mediated by covert shifts of attention from one location to the next (Postle et al., 2004). In contrast, the rehearsal of letters in verbal working memory tasks is based primarily on phonological processes (Sakai & Passingham, 2004). Finally, both LPC and P300 are sensitive to the attentional demands of working memory tasks. Their amplitudes are larger when attention is exclusively focused on analyzing the eliciting stimulus, and smaller when attention is consumed by some other mental activity (Gevins et al., 1996; McEvoy, Smith, & Gevins, 1998). On the basis of the three points, it is possible that negative emotion and spatial working memory competed for attentional resources, such that the influence of negative emotion on the LPC and P300 was greater for the spatial than for the verbal task.

The current density analysis found that frontal–parietal regions were more active for spatial trials in comparison to verbal trials under negative emotion. Neuroimaging studies have demonstrated that superior frontal and parietal cortex are critically involved in the control of visuospatial attention (Corbetta, Miezin, Shulman, & Petersen, 1993; Yantis et al., 2002). Activities of these regions reflect increased frontal–parietal network engagement with increased task-related efforts or working memory demands (Rama et al., 1997). Thereby, we assumed that the process of negative emotion limited visuospatial attention resources during the demanding spatial working memory task. Participants had to make greater efforts to accomplish the task. Hence, frontal-parietal regions were activated more. These findings suggest that frontal-parietal attention control cortical areas may play a key role in the interaction of spatial working memory and negative emotion.

The current density mapping results of Experiment 1 suggested that attention resource competition is more possible underlying mechanism of the selective effect than hemisphere asymmetry hypothesis. Hence, based on the former hypothesis that visuospatial attention is a factor that underlies this selective effect, it is argued that the effect should occur mainly during the phase of information retention, but not during the phases of encoding and retrieval in WM. As with long-term memory systems, WM involves three processes: encoding, retention, and retrieval. Encoding is the process of getting information into the memory, and depends on elaboration, which refers to how extensively information is processed at any given depth in the memory. Retrieval is the process of getting information out of the memory, and is influenced by the presence of cues and the nature of the task (e.g., recognition or recall). Much of the interest in retrieval has focused on long-term memory. Retention is the storage of information over time and the representation of information in the memory (Santrock, 2002). Previous studies have found that information representation at retention in WM is type specific, which means that spatial and verbal information representations are linked to different cognitive strategies and neural mechanisms (Mecklinger & Pfeifer, 1996; Sayala, Sala, & Courtney, 2006). As mentioned, the retention of spatial information relies on spatial selective attention and processes in the visuospatial sketchpad, whereas the retention of verbal information depends on articulatory rehearsal and manipulation in the phonological loop (Ruchkin et al., 1997; Ruchkin et al., 1994).

The purpose of Experiment 2 was to further investigate whether negative emotion induced in healthy people is associated with selective impairment in spatial WM compared with verbal WM, and whether the nature of the impairment is consistent with a retention deficit.

Fifteen students (8M7F) performed spatial and verbal delayed matching-to-sample tasks (DMST) that comprised three phases: target, delay, and probe. Distinct brain processing procedures can be separated by the three phases with this paradigm: information encoding in the target phase, information retention in the delay phase, and information retrieval in the probe phase (D'Esposito, Postle, & Rypma, 2000). All of the trials began with a picture, which remained on the screen for 1000 ms, followed by a short interval (which varied randomly from 400 to 600 ms). Three capital letters at random positions around the cross hairs were then presented for 300ms. After a short delay (which varied randomly from 4000 to 4300 ms), a lowercase letter was presented as a probe stimulus for 300 ms, and the position of this lowercase letter was also picked from the possible 12 positions (see Figure 9. The participants were asked to decide whether or not the lowercase letter was congruent with one of the preceding capital letters, and were instructed to try to respond correctly. The stimulus sets of verbal and spatial WM tasks were equivalent, but different instructions were given to the participants before the beginning of each task. In the verbal task, they were instructed to judge whether the name of the letter in the probe phase was the same as or different from the letter in the target phase, and to ignore the letter's location. However, in the spatial task, only the location of the letter, not its name, was to be remembered and judged. Half of the participants were told to press the "V" key with their left index finger for similar stimuli and the "M" key with their right index finger for different stimuli. Similar and different stimuli were presented in equal proportions. For the other half of participants, the assignment of the response hand was reversed. If no response was given, then the next trial began after 1500 ms. The experiment procedure was as described in the general method, and resulted in 72 trials in each experimental condition (negative-verbal WM, negative-spatial WM, neutral-verbal WM, neutral-spatial WM).

The ERP waveforms were time locked to the onset of the target and probe stimuli, respectively. The averaged epoch for the target stimulus-locked ERP was 4400 ms, ranging from 400 ms before the onset of the target stimuli to 4000 ms after the target stimuli. The averaged epoch for the probe stimulus-locked ERP was 1200 ms, which included a 200 ms pre-probe baseline. The following 21 sites were chosen for statistical analysis for both the target stimulus-locked ERP and probe stimulus-locked ERP components: FPz, Fz, FCz, Cz, AF3, AF4, F3, F4, FC3, FC4, C3, and C4 (12 anterior sites); Pz, POz, Oz, P3, P4, PO3, PO4, O1, and O2 (9 posterior sites). For the target stimulus-locked ERP, the early and lately P3b potentials were measured in time windows of 280-450 ms and 330-770 ms separately over the 9 posterior and 12 anterior sites, as they had different scalp distributions. The negative slow wave (NSW) was broadly distributed over the whole scalp, and was measured by all 21 electrodes in a time window of 1000-4000 ms. For the probe stimulus-locked ERP, the early P3b and late P3b components were mainly distributed over the nine posterior electrodes and measured in 230-460 ms and 460-800 ms time windows, respectively. To demonstrate the scalp distribution of the emotional state effects, topographic voltage maps of the difference waves (obtained by subtracting the averaged ERPs of the neutral trials from those of the negative trials) were generated at intervals of 300-600 ms. An ANOVA of each ERP component was conducted with four factors: emotional state (negative/neutral), task type (spatial/verbal), laterality (left/midline/right), and anterior-posterior scalp location (FP/F/FC/C/P/PO/O).

Based on the self-report changes in emotion, the pictures also induced the expected emotional states. There were no significant statistical effects on response times and accuracy of behavior performance.

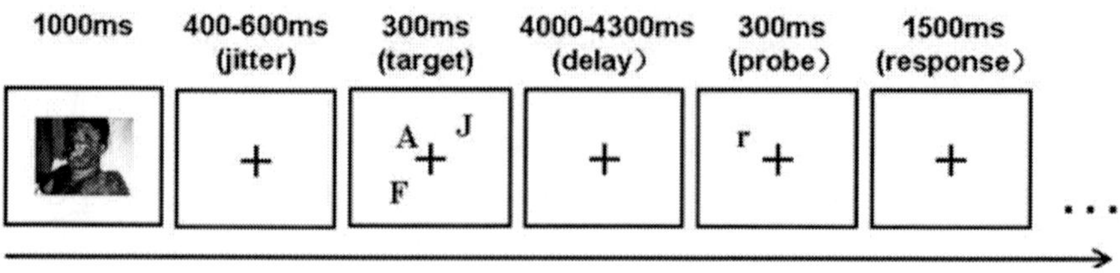

Figure 9. The sequence of events within a single trial of the spatial and the verbal task in Experiment 2.

A four-way ANOVA of the mean amplitudes of early P3b measured at the posterior electrodes revealed significant main effects of emotional state (F(1, 14) = 17.728, p = 0.001), laterality (F(2, 28) = 4.418, p = 0.03), and anterior-posterior electrodes (F(2, 28) = 48.436, p < 0.001). There were also significant interaction effects of emotional state × laterality (F(2, 28) = 4.346, p = 0.037), emotional state × anterior-posterior electrodes (F(2, 28) = 31.231, p < 0.001) and laterality × anterior-posterior electrodes (F(4, 56) = 7.074, p < 0.001). The comparisons of the effects of emotional state at each level of task type, laterality, and anterior-posterior electrodes showed the early P3b amplitudes in the negative emotion condition were smaller than those in the neutral emotion condition for both the spatial and verbal tasks (F(1, 14) = 14.286, p = 0.002; F(1, 14) = 8.2596, p = 0.012). This emotional state effect was larger over the midline and parietal electrodes than over the left-lateral and occipital electrodes (F(1, 14) = 9.452, p = 0.008; F(1, 14) = 75.233, p < 0.001). Overall, early P3b amplitude was largest at the PZ electrode.

An ANOVA of the mean amplitudes of late P3b measured at the anterior electrodes revealed a significant main effect of emotional state (F(1, 14) = 38.151, p < 0.001), a main effect of anterior-posterior electrodes (F(3, 42) = 13.977, p < 0.001), and an interaction effect of task type × emotional state (F(1, 14) = 10.39, p = 0.006). The main effects showed that the amplitude of late P3b in the negative emotion condition was smaller than in the neutral emotion condition for both the spatial and verbal tasks, with the amplitudes increasing along the anterior-posterior dimension and maximal at the central electrodes. The task type × emotional state interaction effect was examined by comparing the effects of emotional state at each level of task type and then comparing the effects of task type at each level of emotional state. The verbal tasks elicited larger late P3b amplitudes than the spatial tasks in the negative emotion condition (F (1, 14) = 9.467, p = 0.008), but not in the neutral emotion condition (F (1, 14) = 0.197, p = 0.664).

Sustained negative slow wave shifts showed condition-related differences over the whole scalp region. The mean amplitudes of the NSW measured at the 21 electrodes indicated an emotional state main effect (F(1, 14) = 3.404, p = 0.086), laterality main effect (F(2, 28) = 3.082, p = 0.062), emotional state × laterality interaction effect (F(2, 28) = 7.169, p = 0.006), and emotional state ×task type interaction effect (F(1, 14) = 17.33, p = 0.001). As with early and late P3b, further analysis of the interaction effects revealed the more important result that spatial tasks in the negative emotion condition elicited a more negative deflection than in the neutral emotion condition (F (1, 14) =13.98, p = 0.002). However, this effect was not observed for the verbal tasks (F (1, 14) =

1.08, p = 0. 317). This emotional state effect was broadly distributed across the whole scalp region, but was relatively larger at the midline electrodes.

There was a significant main effects of emotional state (F (1, 14) = 7.425, p = 0.016), a main effect of task type (F (1, 14) = 14.1, p = 0.002), a main effect of laterality (F (2, 28) = 3.036, p = 0.086), and a main effect of anterior-posterior electrodes (F (2, 28) = 31.918, p < 0.001) for early P3b. No significant interactive effect of emotional state and task type was found. Further analysis found that the probe stimuli in the negative emotion condition elicited a more negative shift than in the neutral emotion condition during an interval of between 230-460 ms, and that the verbal tasks elicited larger amplitudes for early P3b than the spatial tasks. The early P3b amplitudes were relatively larger at the midline and the parietal electrodes.

There were significant main effects of emotional state (F(1, 14) = 3.778, p = 0.072), laterality (F(2, 28) = 7.947, p = 0.002), anterior-posterior electrodes, F(2, 28) = 13.221, p = 0.001), and the emotional state × anterior-posterior electrodes interaction (F(2, 28) = 5.717, p = 0.024). Overall, the late P3b amplitude was larger at the midline and parietal electrodes than at the lateral and occipital electrodes. The emotional state × anterior-posterior electrodes interaction effect was examined by comparing the effects of emotional state at each horizontal axis of electrodes (P/PO/O). Emotional state had a significant effect over the P and PO electrodes (F (1, 14) = 4.854, p = 0.045; F (1, 14) = 5.426, p = 0.035), but not over the O electrodes (F (1, 14) = 0.214, p = 0.651).

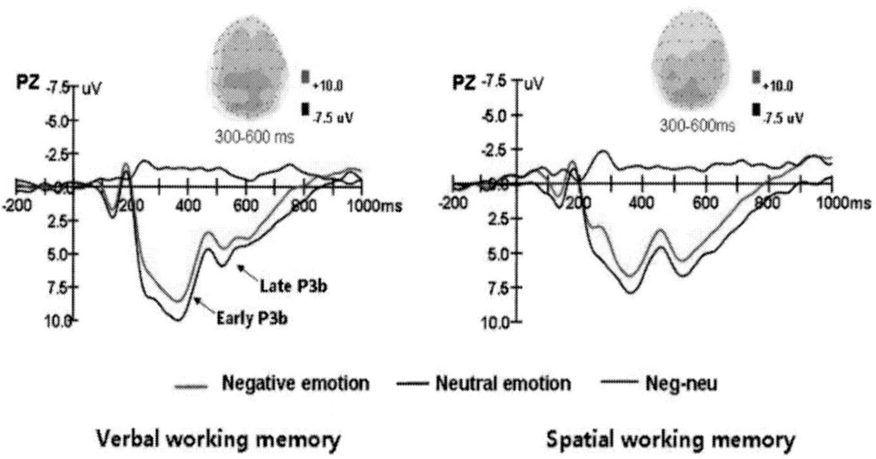

Figure 10. Grand average ERPs in the spatial and verbal tasks in Experiment 2.

The topographic voltage maps of the difference waves revealed that the emotional state effects were mainly distributed over the posterior scalp in both spatial and verbal WM, which is the reason why only the posterior sites were analyzed in the probe phase (see Figure 10).

The aim of this study was to assess whether the nature of the selective impairment is consistent with a retention deficit. We assessed the emotional effects during encoding, retention and retrieval periods of WM and the electrophysiology results give some support to our hypothesis that the selective effect of negative emotion on spatial WM occurs during the period of information retention.

First, the target stimuli-locked early and late P3b potentials showed reduced amplitudes under the negative emotion condition for both the spatial and verbal WM tasks. The P3b peaks, which reached maximum amplitude over the central-parietal region, occurred shortly after the presentation of the target stimuli and several hundred milliseconds before a response was executed. The time course suggests that these signals may reflect encoding and stimulus evaluation processes, rather than activity specifically related to the maintenance of temporary representations in WM. The results suggest that the encoding processes of both spatial and verbal WM are affected by negative emotion. Previous studies have shown that P3b amplitudes are sensitive to the allocation of processing resources, and decrease as the WM load increases. The amplitudes increase when cognitive resources are exclusively focused on analyzing the eliciting stimulus, and decrease when cognitive resources are consumed by other mental activity (Kok, 2001). As aversive information has the ability to draw attention automatically (Huang & Luo, 2006), and the attentional resources taken up by negative emotion may no longer be available for other cognitive processes (Ellis & Ashbrook, 1987), it is obvious from the current results that aversive pictures as exogenous distracters take up more processing resources than neutral pictures. Hence, it is not surprising that the P3b amplitudes for both types of WM task were significantly attenuated under the negative emotion condition.

Second, the most interesting result in this study was the late sustained NSW, which also confirms our hypothesis. The retention-related NSW for the spatial tasks showed a significant negative deflection under the negative emotion condition, but that for the verbal tasks did not, indicating that the induced negative emotion selectively affected the retention function of spatial WM. This may be due to differences in the underlying mechanisms of the maintenance processes of spatial and verbal information in WM. In this experiment, the task required participants to keep the items in mind for a long period. For the spatial tasks, the three locations were probably rehearsed by shifting visual attention from location to location, whereas for the verbal tasks, the relevant information was maintained simply by phonological rehearsal. ERP studies indicate that selective attention is utilized throughout the entire period of active maintenance in spatial WM to keep relevant spatial information in mind (Awh et al., 2000; Awh & Jonides, 2001). In addition, negative stimuli are more capable of capturing attention than neutral stimuli (Huang & Luo, 2006), and the attention taken up by aversive information is known to act as a powerful exogenous cue that can result in the transient involuntary capture of spatial attention and trigger reflexive shifts in spatial attention toward its location (Armony & Dolan, 2002; Egeth & Yantis, 1997). Thus, visuospatial attention may overlap negative emotion and spatial WM, which can lead to affect-induced selective impairment in the retention of spatial information in WM.

Finally, the probe stimuli-locked P3b potentials revealed significant attenuated activity at the posterior poles in the negative emotion condition compared with the neutral emotion condition. In a recent study, Morgan et al. (2008) employed the DMST with faces, and analyzed the ERPs in both the encoding and retrieval phases. In their study, the P3b amplitudes decreased as the WM load increased. It is thought that the P3b amplitude may be suppressed at higher WM loads because the increased cognitive demands of the task leave fewer resources available for stimulus evaluation (Murphy et al., 1999). In this study, the enhanced cognitive demands of the WM tasks in the negative emotion condition left fewer resources for the evaluation of the probe stimulus, and thus the early P3b and late P3b elicited by the probe stimulus were reduced. Both spatial and verbal WM retrieval processes were affected by negative emotion, which is thought to be the consequence of poor encoding processes of both types of WM in the target phase in the negative emotion condition.

According to the self-reported data, the experimental procedure induced a relatively high level of negative emotion. The behavioral data did not show a significant emotional state effect. The absence of an emotional effect is possibly because the negative emotion evoked by the aversive pictures was not sufficiently strong to induce changes in behavioral performance, also possible because the statistical sample is small. Fortunately, the ERP results give more information about the mental activity in emotion-cognition interaction. Both ERP experiments show selective interruption effect between emotional state and memory type, that is, ERP components for spatial working memory are more vulnerable to negative emotion, related to spatial information retention deficit under the negative emotion. The series results also suggest that a common visuospatial attention mechanism underlying anxiety mood and spatial WM plays an important role in this selective effect.

However, the current study was limited by a number of methodological designs. The key issue is that the pictures adopted to induce emotion may have had specific visual interrupt on spatial tasks not on verbal tasks, since pictures themselves were visual stimuli, which challenged the overall hypothesis of the current study. To overcome this challenge, we did additional research using background music to induce emotion. Fifteen participants were exposed in relaxing or horrible background music and performed spatial and verbal n-back task. The methods of first experiment were repeated, including stimuli presentation procedure, ERP recoding and analysis. As expected, the same results as experiment 1 were found on anterior LPC and posterior P300 components, especially, spatial P300 was selectively reduced in horror music background ($F(1, 14) = 12.43$, $p < 0.01$), and this effect wasn't observed for verbal tasks ($F(1, 14) = 0.140$, $p > 0.05$). It can clearly be seen that the selective effect of negative emotion on spatial working memory is stable and not modulated by means of emotion induction (Ouyang, Sun, Li, & Luo, 2010).

In addition, to enable cross-reference with mental disorders, these researches only included negative emotion, which leaves some questions open. Using two emotional states (negative and positive) with two types of WM (spatial and verbal) in a double dissociation design would clarify the relationship between emotion and cognition much better than the single dissociation design. To improve the results, a research including three emotional states (negative, positive and neutral) has been done. The whole experimental methods replicated the experiment 1 too, only positive IAPS was added as another emotional state condition. The ANOVA on anterior LPC and posterior P300 revealed significant interaction effects of emotional state and memory type ($F(2, 38) = 3.414$, $p = 0.046$; $F(2, 38) = 5.861$, $p = 0.006$). Further analysis showed that LPC and P300 amplitudes for spatial trials reduced in both positive and negative emotional states, relative to neutral emotional state. However, these emotion effects were not observed for the verbal trials (X. Li, Ouyang, & Luo, 2010). The result about selective effect of negative emotion on spatial WM was consistent with previous ERP studies. But more interesting result in this study was positive emotion also selectively disturbed the spatial not verbal 2-back tasks. Some studies found positive emotion impaired the performance of the selective attention task, which was interpreted as positive emotion expanded the attention to the surrounding space; therefore the performance of the ongoing task was affected (Rowe, Hirsh, & Anderson, 2007). The other studies believed that attention bias was not only for negative information, but also for positive information. ERP studies on attention bias showed that relative to neutral stimuli, the P2 amplitudes for both positive and negative stimuli increased significantly, which was thought of more attention resource taken up by emotional information. Especially, the late slow waves of positive stimuli were larger than those of negative and neutral stimuli, which was probably because emotion-motivation system played a role and people usually approached the positive emotion (Huang & Luo, 2006). Thereby, pleasing information was also acting as a strong exogenous cue to capture visuo-spatial attention resource just as aversive information. These results gave more supports for attention resource competition hypothesis.

The signal processing technique with low spatial resolution is another limitation. Although source localization techniques have provided some cerebral current activation, the specific cerebral regions involved in processing of emotion-cognition are still questionable. Other neuroimaging methods could be used to more precisely elucidate the involved neural networks. Further studies should investigate cortical contributions to the interaction of negative emotion and working memory and clarify the mechanisms implicated in specific interaction effect. Besides, emotional state is produced by the interaction between individual personality and environment stimulation (Endler & Parker, 1990). Without considering the trait personality, the induced emotional state is considerably unstable. Further studies should also more focus on trait personality, such as trait anxiety and trait depression, which not only betters our understanding of the relationship between emotion and cognition, but also provides the corresponding theoretical basis for anxiety, depression and other mood disorder diagnosis, treatment and intervention.

3. Anxiety and Outcome Evaluation

It has been noted that anxiety affects a variety of cognitive function (Paulus et al., 2004). High-anxious people not only selectively attend to threatening stimuli (Mansell, 2004), but also show some distinctive behavioral tendencies when complex cognitive ability is required. Notably, in decision-making studies, higher levels of (state or trait) anxiety are positively correlated with risk-avoidance. In other words, high-anxious people prefer to avoid risky choices when involved in decision-making tasks (Eisenberg et al., 1998; Miu, Heilman, & Houser, 2008; Wray & Stone, 2005).

To explain the risk-avoidant tendency in high-anxious decision makers, many researchers pay close attention to the relationship between anxiety and the outcome evaluation. Considered the last stage of decision making, the process of outcome evaluation prominently influences future behavior, since choice is always dependent on previous outcomes associated with each alternative (Paulus, 2005; Platt, 2002). According to some researchers, anxious individuals are inclined to feel that negative outcomes are extremely unpleasant. For instance, Mitte (2007) asked participants to choose between different scenarios and found that the subjective cost of negative events increased in concert with trait anxiety score. Taking this a step further, researchers argue that this is the reason why the correlation between the level of anxiety and risk-avoidant tendency is significant (Eisenberg et al., 1998; Maner et al., 2007; Maner & Schmidt, 2006). If that is the case, this phenomenon strongly suggests that the influence of anxiety on the cognitive process is not limited to threat-related stimuli. Rather, anxious people might be overreacting to broadly "negative" information – namely, outcomes that indicate monetary loss.

As an alternative, some researchers emphasize the importance of outcome expectation when investigating this issue. According to their studies, higher levels of anxiety are associated with the expectancy of a more negative outcome in risk-taking tasks (Mitte, 2007; Shepperd, Grace, Cole, & Klein, 2005), and that explains why these subjects were risk-avoidant (Eisenberg et al., 1998; Lauriola & Levin, 2001). This interpretation is also reasonable, since it has been suggested that anxious people are more pessimistic when asked to predict their own future, compared to other person's future (Wray & Stone, 2005). Apparently, it is unnecessary to make an either-or choice between these two theories. Both outcome expectation and outcome evaluation might play important roles in the relationship between anxiety and risk-avoidance.

Nevertheless, it is worth noting that most data in this field came from subjective self-reports. This kind of report is retrospective and might be tied only loosely to the participants' real thoughts during the task (Hajcak, Moser, Holroyd, & Simons, 2007). This point is particularly worth noting when we realize that anxiety strongly influences memory (Reidy & Richards, 1997). In that case, when investigating the process of outcome evaluation (as well as outcome expectation), the validity of retrospective self-reports might be doubtful. We argue that if researchers only rely on self-report in their studies, they would be not able to confirm whether there is really a relationship between anxiety and outcome evaluation (as well as outcome expectation) during risk-taking tasks. Neuroscience technique might be necessary to clarify matters.

Event-related potential (ERP) research has been a non-invasive tool to investigate brain activity. Most critically, it allows us to observe event processing in real-time (Lust & Bartholow, 2009). Thus, it has been noted that ERP studies may provide valuable insights into the nature of outcome evaluation (Yeung, Holroyd, & Cohen, 2005). Among a number of ERP components, feedback-related negativity (FRN) might be most suitable for our research. FRN, also known as medial frontal negativity (MFN; Miltner, Braun, & Coles, 1997), feedback negativity (FN; Yeung & Sanfey, 2004), or feedback error-related negativity (fERN; Holroyd, Coles, & Nieuwenhuis, 2002), is a negative-going component spanning the interval between 200 and 300 ms after the onset of feedback stimuli. It has been confirmed that the FRN becomes larger after losses than after gains in monetary decision-making tasks; this indicates the FRN amplitude is sensitive to the economic valence of outcome (Gehring & Willoughby, 2002; Holroyd, Hajcak, & Larsen, 2006; Yeung & Sanfey, 2004). Accordingly, the FRN amplitude discriminates between favorable and unfavorable outcomes (Nieuwenhuis, Holroyd, Mol, & Coles, 2004).

The purpose of Experiment 1 was to examine if anxious people evaluate negative outcomes disproportionately during decision-making task. A variant of Gehring & Willoughby (2002)'s monetary gambling task was adopted to accommodate an ERP paradigm. In this simple task, which has been shown to consistently elicit FRN, participants were asked to gamble for rewards, and their choices were followed by feedback events. The FRN was used as an objective measure of outcome evaluation process during the task. We hypothesized that the FRN amplitude would be significantly higher for high-anxious participants than low-anxious participants after they received negative outcomes in the task.

33 college students (19 females; mean age = 23.61 ± 1.85 years) participated in the Experiment 1. First, they were asked to fulfill the Chinese version of the trait-anxiety scale from Spielberger's State-Trait Anxiety Inventory (STAI-T), which has demonstrated good internal consistency as well as convergent and discriminant validity (Shek, 1993; Spielberger et al., 1983). According to their score, participants were assigned to the high-trait anxiety (HTA) group (16 persons, 8 females) and low-trait anxiety (LTA) group (17 persons, 11 females), respectively. Pairwise t test showed that the two groups differed significantly in trait anxious scores (58.31 vs. 30.18, $p<0.001$).

Thereafter, participants were involved in a simple monetary gambling task, in which they were asked to try their best to maximize the total score. The higher the score they earned, the more bonus money they would receive at the end of the experiment. For each trial, participants could select one of two alternatives ("5" or "25") to "gamble". The outcome of their choice would then appear on the screen for 1500 milliseconds. If participants get a positive outcome in the current trial (indicated by the "+" symbol), 5 or 25 points (depended on their own choice) would be added to the total score amount; otherwise if they receive a negative outcome (indicated by the "-" symbol), participants would lose 5 or 25 points accordingly. Thus, we defined the choice of "5" as the risk-avoidant choice, predicting that participants would make this choice to avoid the possibility of a large loss ("-25"). However, by making this choice, they also gave up the opportunity to receive the larger reward ("+25"). In contrast, the choice of "25" was defined as the risky choice.

Aside from the positive and negative outcomes, participants might instead receive an "ambiguous outcome" (indicated by the "?" symbol) as well. The probability of receiving positive, negative, or ambiguous outcomes on any given trial was equal (1/3). Before the experiment, the participants were told that the ambiguous outcome was an uninformative outcome of which the valence could be positive or negative. They were asked to guess whether they won or lost in this trial (in fact, the computer counted the "?" as zero score).

Figure 12 (left panels) illustrates the ERP waveforms obtained in Experiment 1 when participants received different kinds of outcomes. The FRN was measured as the maximal negative difference wave, using the ERPs in the condition of positive outcomes as "baseline" (Hajcak et al., 2007; Holroyd, Baker, Kerns, & Muller, 2008; Holroyd & Krigolson, 2007). Following the methods of Holroyd & Krigolson (2007), we created difference waves by subtracting the ERPs on positive outcome trials from the ERPs on negative outcome trials or ambiguous outcome trials. In agreement with previous studies (Gehring & Willoughby, 2002; Yeung et al., 2005), we observed the classic FRN when ERPs were evoked by the presentation of outcome stimuli. The highest peak of the FRN appeared around 300 ms at the FCz electrode site. Thus, the following analysis focused on this electrode. Differences in amplitude were significant between negative and ambiguous trials (negative: -6.21 μV; ambiguous: -10.85 μV).

Most interestingly, we found out that there was a reliable main effect of trait anxiety group on the amplitude of negative-positive difference wave, indicating that the FRN elicited by negative outcomes was significantly larger in the LTA group (-8.06 V) than in the HTA group (-4.21 μV). This phenomenon contradicted our initial hypothesis. In comparison, the ambiguous-positive difference wave did not reveal any intergroup difference.

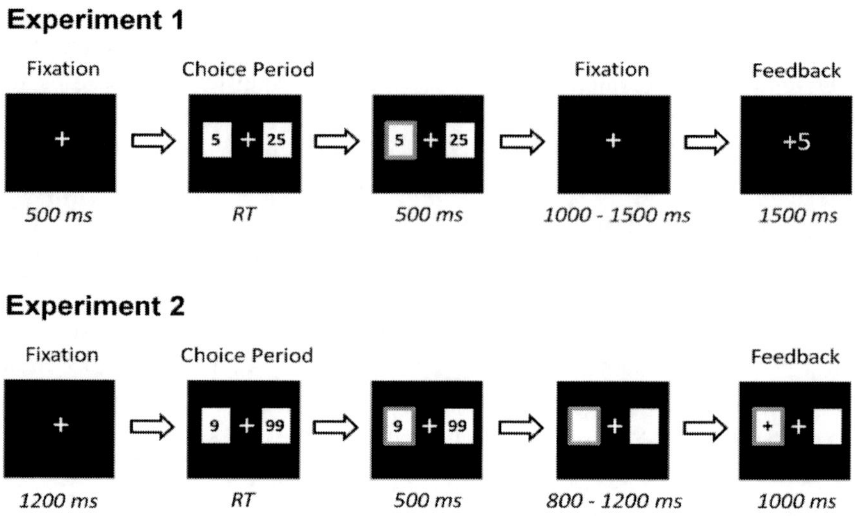

Figure 11. The sequence of events within a single trial of the monetary gambling task, applied in the Experiment 1 (upper panel), and Experiment 2 (lower panel).

The ERP results linked with negative outcomes were inconsistent with our prediction. Since the FRN elicited by negative outcomes were larger in LTA group than HTA group, one might speculate that LTA people, compared to HTA people, evaluate the negative outcome as particularly bad. However, this appears somewhat unlikely, since previous studies do not support this interpretation (Maner et al., 2007; Maner & Schmidt, 2006; Mitte, 2007; Miu et al., 2008). As an alternative, we suggest that these results reflect a difference in expected rather than actual outcome evaluation.

According to researchers, the FRN amplitude depends on the relationship between the actual vs. the expected outcome. That is, the binary evaluation of outcome, indexed by the FRN, is based on the comparison between expectation and actual outcome (Hajcak, Holroyd, Moser, & Simons, 2005; Hajcak, Moser, Holroyd, & Simons, 2006; Nieuwenhuis et al., 2004). For instance, the FRN has been found to be greater for unexpected negative outcomes than expected ones (Bellebaum & Daum, 2008; Hajcak et al., 2007; Yasuda, Sato, Miyawaki, Kumano, & Kuboki, 2004). Hence, it might be the case that HTA participants were more pessimistic than LTA participants when predicting the outcome of their choice. As a result, HTA participants' expectation was much closer to negative outcome compared with LTA participants, indicating by a smaller FRN. This explanation harmonizes previous research that emphasizes the outcome expectation as an important factor in the relationship between anxiety and risk-avoidance (see above).

Also of interest, the FRN elicited by ambiguous outcomes was not significantly different between the LTA and HTA groups. Previous studies have shown that high levels of anxiety are associated with an increased likelihood of negative interpretation of ambiguous stimuli, such as facial expression and lexical information (Bensi & Giusberti, 2007; Blanchette & Richards, 2003; Kverno, 2000; Richards et al., 2002). In our opinion, anxious people are more likely to hold negative interpretation of ambiguous information. Therefore, it is reasonable to expect a larger FRN in the HTA group in the ambiguous outcome condition. Nevertheless, the ERP results in Experiment 1 were surprising.

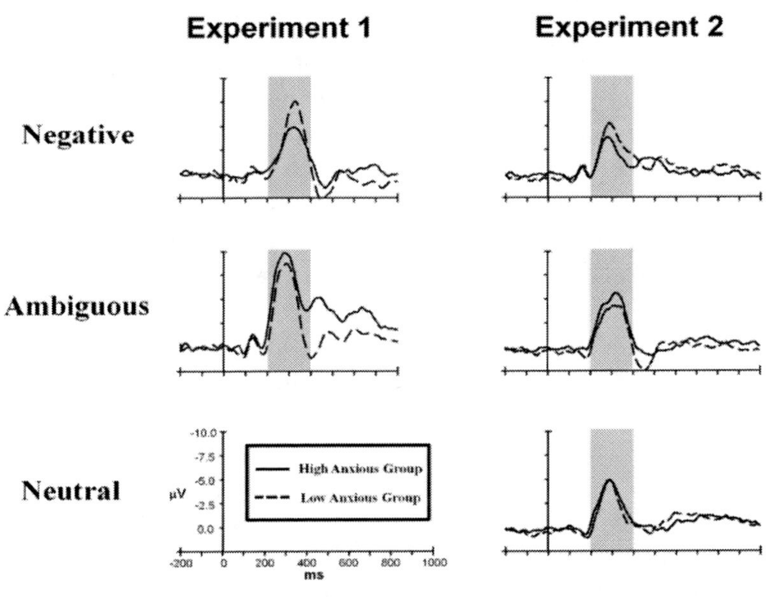

Figure 12. Grand-average ERP difference waves evoked by the presentation of feedback at the FCz recording site, where the FRN reaches its maximum in both experiments. The gray shaded areas indicate the 200–400ms analysis window in which the FRN was quantified. Negative, ambiguous, neutral: valence of the outcome.

Since there was significant difference between the FRN elicited by negative outcomes and that elicited by ambiguous outcomes, we suspected that when we encouraged participants to guess the valence of ambiguous outcomes, the FRN might be intensely influenced by the activity of guessing, and the impact of anxiety on outcome evaluation would be harder to observe in this situation. In other words, the FRN following ambiguous outcomes might be a complex component that reflects guessing and evaluating activity at the same time. Otherwise, if the FRN in this condition was the same with classic research, it should not be larger than that following negative outcomes (Holroyd et al., 2006).

Our interpretation is supported by a study focus on neuroticism. Recently, Hirsh & Inzlicht (2008) reported that uncertain feedback elicited a larger FRN in neurotic individuals compared to non-neurotic individuals. It is worth noting that they did not ask the participants to guess the meaning of uncertain outcomes. Neuroticism is defined as a predisposition toward many kinds of negative affective states, including depression, anxiety, anger, and shame (Miller & Pilkonis, 2006). In light of this discovery, we speculate that the influence of anxiety on ambiguous outcome evaluation should be reflected on the amplitude of FRN, if we could reduce the impact of guessing activity.

Accordingly, we modified the task paradigm and conducted Experiment 2 to determine whether anxious people are more prone to assign negative value to ambiguous outcome during decision-making tasks. Consistent with Experiment 1, the FRN was used to measure the evaluation of different kinds of outcomes. We expected that the impact of anxiety would be significant in both the FRN elicited by negative outcomes and that elicited by ambiguous outcomes. Meanwhile, there should be no intergroup difference in the FRN elicited by neutral outcomes.

34 college students (20 females; mean age = 20.53 ± 2.15 years) participated in the Experiment 2. According to their STAI-T score, participants were assigned to the HTA group (17 persons, 6 females) and LTA group (17 persons, 8 females), respectively. Pairwise t test showed that the two groups differed significantly in trait anxious scores (56.59 vs. 35.29, $p < 0.001$).

The task applied in Experiment 2 was the same with Experiment 1 except for following details (see also Figure 11): (1) participants were told that it was impossible to guess the real valence of ambiguous outcome, so as to exclude the potential impact of guessing activity; (2) the risk-avoidant option and risky the option were changed to "9" and "99" respectively, so as to enlarge the difference between options; (3) since it has been reported that the FRN amplitude is indifferent to outcome magnitude (Holroyd et al., 2006; A. Sato et al., 2005; Yeung & Sanfey, 2004), the way of outcome presentation was changed, so as to highlight the outcome valence; (4) the length of stimulus presentation and interval was slightly changed, so as to increase the number of trials; (5) the neutral outcome was added into the task, so as to compare the evaluation of ambiguous outcome and neutral outcome. Accordingly, there were four kinds of possible outcomes in Experiment 2: "+" (positive), "–" (negative), "*" (ambiguous), and "0" (neutral).

Consistent with Experiment 1, the FRN amplitude was measured as the difference wave between conditions following outcome presentation at the electrode cite with the greatest value (FCz). ANOVA test indicated that there was no significantly difference in the amplitude when we compared three kinds of ERP difference waves (negative-positive, ambiguous-positive, and neutral-positive). The valence x group interaction was significant. Following analysis on this interaction revealed a reliable group effect on the "negative–positive" difference wave, indicating that the FRN elicited by negative outcomes was significantly higher in the LTA group (−7.04 μV) than in the HTA group (−5.10 μV). In contrast, we found that the "ambiguous–positive" difference wave was significantly smaller in LTA group than HTA group (−5.91 μV vs. −7.83 μV). Nevertheless, the group factor did not significantly affect the amplitude of the "neutral–positive" difference wave (−6.20 μV vs. −6.96 μV).

In addition, we separated the sample into HTA group and LTA group and used paired-samples t test to compare the "negative–positive" and "ambiguous–positive" difference wave in both groups. In the HTA group, the "negative–positive" difference wave was significantly smaller than the "ambiguous–positive" one (−4.4 μV vs.−7.5 μV). However, the opposite was true in the LTA group: the 'negative–positive" difference wave was larger than the "ambiguous–positive" one (−6.7 μV vs.−5.3 μV). Recall that the FRN is a negative-going component (i.e. a larger value of amplitude indicates a smaller FRN).

Consistent with Experiment 1, the FRN following negative outcomes was larger in the LTA group than the HTA group. More importantly, the FRN following ambiguous outcomes was significantly smaller in the LTA group than the HTA group, which was different from the results of Experiment 1. We suggest that our methods successfully controlled the influence of guessing in Experiment 2. The FRN following ambiguous outcomes revealed significant difference between groups, indicating that anxiety plays a crucial role in the evaluation of ambiguous outcomes. HTA participants might evaluate ambiguous outcome as negative information, which was even worse than negative outcomes. In contrast, LTA participants evaluate ambiguous outcome as better than negative ones. This viewpoint is supported by the result of comparison of FRN between conditions.

To the best of our knowledge, Experiment 2 is the first study that reports the relationship between level of anxiety and the interpretation of ambiguous outcome in a decision-making task. In previous studies, though it is widely accepted that HTA individuals show increased sensitivity to ambiguous information, most of the results are from attentional studies (e.g. face recognition) (Paulus et al., 2004; Richards et al., 2002). In contrast, the effect of anxiety in the processing of more abstract stimuli has received relatively little attention. In our study, however, the ERP results indicate that anxious people would overreact to not only evolutionary "primary" stimuli, but also stimuli that exist as an idea rather than physical reality (such as stimuli that indicate economic loss). In our opinion, this discovery is related to the finding that the processing of "primary reward" (i.e. food) and that of monetary incentive might located in the same brain region (De Martino, Kumaran, Holt, & Dolan, 2009; Fellows, 2004). This idea is described by Knutson & Bossaerts (2007) in the following way: "humans may use the same neural machinery to surf the stock exchange that they once used to scavenge the savannah."

As an alternative explanation, we shall be aware of the possibility that the intergroup difference in the FRN amplitude did not really have anything to do with the processing of outcome evaluation. In other words, the underlying cognitive function of the FRN might be different from what we had presumed. This explanation might be considered unlikely at the first glance, since the relationship between the FRN amplitude and the binary evaluation of outcomes has been confirmed in the literature (Hajcak et al., 2007; Holroyd & Krigolson, 2007; Polezzi, Sartori, Rumiati, Vidotto, & Daum, 2010; Simons, 2010; Zhou, Yu, & Zhou, 2010). However, our recent studies imply that the cognitive function indicated by the FRN might be different from the classic theory. For instance, we found that when the expected reward (modulated by reward cue) was "0", the high impulsive participants showed larger FRN in response to correct feedback compared with incorrect feedback (manuscript under preparation). The classical RL-ERN theory might not be suitable to explain this phenomenon. Thereby, we call for more studies on the relationship between FRN and different personality types, which may help examine the brain mechanism that generates the FRN.

In conclusion, our studies find that in the decision-making task, the FRN waveforms following negative outcomes (as well as ambiguous outcomes) for HTA and LTA individuals differ significantly. These results indicate that high-anxious people are more likely to (1) hold pessimistic expectation when predicting the outcome of their choice; (2) assign very negative value to the ambiguous outcomes, while guessing or other activity might modulate such negative effect under ambiguity or uncertainty (Gu, Ge, Jiang, & Luo, 2010; Gu, Huang, & Luo, 2010). Further studies in these issues would certainly help us understanding the underlying features of anxiety, and thus prove beneficial to both clinical and nonclinical research.

ACKNOWLEDGMENT

The studies in the chapter are supported by Ministry of Sci & Tech (973 Program, 2011CB711000), the National Natural Science Foundation of China (30930031; 30800298; 30900441), National Key Technologies R&D Program (2009BAI77B01), Global Research Initiative Program, United States National Institute of Health grants (1R01TW007897; P50DA05312), Research Initiation Fund of the Institute of Psychology of the Chinese Academy of Sciences (O9CX083008), and the Fundamental Research Funds for the Central Universities (2009SAP-8).

REFERENCES

Abele, A. (1986). Functions of Gaze in Social-Interaction - Communication and Monitoring. *Journal of Nonverbal Behavior, 10*(2), 83-101.

Albert, M., Gilles, R., Fernando, P. D., Robert, S., Stéphanie, D., Roland, J., & Antoine, P. (2010). Gaze avoidance in social phobia: Objective measure and correlates. *Behaviour Research and Therapy,* 48, 147–151.

Armony, J. L., & Dolan, R. J. (2002). Modulation of spatial attention by fear-conditioned stimuli: an event-related fMRI study. *Neuropsychologia, 40*(7), 817-826.

Aron, A. R., Durston, S., Eagle, D. M., Logan, G. D., Stinear, C. M., & Stuphorn, V. (2007). Converging evidence for a fronto-basal-ganglia network for inhibitory control of action and cognition. *Journal of Neuroscience, 27*(44), 11860-11864.

Awh, E., Anllo-Vento, L., & Hillyard, S. A. (2000). The role of spatial selective attention in working memory for locations: Evidence from event-related potentials. *Journal of Cognitive Neuroscience, 12*(5), 840-847.

Awh, E., & Jonides, J. (2001). Overlapping mechanisms of attention and spatial working memory. *Trends in Cognitive Sciences, 5*(3), 119-126.

Baddeley, A. (1992). Working Memory. *Science, 255*(5044), 556-559.

Bar-Haim, Y., Lamy, D., & Glickman, S. (2005). Attentional bias in anxiety: A behavioral and ERP study. *Brain and Cognition, 59*(1), 11-22.

Bar-Haim, Y., Lamy, D., Pergamin, L., Bakermans-Kranenburg, M. J., & van IJzendoorn, M. H. (2007). Threat-related attentional bias in anxious and nonanxious individuals: A meta-analytic study. *Psychological Bulletin, 133*(1), 1-24.

Bekker, H. L., Legare, F., Stacey, D., O'Connor, A., & Lemyre, L. (2003). Is anxiety a suitable measure of decision aid effectiveness: a systematic review? *Patient Education and Counseling, 50*(3), 255-262.

Bellebaum, C., & Daum, I. (2008). Learning-related changes in reward expectancy are reflected in the feedback-related negativity. *European Journal of Neuroscience, 27*(7), 1823-1835.

Bensi, L., & Giusberti, F. (2007). Trait anxiety and reasoning under uncertainty. *Personality and Individual Differences, 43*(4), 827-838.

Blanchette, I., & Richards, A. (2003). Anxiety and the interpretation of ambiguous information: Beyond the emotion-congruent effect. *Journal of Experimental Psychology-General, 132*(2), 294-309.

Breiter, H. C., Etcoff, N. L., Whalen, P. J., Kennedy, W. A., Rauch, S. L., Buckner, R. L., et al. (1996). Response and habituation of the human amygdala during visual processing of facial expression. *Neuron, 17*(5), 875-887.

Buchsbaum, B. R., Olsen, R. K., Koch, P., & Berman, K. F. (2005). Human dorsal and ventral auditory streams subserve rehearsal-based and echoic processes during verbal working memory. *Neuron, 48*(4), 687-697.

Cabeza, R., & Nyberg, L. (1997). Imaging cognition: An empirical review of PET studies with normal subjects. *Journal of Cognitive Neuroscience, 9*(1), 1-26.

Cacioppo, J. T., Gardner, W. L., & Berntson, G. G. (1999). The affect system has parallel and integrative processing components: Form follows function. *Journal of Personality and Social Psychology, 76*(5), 839-855.

Chiu, P. H., Holmes, A. J., & Pizzagalli, D. A. (2008). Dissociable recruitment of rostral anterior cingulate and inferior frontal cortex in emotional response inhibition. *Psychophysiology, 45*, S115-S116.

Clark, D. M., & Wells, A. (1995). A cognitive model of social phobia. In David M. Clark, Richard G. Heimberg, Michael R. Liebowitz & D. A. Hope (Eds.), *Social Phobia: Diagnosis, Assessment, and Treatment* (pp. 69-93). New York: Guilford Press.

Corbetta, M., Miezin, F. M., Shulman, G. L., & Petersen, S. E. (1993). A Pet Study of Visuospatial Attention. *Journal of Neuroscience, 13*(3), 1202-1226.

D'Esposito, M., Postle, B. R., & Rypma, B. (2000). Prefrontal cortical contributions to working memory: evidence from event-related fMRI studies. *Experimental Brain Research, 133*(1), 3-11.

De Martino, B., Kumaran, D., Holt, B., & Dolan, R. J. (2009). The Neurobiology of Reference-Dependent Value Computation. *Journal of Neuroscience, 29*(12), 3833-3842.

Dillon, D. G., & Pizzagalli, D. A. (2007). Inhibition of action, thought, and emotion: A selective neurobiological review. *Applied & Preventive Psychology, 12*(3), 99-114.

Dimberg, U., & Thunberg, M. (2007). Speech anxiety and rapid emotional reactions to angry and happy facial expressions. *Scandinavian Journal of Psychology, 48*(4), 321-328.

Drevets, W. C., Price, J. L., Simpson, J. R., Todd, R. D., Reich, T., Vannier, M., et al. (1997). Subgenual prefrontal cortex abnormalities in mood disorders. *Nature, 386*(6627), 824-827.

Egeth, H. E., & Yantis, S. (1997). Visual attention: control, representation, and time course. *Annu Rev Psychol, 48*, 269-297.

Eisenberg, A. E., Baron, J., & Seligman, M. E. P. (1998). Individual difference in risk aversion and anxiety. *Psychological Bulletin, 87*, 245-251.

Ellis, H. C., & Ashbrook, P. W. (1987). Resource allocation model of the effects of depressed mood states. In K. Fiedler & J. Forgas (Eds.), *Affect cognition social behavior*. Toronto: Hogrefe.

Endler, N. S., & Parker, J. D. A. (1990). Stress and Anxiety - Conceptual and Assessment Issues. *Stress Medicine, 6*(3), 243-248.

Eysenck, M. W. (1979). Anxiety, Learning, and Memory - Reconceptualization. *Journal of Research in Personality, 13*(4), 363-385.

Eysenck, M. W., & Calvo, M. G. (1992). Anxiety and Performance - the Processing Efficiency Theory. *Cognition & Emotion, 6*(6), 409-434.

Eysenck, M. W., Derakshan, N., Santos, R., & Calvo, M. G. (2007). Anxiety and cognitive performance: Attentional control theory. *Emotion, 7*(2), 336-353.

Falkenstein, M., Hohnsbein, J., & Hoormann, J. (1999). ERP components after motor errors: description, variation and functional significance. *International Journal of Psychophysiology, 33*(1), 43-43.

Fallgatter, A. J., Bartsch, A. J., & Herrmann, M. J. (2002). Electro physiological measurements of anterior cingulate function. *Journal of Neural Transmission, 109*(5-6), 977-988.

Fellows, L. K. (2004). The cognitive neuroscience of human decision making: a review and conceptual framework. *Behav Cogn Neurosci Rev, 3*(3), 159-172.

Fox, E. (2002). Processing emotional facial expressions: the role of anxiety and awareness. *Cogn Affect Behav Neurosci, 2*(1), 52-63.

Fox, E., Russo, R., Bowles, R., & Dutton, K. (2001). Do threatening stimuli draw or hold visual attention in subclinical anxiety? *Journal of Experimental Psychology-General, 130*(4), 681-700.

Fuster, J.M. (1997). The prefrontal cortex : anatomy, physiology, and neuropsychology of the frontal lobe, Lippincott-Raven, Philadelphia, xvi, 333 p. pp.

Garner, M. J., Baldwin, D. S., Bradley, B. P., & Mogg, K. (2006). Impaired recognition of fearful faces in generalized social phobia. *European Neuropsychopharmacology, 16*, S457-S457.

Gehring, W. J., & Willoughby, A. R. (2002). The medial frontal cortex and the rapid processing of monetary gains and losses. *Science, 295*(5563), 2279-2282.

Gevins, A., Cutillo, B., & Smith, M. E. (1995). Regional Modulation of High-Resolution Evoked-Potentials during Verbal and Nonverbal Matching Tasks. *Electroencephalography and Clinical Neurophysiology, 94*(2), 129-147.

Gevins, A., Smith, M. E., Le, J., Leong, H., Bennett, J., Martin, N., et al. (1996). High resolution evoked potential imaging of the cortical dynamics of human working memory. *Electroencephalography and Clinical Neurophysiology, 98*(4), 327-348.

Goldin, P. R., Manber-Ball, T., Werner, K., Heimberg, R., & Gross, J. J. (2009). Neural Mechanisms of Cognitive Reappraisal of Negative Self-Beliefs in Social Anxiety Disorder. *Biological Psychiatry, 66*(12), 1091-1099.

Gray, J. R. (2001). Emotional modulation of cognitive control: Approach-withdrawal states double-dissociate spatial from verbal two-back task performance. *Journal of Experimental Psychology-General, 130*(3), 436-452.

Gray, J. R., Braver, T. S., & Raichle, M. E. (2002). Integration of emotion and cognition in the lateral prefrontal cortex. *Proceedings of the National Academy of Sciences of the United States of America, 99*(6), 4115-4120.

Gu, Ge, Y., Jiang, Y., & Luo, Y.-j. (2010). Anxiety and Outcome Evaluation: The Good, the Bad and the Ambiguous. *Biological Psychology, 85*(2), 200-206.

Gu, Huang, Y. X., & Luo, Y. J. (2010). Anxiety and feedback negativity. *Psychophysiology, 47*(5), 961-967.

Hajcak, G., Holroyd, C. B., Moser, J. S., & Simons, R. F. (2005). Brain potentials associated with expected and unexpected good and bad outcomes. *Psychophysiology, 42*(2), 161-170.

Hajcak, G., Moser, J. S., Holroyd, C. B., & Simons, R. F. (2006). The feedback-related negativity reflects the binary evaluation of good versus bad outcomes. *Biological Psychology, 71*(2), 148-154.

Hajcak, G., Moser, J. S., Holroyd, C. B., & Simons, R. F. (2007). It's worse than you thought: The feedback negativity and violations of reward prediction in gambling tasks. *Psychophysiology, 44*(6), 905-912.

Heinze, H. J., Luck, S. J., Munte, T. F., Gos, A., Mangun, G. R., & Hillyard, S. A. (1994). Attention to Adjacent and Separate Positions in-Space - an Electrophysiological Analysis. *Perception & Psychophysics, 56*(1), 42-52.

Heller, W., & Nitschke, J. B. (1997). Regional brain activity in emotion: A framework for understanding cognition in depression. *Cognition & Emotion, 11*(5-6), 637-661.

Hirsh, J. B., & Inzlicht, M. (2008). The Devil You Know: Neuroticism Predicts Neural Response to Uncertainty. *Psychological Science, 19*(10), 962-967.

Holroyd, C. B., Baker, T. E., Kerns, K. A., & Muller, U. (2008). Electrophysiological evidence of atypical motivation and reward processing in children with attention-deficit hyperactivity disorder. *Neuropsychologia, 46*(8), 2234-2242.

Holroyd, C. B., Coles, M. G. H., & Nieuwenhuis, S. (2002). Medial prefrontal cortex and error potentials. *Science, 296*(5573), 1610-1611.

Holroyd, C. B., Hajcak, G., & Larsen, J. T. (2006). The good, the bad and the neutral: Electrophysiological responses to feedback stimuli. *Brain Research, 1105*, 93-101.

Holroyd, C. B., & Krigolson, O. E. (2007). Reward prediction error signals associated with a modified time estimation task. *Psychophysiology, 44*(6), 913-917.

Horley, K., Williams, L. M., Gonsalvez, C., & Gordon, E. (2004). Face to face: visual scanpath evidence for abnormal processing of facial expressions in social phobia. *Psychiatry Research, 127*(1-2), 43-53.

Huang, Y. X., Bai, L., Ai, H., Li, W., Yua, C., Liu, J., et al. (2009). Influence of trait-anxiety on inhibition function: Evidence from ERPs study. *Neuroscience Letters, 456*(1), 1-5.

Huang, Y. X., & Luo, Y. J. (2006). Temporal course of emotional negativity bias: An ERP study. *Neuroscience Letters, 398*(1-2), 91-96.

Ikeda, M., Iwanaga, M., & Seiwa, H. (1996). Test anxiety and working memory system. *Perceptual and Motor Skills, 82*(3), 1223-1231.

Ilan, A. B., & Polich, J. (1999). P300 and response time from a manual Stroop task. *Clinical Neurophysiology, 110*(2), 367-373.

Kleinke, C. L. (1986). Gaze and Eye Contact - a Research Review. *Psychological Bulletin, 100*(1), 78-100.

Knutson, B., & Bossaerts, P. (2007). Neural antecedents of financial decisions. *Journal of Neuroscience, 27*(31), 8174-8177.

Kok, A. (2001). On the utility of P3 amplitude as a measure of processing capacity. *Psychophysiology, 38*(3), 557-577.

Kusak, G., Grune, K., Hagendorf, H., & Metz, A. M. (2000). Updating of working memory in a running memory task: an event-related potential study. *International Journal of Psychophysiology, 39*(1), 51-65.

Kverno, K. S. (2000). Trait anxiety influences on judgments of frequency and recall. *Personality and Individual Differences, 29*(3), 395-404.

Lane, R. D., Reiman, E. M., Bradley, M. M., Lang, P. J., Ahern, G. L., Davidson, R. J., et al. (1997). Neuroanatomical correlates of pleasant and unpleasant emotion. *Neuropsychologia, 35*(11), 1437-1444.

Lang, P. J., Bradley, M. M., & Cuthbert, B. N. (2008). *International affective picture system (IAPS): Affective ratings of pictures and instruction manual* (Technical Report A-8). Gainesville, FL: University of Floridao. Document Number)

Lauriola, M., & Levin, I. P. (2001). Personality traits and risky decision-making in a controlled experimental task: an exploratory study. *Personality and Individual Differences, 31*(2), 215-226.

Lavric, A., Rippon, G., & Gray, J. R. (2003). Threat-evoked anxiety disrupts spatial working memory performance: An attentional account. *Cognitive Therapy and Research, 27*(5), 489-504.

Lavric, A., Shackman, A. J., Sarinopoulos, I., Sarinopoulos, A. P., & Davidson, R. J. (2000). Effects of threat-of shock on verbal and spatial working memory. *Psychophysiology, 37*, S62-S62.

Lerner, J. S., & Keltner, D. (2000). Beyond valence: Toward a model of emotion-specific influences on judgement and choice. *Cognition & Emotion, 14*(4), 473-493.

Li, X., Ouyang, Z., & Luo, Y.-J. (2010). The Effect of Cognitive Load on Interaction Pattern of Emotion and WM. *Proceedings of ICCI'10, IEEE Press*.

Li, X. Y., Li, X. B., & Luo, Y. J. (2005). Anxiety and attentional bias for threat: an event-related potential study. *Neuroreport, 16*(13), 1501-1505.

Liotti, M., Woldorff, M. G., Perez, R., & Mayberg, H. S. (2000). An ERP study of the temporal course of the Stroop color-word interference effect. *Neuropsychologia, 38*(5), 701-711.

Loewenstein, G. F., Weber, E. U., Hsee, C. K., & Welch, N. (2001). Risk as feelings. *Psychological Bulletin, 127*(2), 267-286.

Lust, S. A., & Bartholow, B. D. (2009). Self-reported and P3 event-related potential evaluations of condoms: Does what we say match how we feel? *Psychophysiology, 46*(2), 420-424.

Maner, J. K., Richey, J. A., Cromer, K., Mallott, M., Lejuez, C. W., Joiner, T. E., et al. (2007). Dispositional anxiety and risk-avoidant decision-making. *Personality and Individual Differences, 42*(4), 665-675.

Maner, J. K., & Schmidt, N. B. (2006). The role of risk avoidance in anxiety. *Behavior Therapy, 37*(2), 181-189.

Mansell, W. (2004). Cognitive psychology and anxiety. *Psychiatry, 3*(4), 6-10.

Martinez, A., Anllo-Vento, L., Buxton, R., Wong, E., & Hillyard, S. (1998). Spatio-temporal analysis of brain activity during visual spatial attention. *Journal of Cognitive Neuroscience*, 74-74.

Mathews, A., & Mackintosh, B. (1998). A cognitive model of selective processing in anxiety. *Cognitive Therapy and Research, 22*(6), 539-560.

McEvoy, L. K., Smith, M. E., & Gevins, A. (1998). Dynamic cortical networks of verbal and spatial working memory: Effects of memory load and task practice. *Cerebral Cortex, 8*(7), 563-574.

McNaughton, N., & Gray, J. A. (2000). Anxiolytic action on the behavioural inhibition system implies multiple types of arousal contribute to anxiety. *J Affect Disord, 61*(3), 161-176.

Mecklinger, A., & Pfeifer, E. (1996). Event-related potentials reveal topographical and temporal distinct neuronal activation patterns for spatial and object working memory. *Cognitive Brain Research, 4*(3), 211-224.

Miller, J. D., & Pilkonis, P. A. (2006). Neuroticism and affective instability: The same or different? *American Journal of Psychiatry, 163*(5), 839-845.

Miltner, W. H. R., Braun, C. H., & Coles, M. G. H. (1997). Event-Related Brain Potentials Following Incorrect Feedback in a Time-Estimation Task: Evidence for a "Generic" Neural System for Error Detection. *Journal of Cognitive Neuroscience, 9*(6), 788-798.

Mitte, K. (2007). Anxiety and risk decision-making: The role of subjective probability and subjective cost of negative events. *Personality and Individual Differences, 43*(2), 243-253.

Miu, A. C., Heilman, R. M., & Houser, D. (2008). Anxiety impairs decision-making: Psychophysiological evidence from an Iowa Gambling Task. *Biological Psychology, 77*(3), 353-358.

Mogg, K., & Bradley, B. P. (1998). A cognitive-motivational analysis of anxiety. *Behav Res Ther, 36*(9), 809-848.

Mogg, K., Bradley, B. P., Williams, R., & Mathews, A. (1993). Subliminal processing of emotional information in anxiety and depression. *J Abnorm Psychol, 102*(2), 304-311.

Mogg, K., Millar, N., & Bradley, B. P. (2000). Biases in eye movements to threatening facial expressions in generalized anxiety disorder and depressive disorder. *J Abnorm Psychol, 109*(4), 695-704.

Morgan, H. M., Klein, C., Boehm, S. G., Shapiro, K. L., & Linden, D. E. J. (2008). Working memory load for faces modulates P300, N170, and N250r. *Journal of Cognitive Neuroscience, 20*(6), 989-1002.

Morita, Y., Morita, K., Yamamoto, M., Waseda, Y., & Maeda, H. (2001). Effects of facial affect recognition on the auditory P300 in healthy subjects. *Neuroscience Research, 41*(1), 89-95.

Moser, J. S., Hajcak, G., Bukay, E., & Simons, R. F. (2006). Intentional modulation of emotional responding to unpleasant pictures: an ERP study. *Psychophysiology, 43*(3), 292-296.

Murphy, F. C., Sahakian, B. J., Rubinsztein, J. S., Michael, A., Rogers, R. D., Robbins, T. W., et al. (1999). Emotional bias and inhibitory control processes in mania and depression. *Psychol Med, 29*(6), 1307-1321.

Nesse, R. M. (2006). Darwinian medicine and mental disorders. *International Congress Series, 1296*, 83-94.

Newman, J. P., Wallace, J. F., Schmitt, W. A., & Arnett, P. A. (1997). Behavioral inhibition system functioning in anxious, impulsive and psychopathic individuals. *Personality and Individual Differences, 23*(4), 583-592.

Nieuwenhuis, S., Holroyd, C. B., Mol, N., & Coles, M. G. H. (2004). Reinforcement-related brain potentials from medial frontal cortex: origins and functional significance. *Neuroscience and Biobehavioral Reviews, 28*(4), 441-448.

Ouyang, Z., Sun, S., Li, X., & Luo, Y.-J. (2010). The different effect of negative emotion induced by background music on verbal and spatial working memory: evidence from ERP study. *Chinese Journal of Behavioral Medicine and Brain Science, 19*(9), 813-816.

Paulus, M. P. (2005). Neurobiology of decision-making: Quo vadis? *Cognitive Brain Research, 23*(1), 2-10.

Paulus, M. P., Feinstein, J. S., Simmons, A., & Stein, M. B. (2004). Anterior cingulate activation in high trait anxious subjects is related to altered error processing during decision making. *Biological Psychiatry, 55*(12), 1179-1187.

Pessoa, L. (2008). On the relationship between emotion and cognition. *Nature Reviews Neuroscience, 9*(2), 148-158.

Platt, M. L. (2002). Neural correlates of decisions. *Current Opinion in Neurobiology, 12*(2), 141-148.

Polezzi, D., Sartori, G., Rumiati, R., Vidotto, G., & Daum, I. (2010). Brain correlates of risky decision-making. *Neuroimage, 49*(2), 1886-1894.

Postle, B. R., Awh, E., Jonides, J., Smith, E. E., & D'Esposito, M. (2004). The where and how of attention-based rehearsal in spatial working memory. *Cognitive Brain Research, 20*(2), 194-205.

Pourtois, G., Grandjean, D., Sander, D., & Vuilleumier, P. (2004). Electrophysiological correlates of rapid spatial orienting towards fearful faces. *Cerebral Cortex, 14*(6), 619-633.

Quartz, S. R. (2009). Reason, emotion and decision-making: risk and reward computation with feeling. *Trends in Cognitive Sciences, 13*(5), 209-215.

Quraishi, S., & Frangou, S. (2002). Neuropsychology of bipolar disorder: a review. *J Affect Disord, 72*(3), 209-226.

Rama, P., Kesseli, K., Reinikainen, K., Kekoni, J., Hamalainen, H., & Carlson, S. (1997). Visuospatial mnemonic load modulates event-related slow potentials. *Neuroreport, 8*(4), 871-876.

Reidy, J., & Richards, A. (1997). A memory bias for threat in high-trait anxiety. *Personality and Individual Differences 23*(4), 653-663.

Richards, A., French, C. C., Calder, A. J., Webb, B., Fox, R., & Young, A. W. (2002). Anxiety-related bias in the classification of emotionally ambiguous facial expressions. *Emotion, 2*(3), 273-287.

Rowe, G., Hirsh, J. B., & Anderson, A. K. (2007). Positive affect increases the breadth of attentional selection. *Proceedings of the National Academy of Sciences of the United States of America, 104*(1), 383-388.

Ruchkin, D. S., Berndt, R. S., Johnson, R., Ritter, W., Grafman, J., & Canoune, H. L. (1997). Modality-specific processing streams in verbal working memory: evidence from spatio-temporal patterns of brain activity. *Cognitive Brain Research, 6*(2), 95-113.

Ruchkin, D. S., Grafman, J., Krauss, G. L., Johnson, R., Canoune, H., & Ritter, W. (1994). Event-Related Brain Potential Evidence for a Verbal Working-Memory Deficit in Multiple-Sclerosis. *Brain, 117*, 289-305.

Sakai, K., & Passingham, R. E. (2004). Prefrontal selection and medial temporal lobe reactivation in retrieval of short-term verbal information. *Cerebral Cortex, 14*(8), 914-921.

Santrock, J. W. (2002). *Psychology* (7th ed.). New York: McGraw-Hill Humanities.

Sato, A., Yasuda, A., Ohira, H., Miyawaki, K., Nishikawa, M., Kumano, H., et al. (2005). Effects of value and reward magnitude on feedback negativity and P300. *Neuroreport, 16*(4), 407-411.

Sato, W., Kochiyama, T., Yoshikawa, S., & Matsumura, M. (2001). Emotional expression boosts early visual processing of the face: ERP recording and its decomposition by independent component analysis. *Neuroreport, 12*(4), 709-714.

Sayala, S., Sala, J. B., & Courtney, S. M. (2006). Increased neural efficiency with repeated performance of a working memory task is information-type dependent. *Cerebral Cortex, 16*(5), 609-617.

Shackman, A. J., Sarinopoulos, I., Maxwell, J. S., Pizzagalli, D. A., Lavric, A., & Davidson, R. J. (2006). Anxiety selectively disrupts visuospatial working memory. *Emotion, 6*(1), 40-61.

Shek, D. T. (1993). The Chinese version of the State-Trait Anxiety Inventory: its relationship to different measures of psychological well-being. *J Clin Psychol, 49*(3), 349-358.

Shepperd, J. A., Grace, J., Cole, L. J., & Klein, C. (2005). Anxiety and outcome predictions. *Personality and Social Psychology Bulletin, 31*(2), 267-275.

Simon-Thomas, E. R., Role, K. O., & Knight, R. T. (2005). Behavioral and electrophysiological evidence of a right hemisphere bias for the influence of negative emotion on higher cognition. *Journal of Cognitive Neuroscience, 17*(3), 518-529.

Simons, R. F. (2010). The way of our errors: Theme and variations. *Psychophysiology, 47*(1), 1-14.

Smith, E. E., & Jonides, J. (1998). Neuroimaging analyses of human working memory. *Proceedings of the National Academy of Sciences of the United States of America, 95*(20), 12061-12068.

Smith, E. E., & Jonides, J. (1999). Neuroscience - Storage and executive processes in the frontal lobes. *Science, 283*(5408), 1657-1661.

Smith, E. E., Jonides, J., & Koeppe, R. A. (1996). Dissociating verbal and spatial working memory using PET. *Cerebral Cortex, 6*(1), 11-20.

Spielberger, C. D., Gorsuch, R. L., Lushene, R., Vagg, P. R., & Jacobs, G. A. (1983). Manual for the state-trait anxiety inventory. *Palo Alto, CA: Consulting Psychologist Press.*

Straube, T., Kolassa, I. T., Glauer, M., Mentzel, H. J., & Miltner, W. H. R. (2004). Effect of task conditions on brain responses to threatening faces in social phobics: An event-related functional magnetic resonance Imaging study. *Biological Psychiatry, 56*(12), 921-930.

Swick, D., & Jovanovic, J. (2002). Anterior cingulate cortex and the Stroop task: neuropsychological evidence for topographic specificity. *Neuropsychologia, 40*(8), 1240-1253.

Tallis, F. (1997). The neuropsychology of obsessive-compulsive disorder: a review and consideration of clinical implications. *Br J Clin Psychol, 36 (Pt 1)*, 3-20.

Watson, D., Clark, L. A., & Tellegen, A. (1988). Development and Validation of Brief Measures of Positive and Negative Affect - the Panas Scales. *Journal of Personality and Social Psychology, 54*(6), 1063-1070.

Weiland-Fiedler, P., Erickson, K., Waldeck, T., Luckenbaugh, D. A., Pike, D., Bonne, O., et al. (2004). Evidence for continuing neuropsychological impairments in depression. *J Affect Disord, 82*(2), 253-258.

Wheeler, R. E., Davidson, R. J., & Tomarken, A. J. (1993). Frontal Brain Asymmetry and Emotional Reactivity - a Biological Substrate of Affective Style. *Psychophysiology, 30*(1), 82-89.

Wieser, M. J., Muhlberger, A., & Pauli, P. (2007). Eye to eye contact in social anxiety: New insights from eye-tracking and psychophysiological data in a mutual gaze design. *Psychophysiology, 44*, S35-S35.

Wilson, E., & MacLeod, C. (2003). Contrasting two accounts of anxiety-linked attentional bias: selective attention to varying levels of stimulus threat intensity. *J Abnorm Psychol, 112*(2), 212-218.

Wray, L. D., & Stone, E. R. (2005). The role of self-esteem and anxiety in decision making for self versus others in relationships. *Journal of Behavioral Decision Making, 18*(2), 125-144.

Yamasaki, H., LaBar, K. S., & McCarthy, G. (2002). Dissociable prefrontal brain systems for attention and emotion. *Proceedings of the National Academy of Sciences of the United States of America, 99*(17), 11447-11451.

Yantis, S., Schwarzbach, J., Serences, J. T., Carlson, R. L., Steinmetz, M. A., Pekar, J. J., et al. (2002). Transient neural activity in human parietal cortex during spatial attention shifts. *Nature Neuroscience, 5*(10), 995-1002.

Yasuda, A., Sato, A., Miyawaki, K., Kumano, H., & Kuboki, T. (2004). Error-related negativity reflects detection of negative reward prediction error. *Neuroreport, 15*(16), 2561-2565.

Yeung, N., Holroyd, C. B., & Cohen, J. D. (2005). ERP correlates of feedback and reward processing in the presence and absence of response choice. *Cerebral Cortex, 15*(5), 535-544.

Yeung, N., & Sanfey, A. G. (2004). Independent coding of reward magnitude and valence in the human brain. *Journal of Neuroscience, 24*(28), 6258-6264.

Yiend, J., & Mathews, A. (2001). Anxiety and attention to threatening pictures. *Q J Exp Psychol A, 54*(3), 665-681.

Zhou, Z., Yu, R., & Zhou, X. (2010). To do or not to do? Action enlarges the FRN and P300 effects in outcome evaluation. *Neuropsychologia, 48*(12), 3606-3613.

In: Trait Anxiety
Editor: Anna S. Morales
ISBN 978-1-61324-551-4

Chapter 2

AN INNOVATIVE APPROACH TO EXPLORE PERINATAL ANXIETY

Irène Capponi
Université de Nantes, Nantes Atlantique Universités
Laboratoire "Education, Cognition, Développement" EA 3259,
B.P. 81227, F-44000 Nantes Cédex 3, France

ABSTRACT

Although anxiety is the most common phenomenon among women during the transition to motherhood (Wenzel, Haugen, Jackson & Brendle, 2005), equivocal results have been reported in studies both on the relationships between situational (state) and dispositional (trait) anxiety, on effects of maternal anxiety, and on treatment evaluation. The purpose of this chapter is to present a new way of examining and understanding maternal anxiety in healthy primiparous women from the idea that "inter-individual differences cannot be understood without reference to intra-individual differences" (Apter, 2003). Changes in anxiety were explored from intra-individual differences in terms of gap (discrepancy) between state anxiety at different time points and between dispositional and situational anxiety. In others words, take a fresh look at measures of anxiety to see things differently.

A sample of 77 participants were administered the French version of the Spielberger State-Trait Anxiety Inventory Form Y (STAI-Y) during the eighth month of pregnancy (A-trait and A-state) and the first and third month after birth (A-state). The main result has related to the women characterized by an extreme trait-anxiety score. Those with the highest (vs. lowest) dispositional anxiety had state-anxiety scores significantly lower (vs. higher) than their A-Trait. These findings indicate a self-regulation of anxiety and even a normalization of mood variation during the perinatal period.

Findings in this chapter show an alternative at the common assumption that individuals high in trait anxiety are expected to respond to new/stressful situations with elevated state anxiety. Here, it is as though women were adapting to the new situation – becoming a mother-by adjusting their level of anxiety through a reversal process. Studies in animals, cognitive psychology of affective disorders, and part of Apter's theory, provide evidence to support my interpretative hypothesis, and an explanation for the function of perinatal anxiety.

Several implications can be considered. Lack of knowledge about this normalization could explain the heterogeneity of the results reported in the literature and why there is little evidence of improved outcomes for mothers within professional intervention groups. Women's groups with a high level of anxiety may be heterogeneous, i.e. composed of women who experience normalization of their anxiety and of women who suffer from occasional anxiety disorders.

INTRODUCTION

Becoming a mother is a major life event with changes in biology, roles, social context, intra-psychic, and interpersonal adjustment (Poussin, 1993). The transition to motherhood is a "period of exceptional vulnerability" (Dugnat, 2002), which can be a stressful transition time (Goldstein, Diener, & Mangelsdorf, 1996) with an increased risk of psychiatric morbidity (Dollander & Tichey, 2002). Most research into mood changes in the peripartum period have investigated maternal depression, but less is known about anxiety (Capponi & Horbacz, 2005; Heron, O'Connor, Evans, Golding, & Glover, 2004) because measurements of anxiety have often been examined as being an aspect of postpartum depression (Wenzel, Haugen, Jackson, & Robinson, 2003). However, some studies reported that anxiety disorders were distinct from depression (Matthey, Barnett, Howie & Kavanagh, 2003; Wenzel et al., 2003; Brown et al., 2001 cited by Wenzel et al., 2003), and that the symptom profiles of mothers with depression and of those with anxiety disorder were independent (Ballard, Davis, Handy & Mohan, 1993). Moreover, some have indicated that anxiety is the most common emotional dysregulation during the perinatal period (Wenzel, Haugen, Jackson, & Brendle, 2005). On the other hand, several studies have reported that high anxiety is associated with negative effects both on pregnancy outcomes and child development; unfortunately, a recent study has revealed that rates of detection and treatment have been "alarmingly low" (Goodman & Tyer-Viola, 2010).

Even less attention has been focused on the course of anxiety across the transition to motherhood to differentiate normal (or non-pathological) anxiety modification from anxiety disorder, while this concerns each specialist involved in perinatal care (Glazier, Elgar, Goel, & Holzapfel, 2004; Mertesacker, Bade, Haverkock, & Pauli-Pott, 2004; Ross & Mclean, 2006). Indeed, when anxiety is detected, little evidence of improved outcomes for mothers within professional intervention groups has been reported. Accordingly, more studies are needed into anxiety changes in *healthy* women to improve our understanding of normal individual differences, keeping in mind that "inter-individual differences cannot be understood without reference to intra-individual differences" (Apter, 2003).

The aim of this chapter is to focus on anxiety variations in a sample of healthy primiparous women, using a novel approach. I used the STAI-Y (State-Trait Anxiety Inventory Form Y, Spielberger, Gorsuch, & Lushene, 1983), which differentiates anxiety as a transitory emotional state (A-state) from individual differences in anxiety proneness as a relatively stable personality trait (A-trait). A novel design is proposed by exploring intra-individual differences in terms of the gap (discrepancy) both between dispositional and situational anxiety and between situational anxiety scores at different time points. In others words, take a fresh look at perinatal anxiety measurements from a novel viewpoint.

Studies on Maternal Anxiety

Studies on maternal anxiety have dealt with prevalence assessment, factor identification, effect purposes, and treatment evaluation.

Although the evolution and detection of anxiety have been paid little attention in the literature (as pointed out by Grant, McMahon & Austin, 2008, Heron et al., 2004, Jomeen, 2004), particular interest in the question of specificity of anxiety dysregulation across the perinatal period has been shown. Some limited research compared scores of a perinatal sample with a control group (no perinatal sample). Regarding the level of trait anxiety (A-Trait), i.e. the dispositional indicator provided by a subscale of the STAI-Y, no significant difference was found between the group in the immediate postpartum period and the control group (Knight & Thirkettle, 1986). Using the two subscales of the STAI Form Y, which differentiates between temporary or emotional state anxiety versus long standing personality trait anxiety, Bhagwanani, Seagraves, Dierker & Lax (1997) reported average A-state and A-trait scores throughout pregnancy that were similar to those in non pregnant women. Similarly, Breitkopf et al. (2006) revealed no mean differences in state anxiety (with the STAI-Y) between pregnant and non-pregnant women; but they found a significantly lower mean A-state in postpartum women compared to pregnant and non pregnant groups. Nevertheless, Lonstein (2007) indicated that "the reported rate of elevated anxiety or diagnosable anxiety disorders in postpartum women is significantly underestimated". Using the STAI-Y and a cut-off to define cases and non-cases, the studies on prevalence referring to the number of cases that arise within a specific time period (pregnancy and postpartum period) have revealed a prevalence of A-State ranging from 12 % (Skari et al., 2002) to 59 % during pregnancy (Faisal-Cury & Rossi Menezes, 2007) and from 21% to 35% during the postpartum period. These rates are greater than those for depression, which range from 5% to 12-25% (Banti et al., 2009; Lee et al., 2007; Matthey et al., 2003; Austin et al., 2008). However, Austin et al. (2010) referred to other studies showing a similar prevalence of anxiety disorders and depressive disorders. Therefore, there is little agreement about the prevalence of anxiety state during the perinatal period. On the other hand, some studies into the course of anxiety during this period report an improvement in anxiety symptoms (Altshuler, Hendrick, & Cohen, 2000; Austin et al., 2008; Fleming, Flett, Ruble &Van Wagner, 1990; Sjögren, Widström, Edman & Uvnäs-Moberg, 2000). In contrast, other studies indicate that anxiety levels remain stable across motherhood (Austin, 2004; Grant et al., 2008; Keeton, Perry-Jenkins, & Sayer, 2008). So, although the data from Ballard et al. (1993) or Wenzel et al. (2005) have led to consider anxiety disturbances as the most common phenomenon related to childbearing, the impact of the peripartum period on the course of anxiety is unclear.

The second approach, with studies on factor identification and effect purposes, was founded on constructing subgroups a posteriori, usually based on three anxiety levels (high, moderate, and low). Despite the use of different tools for measuring anxiety, numerous studies have reported the same factors (predictors) related with anxiety levels. Associations between high anxiety and concerns for fetal integrity, health and safety (Brockington, Macdonald, & Wainscott, 2006, with Birmingham Interview whose score seemed to reflect an anxiety state), feelings of inadequate social support (Barnett & Parker, 1985,

1986, A-trait with the STAI-Y; Capponi & Horbacz, 2008, with A-state of the STAI-Y; review of Jomeen, 2004), poor self-esteem, and self-efficacy (Sayil, Güre, & Uçanok, 2006, A-Trait with STAI-Y) have been shown. This could be helpful for identifying women at risk for developing anxiety and to implement targeted interventions.

On the other hand, recent literature into the effects of perinatal anxiety has received increased attention owing to:

its negative impact on pregnancy outcomes (Hosseini, Biglan, Larkby & Gorin, 2009, with trait anxiety of STAI-Y; Orr, Reiter, Blazer & Sherman, 2007, with pregnancy-related anxiety): premature birth, cesarean section, length of labour, low birth weight, and postnatal complications (see reviews of Banti et al., 2009; Littleton, Breitkopf & Berenson, 2007);

its implications on maternal qualitative interactive characteristics in child rearing such as adjustment to the infant: high anxiety was related to insensitive, intrusive, controlling, or overprotective behaviour (see review of Kaitz & Maytal, 2005; Nicol-Harper, Harvey & Stein, 2007, with trait anxiety of STAI-Y);

and its links with the somatic and psychological development of the offspring (Brouwers, Van Baar, & Pop, 2001, with STAI-Y but high anxiety was defined on the basis of either state or trait anxiety or both; Davis et al., 2004; O'Connor et al., 2007, with the Crown-Crisp experiential index; Glasheen, Richardson & Fabio, 2010 for review). A number of studies have also indicated that high maternal trait anxiety in *pregnancy* was associated with both difficult infant temperament (Austin et al., 2005, with trait anxiety of STAI-Y) and behavioural difficulties in childhood (O'Connor et al., 2002).

Thus, according to Zelkowitz and Papageorgiou (2005) it is warranted to develop programmes to detect anxious mothers and thus assist them, including targeting women who might benefit from preventive services. This recommendation is laudable, but further studies on perinatal anxiety are needed. Indeed, prevalence and incidence vary "depending on the sampling methods, the criteria for diagnosis, the measures used, and the timing of assessments" (Austin et al., 2010). One meta-analysis and one systematic review found no evidence of an association between anxiety and adverse perinatal outcomes (Littleton et al., 2007), or between postnatal anxiety and child development (Glasheen et al., 2010). Furthermore, from the research currently available, it is difficult to draw accurate conclusions about the *type* of anxiety (clinical versus subclinical anxiety, trait or state anxiety, chronic versus transient anxiety) that is associated with these potential factors.

Finally, relating to the third area on impact of interventions, as noted by Austin et al. (2008), there is little evidence of improved outcomes for mothers within professional intervention groups (Barnett, Schaafsma, Guzman, & Parker, 1991; Teixeira et al. 2005; Shaw et al., 2006 for review). For example, Austin et al. (2008) failed to demonstrate a significant effect of treatment on state anxiety as measured either by the STAI-Y or the Mini International Neuropsychiatric Interview (MINI; Lecrubier et al., 1997 cited by Austin et al.); the differences between the intervention and control groups were not significant. The failure of these programmes can come either from inappropriate intervention or targeting of anxious women. The latter is likely because anxiety may be unapparent to specialists in nursing services, according to some authors (Barnett & Parker, 1986; Dayan, Andro, & Dugnat, 1999). Recent reports (Coates, Schaefer & Alexander, 2004; Goodman & Tyer-Viola; 2010) have shown that the majority of women who screened positive for anxiety (with the Patient Health Questionnaire) were not identified by their obstetrical providers during pregnancy or the postpartum period. Thus, a related issue requiring further attention is the criteria used to diagnose women with anxiety during the perinatal period (Austin, 2004).

MEASURING MATERNAL ANXIETY

A central purpose in the evaluation of diagnostic scales is to identify the optimal cut-point for probable cases and to distinguish persons with emotional disorders from those without. Numerous studies on screening for mood have included both depression and anxiety disorders, thus potentially obscuring the detection of anxiety symptoms and disorders (like Austin et al., 2010). I will therefore continue this chapter on maternal anxiety using the STAI-Y scale (Spielberger et al., 1983). This scale has been widely used in perinatal research (Gunning et al., 2010); it is quick and easy and provides separate self-report measures of state and trait anxiety, thus respecting the importance of distinguishing between anxiety as a transitory emotional state and anxiety proneness as a relatively stable personality trait (Spielberger et al., 1983; Sveback & Apter, 1997).

Authors have frequently used a derived cut-off score of 40 defined statistically on both state and trait scales (Barnett & Parker, 1986; Hart &

McMahon, 2006; Faisal-Cury & Rossi Menezes, 2007). However, there is no official standardized cut-off score for the STAI instrument (Glasheen et al., 2010; Persson & Dykes, 2009). A variety of cut-off points have also been used to indicate high anxiety; "the STAI has been used in perinatal samples with cut-offs of >40 (Grant et al., 2008) to >45 (Moss et al., 2009) or >48 (Field et al., 2010) to indicate disorder, without prior validation in this population" (Meades & Ayers, 2010). This procedure could in part explain both the minimal effect of interventions due to poorly targeted anxious women and the discrepancies between the aforementioned prevalence studies.

Concerning anxiety changes across motherhood, the use of mean scores may obscure some substantial changes. State anxiety may decrease for some mothers while an increase in anxiety may be experienced by others, causing mean scores to appear unchanged over time and significant but moderate correlations (Capponi & Horbacz, 2007; Coplan, O'Neil, & Arbeau, 2005 ; O'Connor et al., 2003). Then, the analysis of the directional changes in state anxiety scores over time may be of interest for exploring intra-individuals changes.

A better understanding of maternal anxiety may also be impaired because of the partial assessment of anxiety. Some studies reported data on either dispositional anxiety (Persson & Dykes, 2009; Sayil et al., 2006) or situational anxiety (Glazier et al. 2004; Keeton et al., 2008; Norbeck & Anderson, 1989; Skari et al., 2002), making comparisons difficult. High correlation coefficients were found between A-Trait and A-State in some studies including both types of anxiety with primiparous *pregnant* women (Brouwers et al., 2001; Hart & McMahon, 2006; Bhagwanani et al., 1997; .74, .77, and .75, respectively). Coplan et al. (2005) also found that *postnatal* A-trait and A-state were highly inter-correlated (.77) with participants who were not solely first-time mothers. Results from Coplan et al. (2005) revealed a significant but moderate (.47) association between *prenatal* A-State and *postnatal* A-Trait. Recent research on nulliparous and parous women (Robert, David, Reeves, Goron, & Delfosse, 2008) indicated that antenatal A-Trait was highly associated with antenatal A-State (.68), but the correlation with postnatal A-State was quite modest (.28). Existing studies on the association between A-trait and A-state seem equivocal during the perinatal period. Nevertheless, we notice that high correlations between A-Trait and A-State have only been shown for concurrent measurements. Further research in this area is therefore needed to understand the nature of the relationships between the two types of anxiety during the transition to motherhood. It could be interesting to take the subject of maternal anxiety one step further by examining it from a different angle.

An Innovative Approach to Perinatal Anxiety?

High anxiety trait is usually associated with a higher vulnerability in response to new, altered, or stressful situations. Two types of findings have been reported. First, several empirical findings on different populations have produced consistent evidence of a strong association between A-trait and A-state. However, as noted previously, this association is less obvious during the perinatal period despite the fact that the events of birth and the postpartum period are considered as the most demanding and stressful moments of life (Cowan & Cowan, 2000 cited by Keeton et al., 2008). Second, Spielberger (1983) indicated that A-state scores were higher than A-trait scores during a stressful situation (in military people); there was a discrepancy of around 7 points. As far as I am aware, there are no published reports examining the gap between the two types of anxiety during the transition to motherhood (except one of our previous publications in a French journal, Capponi & Horbacz, 2007). This gap should provide information on how anxiety states vary with respect to trait anxiety from both a synchronic and diachronic perspective, while preserving information on intra and inter-individual differences. On the other hand, the gap between state anxiety measurements over the maternal period, which provides the direction of change between time points, has already been explored (Capponi & Horbacz, 2007) and used as a predictor of preterm delivery (Glynn, Dunkel-Schetter, Hobel, & Sandman, 2008). I quote the latter: "Whether or not a woman reported an increase in perceived stress or state anxiety during pregnancy was a better predictor of preterm birth than levels of these variables at either of the gestational time points under study. In this study, the size of the change was not as important as the simple presence of an increase or decrease".

It is therefore appropriate (1) to explore the directional changes in state anxiety scores over time from pregnancy to the postnatal period, (2) to examine the variation of A-State compared to A-Trait using the gap between them rather than simple correlations between the two. This disparity between A-Trait and A-State may be an indicator of adjustment to the new situation because the trait scale measures a relatively stable disposition of personality and the state scale a transitory psychological state related to a specific situation or time period (Spielberger et al., 1983). Without such a comparison, we are unable to draw any conclusions about episodic perinatal anxiety as anything other than the usual anxiety experienced by women in their everyday life. To carry out this approach, T-scores (not raw scores) are required to compare the two types of anxiety. In addition, an initial assessment of dispositional anxiety is necessary to obtain a baseline and the question is to determine the exact time to do it. Indeed, some studies have shown that the A-Trait is unstable during the immediate post-partum period (Barnett & Parker 1985; Hundley, Gurney, Graham, & Rennie, 1998), but that successive A-Trait scores are highly correlated during pregnancy (Bhagwanani et al., 1997). Given these findings, it would be interesting to explore how the anxiety state varies across the transition to motherhood, as a function of the anxiety trait measured before delivery.

Aims

The purpose of the present chapter is to investigate, using a novel approach, the anxiety changes during the transition to motherhood and especially the relationships between STAI-Y scores (Spielberger et al., 1983). This chapter presents a modest prospective longitudinal study in a healthy, low-risk sample of primiparous women. Given the exploratory nature of the research, no a priori hypothesis is made regarding either individual changes (intra and inter) in state anxiety, or discrepancy between trait and state anxiety, and therefore no examination of predictors.

Methods

Participants

Nulliparous women attending ante-natal classes with midwives were asked to participate. The inclusion criteria were: woman between 20 and 40 years of age, with good comprehension of the French language, experiencing a normal single pregnancy with less than one week's hospitalization, and with no known psychiatric disorder (such as clinical depression). Each subject was assured confidentially and freedom to withdraw from the study any time.

The longitudinal sample consisted of seventy-seven women from North West France; 53% percent of the participants were from rural areas, and the remainder were city-dwellers. Three women were excluded from the analyses due to technical problems (missing data) and three others dropped out of the study for health reasons (breast cancer, outcome of delivery). A total of 71 prospective first-time mothers completed the study. The mean age was 28 years (*SD* = 3.8). Four participants were hospitalized during pregnancy but only over a period of one or two days for diabetes (1), painful fibroma (1), and for contractions during the 5th month of pregnancy (2). Twenty-two point five (22.5) percent did not graduate from high school, 7% were high school graduates, 31% had a university degree or undergraduate studies, and 39.5% had a Master's Degree or above. All participants gave birth to a healthy, full-term baby. Consent was obtained from all study participants, and no remuneration was given.

Materials and Procedure

Participants were met individually at three different times. The first time was late into pregnancy, i.e. during the 8th month (T1, *M* = 38 days before scheduled term, *SD* =10 days), this was justified by reports that have demonstrated higher anxiety symptoms (A-state) in the 1st and 3rd pregnancy trimesters compared to the 2nd (Bhagwanani et al., 1997; confirmed by Lee et al., 2007; Texiera et al, 2009). The third trimester was chosen to maximize ongoing participation after childbirth. The second visit took place between 15 and 30 days after delivery (T2, *M* = 23 days after birth, *SD* = 8 days), i.e. after the potential post partum blues period (Sutter & Bourgeois, 1995), and the third during the baby's third month (T3, *M* = 81 days after birth, *SD*=13 days) at the end of the official state-supported maternity leave. A background questionnaire was administered at the beginning of each visit and participants were asked to complete several self-administered questionnaires (STAI-Y for anxiety cf. hereafter; a modified version of Social Support Questionnaire of Sarason, Levine, Basham & Sarason, 1983; and the questionnaire on maternal feelings of Bourgeois et al., 1998). The full interview was lengthy, requiring 1 to 1½ hrs. Only the results from the questionnaire on anxiety are presented here.

The participants completed the French version of the Spielberger State-Trait Anxiety Inventory (STAI-Y, Bruchon-Schweitzer & Paulhan 1993), which is usually administered as a self-completion questionnaire. A general anxiety measure such as the STAI-Y is by far the most commonly used in antenatal and postpartum research (Littleton et al., 2006 cited by Gunning et al., 2010; van Bussel, Spitz, Demyttenaere, 2008). A recent study concluded that "STAI may be used during pregnancy with some confidence regarding its validity for pregnant women" (Gunning et al., 2010). STAI-Y (French version) is a reliable and valid scale that has been used with both clinical and non clinical populations (Bruchon-Schweitzer & Paulhan 1993; Spielberger et al., 1983). This inventory is a well-known 40-item scale, measuring transient and enduring levels of anxiety respectively; it is the only measure that separates state from trait anxiety (Meades & Ayers, 2010). The scale therefore comprises two subscales, the first measuring state anxiety and the second trait anxiety. State anxiety is conceptualized "as a transitory emotional state or condition of the human organism that is characterized by subjective, consciously perceived feelings of tension and apprehension and heightened autonomic nervous system activity" (Hersen, 2004, p. 71). Trait anxiety is defined as a long standing personality anxiety in adults. A 20-item state measure (A-State) instructs participants to report how they are feeling "now" (e.g. "I feel calm", "I feel tense") and a 20-item trait measure (A-Trait) evaluates how respondents "generally feel" (e.g. "I worry too much about something that does not really matter"). The measure is rated on a four point scale from "not at all" to "very much so" for A-State and from "almost never" to "almost always" for A-Trait, with high scores indicating high state or trait anxiety. The range of raw scores is 20-80 for each subscale.

To determine changes in state anxiety depending on the dispositional anxiety, A-Trait was measured only during pregnancy and the A-State at the three different times (pregnancy and twice in postpartum). Indeed, as noted previously, anxiety trait seems to be unstable over the close post-partum because childbirth appears to upset the equilibrium of the mothers' mood (Hundley et al., 1998). Thus, it seemed reasonable to consider A-Trait score measured before childbirth as a baseline (dispositional anxiety) because the women were still in a dyadic situation (with their partner) not involving adjustment to the baby. This can be supported by the findings of Grant et al. (2008) who indicated considerable stability in trait anxiety from the third trimester of pregnancy to the seventh postnatal month ($r = .76$), i.e. when the interval between the two measurements was longer than that of Hundley et al. (roughly 10 days postpartum). Also, recent studies with pregnant women reported that trait scores did not differ from one trimester to the next (Gunning et al., 2010). Here, *raw scores were converted into T-scores* from the French version of the STAI-Y (Bruchon-Schweitzer & Paulhan, 1993); for the women who participated in its validation and standardization, the T-Scores ranged from 35 to 93 for A-State and from 25 to 87 for A-Trait. The French version has shown good internal consistence (Trait and State split-half =.78 for both).

Data Analysis

First, descriptive statistics for anxiety scores were computed using mean and standard deviation. Anxiety variables were normally distributed (Kolmogorov-Smirnov test, Dmax=.119 for A-Trait; Dmax=.148 for A-State at T1, Dmax=.108 for A-State at T2, and Dmax=.118 for A-State at T3; all *p* ns). Pearson correlations and Paired *t*-tests were conducted to test associations between anxiety scores (A-State at T1, T2, and T3, A-Trait at T1).

Second, the change in state anxiety was assessed both as a continuous (A-state score at T1 minus A-state score at T2, A-state at T2 minus at T3, and T1-T3) and a dichotomous (direction of the change between time points, i.e. an increase or a decrease) variable.

Similarly, to explore individual differences in situational anxiety on the basis of dispositional anxiety (deviation from A-trait), I used differences between A-Trait and A-State scores, and variance analyses were computed with two groups contrasted on A-Trait level (using quartile values).

In addition, hierarchical multiple regression analyses were included to explore whether any association between antenatal anxiety measures could predict the postnatal variation of state anxiety.

Results

Evolution of Situational Anxiety from Prepartum to Postpartum

A-State scores ranged from 35 to 84 (M = 48.4, SD = 9.6; Table 1). Interrelations between A-State scores were significant and positive (Table 2), but moderate (from .42 to .47). Mean scores neither fluctuated significantly from pregnancy (S1 for State at T1) to one month after delivery (S2) or three months later (S3), nor over the postpartum time (S1, S2: t = .74; S1, S3: t = 1; S2, S3: t = .30; all df= 70, all p-values ns). These findings may be the result of the change in direction of state anxiety scores between the times of measurement.

Table 1. T-scores of the STAI-Y: descriptive statistics at each time

	Mean	SD	Median	Range
Time 1				
A-Trait	46.86	9.72	45	26-74
A-State	49.13	10.06	48	35-84
Time 2				
A-State	48.24	8.71	46	35-73
Time 3				
A-State	47.87	10.1	46	35-74

Note: N = 71; Time 1= pregnancy; Time 2 = post-partum (1st month); Time 3 = post-partum (3rd month).

So, I calculated compounded scores comprised of the difference between state anxiety scores (DSS for Difference State-State): the score at the time of the 1st meeting (S1) minus the score at the time of the second meeting (S2) named DS1S2, and S2 minus A-State at time 3 (S3) named DS2S3. The DS1S2 ranged from -24 to +46, DS2S3 from -22 to +27, and DS1S3 from -25 to +40 (Table 3). Scores increased (difference < 0) for 47.9 % of participants from pregnancy to one month after delivery and for 43.7 % from time 2 to time 3 (Table 3). Mean scores of DS1S2 and DS2S3 in women with a decrease (difference $>= 0$) were significantly different from those of women with an increase ($F(1,69) = 70$ to DS1S2; $F(1,69) = 120$ to DS2S3; all $p <.0001$). The proportion of participants who presented the same change in direction (twice an increase; twice a decrease or matching) was 33.8% and the remaining women had changes in the two directions. These findings suggested an *inter- and intra-women variability*, explained the moderate associations between measures of anxiety state, and the absence of significant differences between the mean scores for A-state over time.

Table 2. Correlations between anxiety T-scores (N=71)

Variables	A-State 1	A-State 2	A-State 3
A-Trait	.55*	.45*	.45*
A-State 1	-	.43*	.47*
A-State 2		-	.42*

Note: A-State 1 = pregnancy anxiety state.
A-State 2 = A-state at 1st month after birth.
A-State 3 = A-state at 3rd month after birth.
* p < .0001.

Table 3. Descriptive statistics on Differences between anxiety-State Scores (DSS), with T-scores

	Differences between anxiety-State Scores					
	DS1S2		DS1S3		DS2S3	
Direction	< 0	>= 0	< 0	>= 0	< 0	>= 0
n	34	37	26	45	31	40
Mean	- 6.6	7.7	- 8.35	6.8	- 8.8	7.5
Median	- 5.0	5.0	- 7.0	4.0	- 7.0	6.0
Mini	- 24	0	- 25	0	- 22	1
Maxi	- 1	46	- 1	40	- 1	27
SD	4.9	8.7	5.9	8.1	6.3	6.2

Note: S1= pregnancy A-State; S2 = A-state at first post-partum time (1st month); S3 = A-state at second post-partum time (3rd month).

Individual Differences of A-state on the Basis of A-trait

Prenatal trait anxiety scores ranged from 26 to 74 (M = 46.9, SD = 9.7; Table 1). The mean A-state score was higher than the mean A-trait score in the prenatal period (t = 2.03, df = 70, p = .05), but no difference was found between the mean postnatal A-State score and the mean prenatal A-Trait score (S2: t = 1.2; S3: t = .82, df = 70, p ns). The data on interrelations between A-states and A-trait showed significant and positive, but moderate, associations (from .45 to .55, Table 2).

To explore changes in direction between A-trait and A-state, I calculated compounded scores comprised of the differences between anxiety-trait score minus each anxiety-state score named DTS (for Difference Trait-State). The proportion of women who experienced an increase in A-State compared to their A-Trait (difference < 0; ranged from -1 to -31) were 56.3% at time 1, 57.7% at time 2, and 52.1% at time 3 (Table 4). Mean scores of DTS1, DTS2, and DTS3 between women with a decrease or matching scores and those with an increase were significantly different (respectively: $F(1,69) = 97$; $F(1,69) = 90$; $F(1,69) = 99$; all $p < 0001$). Globally, 50.7% of women presented the same change in direction (three times an increase: 31%, three times a decrease or match: 19.7%) and the remaining women were characterized by changes in the two directions. Looking at the figure data, the participants who obtained a higher A-state score than their own A-trait score (i.e. negative number) were those who were characterized by the lowest A-Trait score. Conversely, the participants who obtained a lower A-state score than their own A-trait score (i.e. positive number) were those who were characterized by the highest A-Trait score. So, further investigation is needed.

I conducted analyses with two groups of women, a posteriori, on the basis of quartile values of the A-Trait score. One group had scores lower or equal to the first quartile (40, n = 21) and the other had scores above or equal to the third quartile (53, n = 23). The dependent variables were the differences between trait and state scores (DTS). I focused on the variation in state anxiety relative to habitual mood (A-Trait), therefore changes over time in DTS were examined with repeated measurements (MANOVA test). A significant difference appeared between the groups ($F(1,42) = 17.7$; $p < .001$) but not over the three testing periods (pregnancy, 1 and 3 months post; Figure 1). The more anxious women on the A-Trait presented positive DTS, which means their current anxiety state scores were lower than their usual anxiety score, while the women with the lowest A-Trait scores have experienced more anxiety than usually (i.e. negative DTS). Planned contrasts confirmed these findings at the three times (T1: $F = 6.43$; $p < .02$; T2: $F = 21.3$; $p < .0001$; T3: $F = 7.87$; $p < .01$; *df* 1, 42). Thus, it appears that healthy mothers adjusted their level of state anxiety to the situation. This finding could explain the prior moderate associations between A-Trait and A-States. In order to explain these moderate but not poor relations, we can assume that, despite their adjustment, women with high trait anxiety obtained higher state anxiety scores than those characterized by low A-Trait.

Table 4. Descriptive statistics on Differences between Trait and State anxiety scores (DTS), with T-scores

	Differences between Trait and State anxiety scores					
	DTS1		DTS2		DTS3	
Direction	< 0	>= 0	< 0	>= 0	< 0	>= 0
n	40	31	41	30	37	34
Mean	- 8.6	5.8	- 7.6	7.1	- 8.6	7.2
Median	- 7.0	4.0	- 6.0	4.0	- 8.0	5.0
Mini	- 31	0	- 26	0	- 24	0
Maxi	- 1	18	- 1	23	- 1	32
SD	6.6	5.3	6.1	6.9	5.8	7.5

DTS 1 = prenatal difference between A-Trait and A-State scores.

DTS2 = difference between antenatal A-Trait score and A-State score at first post-partum time.

DTS3 = difference between antenatal A-Trait score and A-State score at second post-partum time.

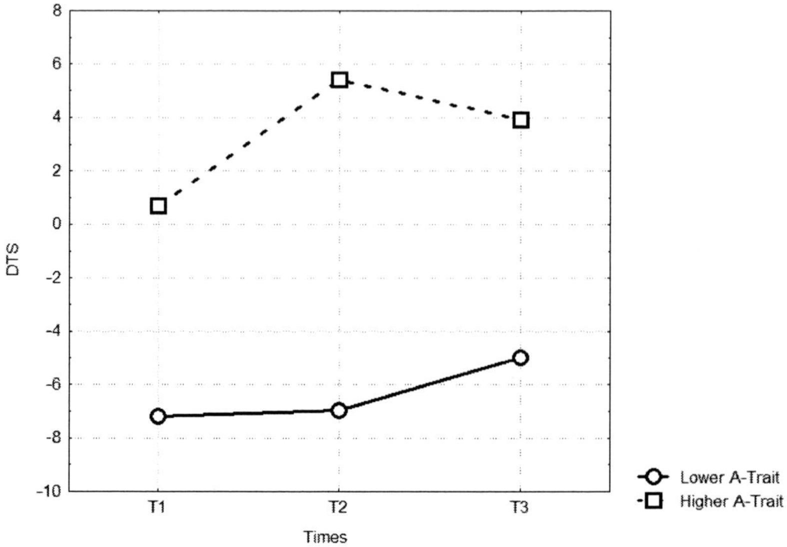

Figure 1. Mean of DTS scores (A-Trait minus A-State) according to anxiety trait level over time.

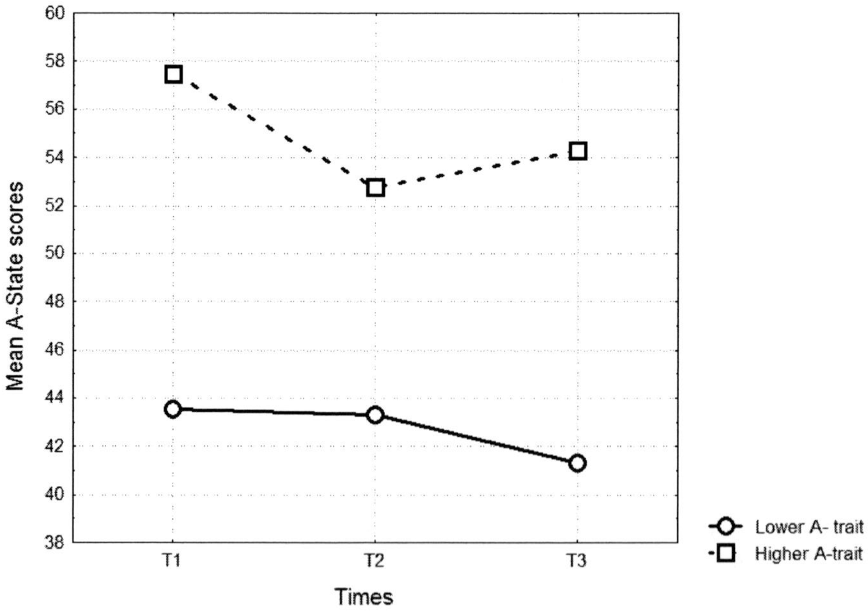

Figure 2. Mean of A-state scores according to levels of A-Trait over time.

So, a MANOVA test was conducted with these same two groups and A-state scores as dependent variable. A significant difference appeared between the groups (repeated measures: $F(1,42) = 44.92$; $p < .00001$) but not over the testing period. Planned contrasts showed that women with high trait anxiety obtained higher A-state scores than those with low A-Trait (Figure 2) at the three times (T1: $F= 24.46$; T2: $F= 14.66$; T3: $F = 25.02$; all $p < .001$, df 1, 42).

The Gap between Trait and State Anxiety Scores before Birth Could Predict the Gap between Antenatal Trait Score and Postnatal State Scores?

To achieve a further investigation of the relationship between A-trait and A-state on the *full sample*, I examined whether the difference between the two prenatal scores (DTS1: antenatal trait score minus state anxiety score) was maintained after birth (DTS2 and DTS3). Referring to the prior results on the effect of the A-Trait level, I included A-trait scores in the hierarchical regression model along with DTS1. I estimated the detection tolerance for multicollinearity (Howell, Rogier, Yzerbyt & Bestgen, 2007) in the regression analysis because of the correlation between the two explanatory variables (A-trait and DTS1: $r = .44$; $p < .0001$). Tolerance was .80 ($p < .001$), so little overlap was observed and the model could be viewed as valid and stable. The model was significant in each case (Table 5), i.e. to determine the discrepancies between A-Trait and A-State scores one month after birth (adjusted $R^2 = 0.40$; $F(2,68) = 22.41$, $p < .00001$) and three months after (adjusted $R^2 = 0.32$; $F\ (2,68) = 15.46$; $p < .00001$) . Nevertheless, the slope (β) of A-Trait factor was greater than that for the other factor.

Table 5. Regression analysis of factors related to DTS (Difference between anxiety Trait and State scores; full sample)

	Difference between anxiety Trait and State scores					
	DTS2[b]			DTS3[c]		
Pregnancy Variable	Beta	R^2 *Change*	*p*	Beta	R^2 *Change*	*p*
A-Trait	.50	.36	<.0001	.37	.25	< .0001
DTS1[a]	.23	.04	<.04	.29	.07	<.02

[a] Pregnancy difference between anxiety Trait and State scores (time 1).
[b] Difference between prenatal A-Trait score and A-State score at time 2.
[c] Difference between prenatal A-Trait score and A-State score at time 3.

The same set of analyses was conducted but only with mothers who presented an extreme A-Trait *and* a prenatal adjustment of mood. The same dependent variables were used (DTS2 and DTS3 respectively). However, the A-Trait as independent variable was not retained in so far as the tolerance with the other independent variable (DTS1) was .22; therefore, a large overlap was observed. Selected cases were 31 women reporting either a high A-Trait score (>= third quartile) *and* A-State score lower than their A-Trait (difference >= 0), or a low A-Trait score (< first quartile) *and* A-State score (difference < 0) higher than their A-Trait. The model was highly significant with predictor explaining 65% of the variance of DTS2 ($F(1,29) = 53$; $p <.00001$; $\beta = .81$, $R^2 = .65$) and 53% of DTS3 ($F(1,29) = 33$; $p < .00001$; $\beta = .74$, $R^2 = .53$). This result indicated that even women with an *extreme* A-Trait (and an adaptation during pregnancy) showed, after delivery, a substantial stability of the difference between prenatal A-trait and A-state, confirming previous results with MANOVA test.

Now, Would it Be Possible to Predict the Evolution of A-State Scores ?

The next question to be addressed was whether A-Trait and prenatal DTS were associated with evolution of A-State from pregnancy to postnatal period. Regression analyses were computed (full sample) with the differences between antenatal A-state score and those measured after birth (DS1S2 and DS1S3) as dependent variables. The independent variables included trait anxiety and DTS1. The model was significant explaining 44% of the variance of DS1S2 and 31% of DS1S3 (respectively $F = 26.73$ and $F = 15.57$, all $p <. 00001$; df 2, 68). The amount of R^2 change attributed to the two variables was significant (Table 6). The slope of the factor for discrepancy (DTS1) was greater than that for A-Trait; associations were negative with the DTS1 and positive with A-Trait. Explanations for this finding are more difficult.

Therefore, further analyses using *contrasting groups* had to be carried out. The two independent variables were the level of trait (seen previously: quartiles, n=44) and DTS1. DTS1 has been transformed into a categorial variable with one subgroup characterized by positive differences (A-Trait score was above or equal to A-State score during pregnancy) and the other by negative differences (A-Trait was lower than A-State). A MANOVA test with repeated measures was performed with DS1S2 and DS1S3 as dependent variables (Figure 3).

Table 6. Regression analysis of factors associated with variation of A-state from pregnancy to postpartum

	Difference between anxiety Trait and State scores					
	DS1S2[b]			DS1S3[c]		
Pregnancy Variable	Beta	R^2 *Change*	*p*	Beta	R^2 *Change*	*p*
DTS1[a]	-.72	.25	<.0001	-.62	.21	< .0001
A-Trait	.48	.19	<.0001	.37	.11	= .02

[a] Pregnancy difference between A-Trait and A-State scores.
[b] Difference between prenatal and one month after delivery A-State Scores.
[c] Difference between prenatal and third month after delivery A-State Scores.

Planned comparisons showed that DS1S2 was equivalent to DS1S3 for the two subgroups characterized by an adjustment during the pregnancy (subgroup A in the Figure 3: women with low A-Trait and negative scores on DTS1, n=18, $F(1,40) = 1.33$; *p* ns; subgroup A': women with high A-Trait and positive DTS1, n=13, $F(1,40) = 0.34$; *p* ns). This finding was consistent with previous results on stability of adaptation.

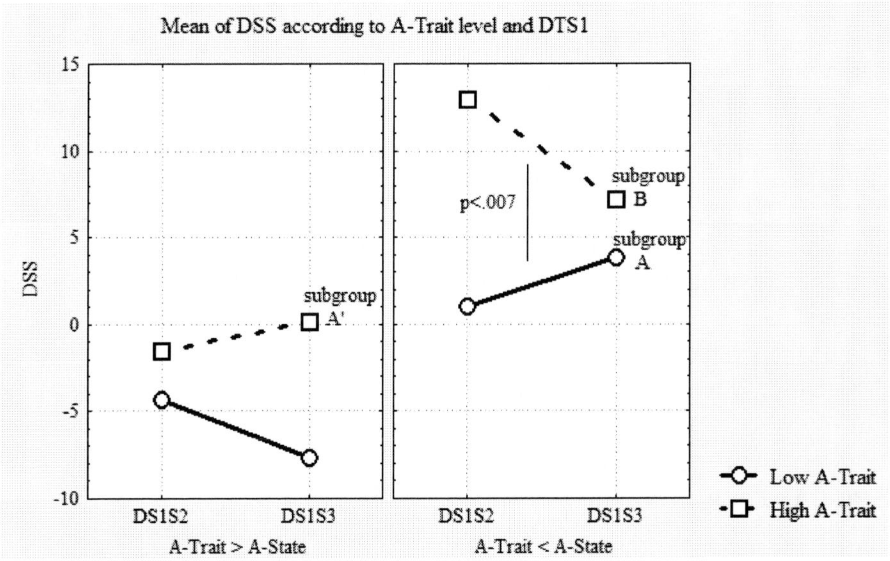

Figure 3. Mean of DSS[a] according to levels of A-Trait and DTS1[b].
[a] Difference between prenatal and postnatal A-State scores.
[b] Pregnancy difference between anxiety trait and state scores.

For the subgroups with high A-Trait, planned comparisons indicated a significant effect of DTS1 ($F(1,40) = 8,23$; $p < .007$): women with prenatal A-State score *above* their own A-Trait experienced positive scores on DSS (subgroup B on the Figure 3, n = 10; mean scores = 13), but women who presented adaptation during pregnancy had scores on DSS close to zero (group A', mean scores = -1.35). In other words, women with high A-Trait and A-State *above* A-Trait before delivery experienced a decrease of their level in situational anxiety *after birth* (for this subgroup B planned comparisons showed that DS1S2 did not differ significantly from DS1S3: $F(1,40)=3$; $p=.09$). Finally, regarding the last subgroup with low A-Trait and A-State below A-Trait, I cannot say anything because there were only three women.

CONCLUSION

This chapter examined an unexplored approach to dimensions of anxiety in healthy primiparous women from pregnancy to the third month after birth. To achieve a greater understanding of the variations in perinatal anxiety measured with STAI-Y, I analysed the evolution of A-state over time and its relation to A-trait both in a traditional framework and a new intra-individual design, that of discrepancy between measures. Although the results seem interesting, some limitations need to be considered. First, the study was conducted on a homogeneous sample of volunteers (living with their partner and most being at least high school graduates). Thus, the nature of this sample minimizes the possibility of generalising the findings. Second, this exploratory study employed new compounded measures that could be improved. The magnitude of anxious variation measures could be sharpened with a larger sample to shed additional light on the evolution in patterns of anxiety. Further research is needed to confirm and develop these findings. Finally, I have limited the explanation for maternal self-regulation to anxiety; I did not study depression, which is a co-morbid symptom.

State Anxiety

First, I found that the mean A-State scores did not differ significantly across the different time points (8th months of pregnancy, first and third months after birth). These findings could be interpreted as stability in individual differences and are consistent with some studies (Grant et al., 2008, with STAI-Y; Heron et al., 2004, using the anxiety items from the Crown–Crisp experiential index; Keeton et al., 2008, with STAI-Y), but give no additional information.

Second, depending on the study, associations between antenatal and postnatal A-State scores (from STAI-Y) were relatively high (.64 for Grant et al. 2008), moderate (.45 for Coplan et al., 2005) as with our results, or not significant (.07 for Robert et al., 2008). These latter reports suggested some discontinuity during the transition to parenthood (Robert et al., 2008) and required more investigation. Some authors have started to show interest in reporting longitudinal patterns of anxiety, and although these studies were well designed with large samples, intra-individual differences still seem neglected. For example, when Heron et al. (2004) reported that "most (64%) of women who reported elevated levels of anxious symptoms in pregnancy also reported elevated levels of anxiety postpartum", because researchers are taught to look at and process data from a statistical standpoint, they concluded that individual differences in anxiety symptoms were stable from pregnancy through to the postpartum period. What about the remaining percentages ? In Heron et al.'s study, women who only had high levels of anxiety in the antenatal period represented 13% of their cohort, and 35.7% of women whose score was above the cut-off on at least one postnatal assessment did not report anxiety before birth. In my opinion these percentages are not marginal and it would be useful to continue to study patterns of anxiety whilst overcoming our tendency to look first at the work of previous researchers.

Third, intra-individual changes in state anxiety were evaluated using both continuous (differences between each occasion of measurements) and dichotomous (direction of the change between time points, i.e., an increase or a decrease) variables, revealing significant individual changes. The discrepancy between A-state scores from one time point to another varied from -22 to +46; overall, scores increased (difference < 0) for approximately 46% of participants (so decreased for 54%), however, 66.2% of women had changes in both directions (so 44.8% in the same direction, either an increase or a decrease). This first interesting result was to highlight the intra- and inter-individual differences, which is an important issue. Indeed, support for the distinction between "intensity" and "direction" of anxiety symptoms has been provided in some empirical investigations, essentially in the field of sport research (Jones, 1995), but also recently during pregnancy (Glynn et al., 2008). The use of intra-individual discrepancy between measures seems to be relevant because the findings reported by Jones showed that cognitive anxiety direction was a better predictor of performance than cognitive anxiety intensity; and according to Glynn et al. (ibid) "had we not taken change in stress [or anxiety] responding into account and simply looked at the average of our prenatal stress [or anxiety] measures, or at the levels at individual time points, we would not have detected a relation between prenatal stress [or anxiety] and shortened gestation". Thus, the use of intra-individual differences in this way may be a promising approach for future research to reveal differences among individuals.

Deviation of State from Trait Anxiety

First, empirical findings stemming from different perspectives have produced consistent evidence of a strong association between A-trait and A-state. Examination of this relation during the perinatal period has been rare and findings equivocal. In the present chapter, the strength of the relationships between A-trait and A-state scores were, even if significant, moderate (from .45 to .55). These findings may be due to the time interval between the measurements. Indeed, in the literature, high correlations between A-Trait and A-State were only observed for concomitant measures (as in the study of Hart & McMahon, 2006). However, Brouwers et al. (2001) reported that 30% of a sample of pregnant women had high state anxiety scores but not for trait anxiety, but they did not explore this. Given these findings, the next step was to determine whether meaningful individual differences in anxiety responses (A-state) in relation to A-trait level existed during the perinatal period.

Second, my purpose was to investigate new aspects of anxiety that seem to have been overlooked in previous studies. To explore the changes in A-state relative to A-trait, I used a novel compounded measurement: "Difference between the anxiety Trait and State scores" (DTS), i.e. the anxiety state score at each time point was subtracted from the anxiety trait score measured prenatally. The results support the dynamic aspect of transition to motherhood by revealing another feature of inter-individual differences. Irrespective of the time point, roughly half of the mothers showed an increase in their state anxiety compared to their usual anxiety (the gap varied from -1 to -31), whilst the remainder showed a decrease (or matching scores: from 0 to 32). This supports the existence of different anxiety patterns and is incongruent with theoretical predictions (Spielberger et al., 1983), but congruent with some studies (Brouwers et al., 2001; Heron et al., 2004; although they did not explore these data as such because it was not the objective of their study). Further, by contrasting groups in terms of A-Trait level (n=44), I observed a reduction in anxiety for mothers with the highest A-Trait scores but an increase for those with the lowest A-trait scores (with the Manova test). With respect to the assessment time points, the mean magnitude of the gap varied as follows: -7, -7, -5 in the subgroup with an increase in anxiety, and +0.7, +5, +4 in the subgroup with a decrease in anxiety. These new results are at odds with the widely held view that the characteristic stress of the peripartum period would increase the risk of vulnerable women developing state anxiety during this time (Wenzel et al., 2003). Here, the anxiety of some women - who could be considered vulnerable because of their high A-trait level, traditionally associated with an increase in A-state anxiety during this maternal period - did not develop or was not exacerbated but conversely decreased; and reciprocally for women with low trait anxiety. This finding supports the idea of a normalization of mood variation during the perinatal period amongst women with an extreme A-trait score. From this perspective, these variations in anxiety seem to reflect self-regulation (please refer to the next section). However, women with the highest A-trait scored higher in A-State than those with the lowest A-Trait, which explains why previous correlations between A-Trait and A-State scores were moderate although not poor. Even though this latter result has been commonly observed, it underlines the importance of taking the discrepancy between the A-state and A-trait into consideration, and not just the intensity of the state or trait anxiety. Indeed, a high A-state does not represent "anxiety" *per se* since according to our findings, women with a high trait anxiety can show a decline of A-state compared to their A-trait. Therefore, high anxiety (trait or state) might not always be regarded as negative during the transition to motherhood thus suggesting the existence of false positive cases. One of the regression analyses that I performed, on selected cases comprising only the women characterized by an extreme A-trait *and* a regulation during pregnancy (n=31, i.e. 43.6% of full sample), showed that individual differences in the gap between A-Trait and A-State were relatively stable from pregnancy to postpartum period (DTS1 explained 65% of the variance of DTS2 and 53% of DTS3). The last main finding indicated that women with high A-Trait *and* A-State above A-Trait before delivery experienced a decrease in their level of situational anxiety after birth (gap between A-state scores; n=10, i.e. 14% of full sample). Additional analysis indicates also a regulation of anxiety in terms of the gap between trait and state, these mothers were characterized by an average deviation of -10 during pregnancy, but of +2.5 in the first month after birth (t=2.64; p<.03). So, for these women, the self-regulation process occurred at a different time, only once the baby was present. Altogether, 93.2% (((31+10)/44) x 100) of the two subgroups with an extreme A-trait presented a regulation during the transition to motherhood.

Why Defend the Idea of a Normalization of Anxiety?

The anxiety variation as underlined here could be regarded as an indicator of psychological adjustment such as a self-regulation process. I will give some evidence in support of this interpretative hypothesis, mainly relying on the results of studies in animals, cognitive theories of affective disorders, and part of Apter's theory. Although researchers still do not know the relative contribution of biological or environmental factors to peripartum anxiety, it appears that becoming a mother may produce some beneficial changes to women and non-human animals in terms of lowering the anxiety response (see reviews of Lonstein, 2007; Macbeth & Luine, 2010). Consistent research evidence supports the existence of several hormones during pregnancy and the postpartum period that are related to lowering anxiety, i.e. motherhood has anxiolytic effects. From these findings, it is possible to explain why, in our results, mothers with the highest A-trait scores had lower A-state scores than their own A-trait score from pregnancy. Regardless of this approach, another body of literature has provided interesting reports on the relationships between anxiety and psychological adjustment to pregnancy. Anxiety proneness was highly inversely correlated with optimism (Catov, Abatemarco, Markovic & Roberts, 2010) and the women reporting “high” attachment or more positive feelings and cognitions to the foetus demonstrated lower trait and state anxiety compared to those with negative attachment (Hart & McMahon, 2006). So, lowering ones level of anxiety may be considered as an indication of natural adjustment to the new situation. Concerning the women of our sample who only showed regulation after birth, Heron et al. (2004) provides an explanation regarding both physiological and social-psychological factors, for example, “anxiety would be resolved by a healthy birth”. Furthermore, our data concur with Lonstein's (2007) animal model; the latter reported how postpartum anxiety can be mitigated by contact with infants, resulting in a reduction in anxiety.

How then, can we explain the fact that anxiety decreases in some women, especially for those with the highest A-trait scores, but increases in others, especially those with lowest A-trait ? It is not conventional to consider that the interaction of affect and cognition which changes over time produces different types of experience. Yet, it has been argued that behaviour is not determined solely by traits of personality but also by the interaction between personality and characteristics of the task (Apter, 2001, p.27; Delignières, D., 2008). Women during the transition to motherhood "are adjusting to a new set of expectations for themselves, a new set of others' expectations for them" (Wenzel et al., 2003), and also display a number of new activities and thoughts (preoccupation for the infant). The exclusive focus on the baby characterizing most of these women requires the ability to anticipate the difficulties ahead and prepare for them, which is enabled by mobilizing anxiety. The notion of debilitating dimensions of the anxiety response has been prominent in the literature on maternal anxiety, but not as facilitating the attentional process by selectively concentrating on one aspect of the environment while ignoring other things. Eysenck (1984) proposed that the positive effect of anxiety could serve to increase the attentional resources allocated to performance. On the other hand, the general framework of Apter's theory (Apter, 2001) represents an interesting approach, which potentially provides an integrative framework to explain the results of this chapter and overcome the limitations of current studies into perinatal anxiety. This theory, named "reversal theory" or "motivational style theory" provides a general structure for understanding subjective experience by going beyond the overt problem behaviour. This approach has important methodological implications since it is dependent upon an experimental design with repeated measures which emphasizes within-subject variation. The theory, which is primarily concerned with the experience of motivation, argues that individuals are inherently inconsistent over time. Although people have a tendency to be predominantly in a goal-directed, arousal-avoidant mode versus arousal-seeking mode (Murgatroyd, Rushton, Apter & Ray, 1978), there are also involuntary transactional states depending on their needs determined by the present situation. These states are achieved by switching between the members of the pairs of motivational modes/styles ("reversing") (Apter, Mallows & Williams, 1998), only one level of the arousal system is preferred with one being "operative" at a given time (Apter, 1989, 1997). The data in this chapter show a similar trend, it is as though women with an extreme A-trait are adapting to the new situation – becoming a mother– by adjusting their level of anxiety through a reversal process. Furthermore, Apter's approach can be compared with Mogg and Bradley's (1998) cognitive motivational model, which assumes that the motivational processes and objectives of a person affect information processing. Emotional states that reflect an active motivational system should orient selective attention by prioritizing the processing of motivationally-relevant information. According to numerous cognitive psychology studies, although they do not all concur on the stages of processing and thus the underlying mechanisms, there is substantial evidence for the effects of anxiety on attention to threatening stimuli (for a review see Ouimet, Gawronski & Dozois, 2009). This is a core feature of anxiety in general, because these results have been found in comparisons between low-anxious with high-anxious participants (often with the STAI-Y), in studies comparing anxiety patients with healthy control persons, and also in patients with different anxiety disorders (Bar-Haim et al., 2007). It has been argued that high anxiety is associated with attentional processing which *favours* the processing of emotional stimuli, but some studies support the assumption that low anxious individuals show *avoidance* of threat-related stimuli and shift attention away from them (MacLeod et al., 1986; Williams et al., 1988, all cited by Bar-Haim et al., 2007). Both Mogg and Bradley (1998) and Williams et al. (1988; 1997 cited by Mitte, 2008) assumed that state anxiety was involved in the evaluation of new stimuli. It would be difficult to refute that a baby is an emotionally-laden new "stimulus" for primiparous women. Thus, my interpretative hypothesis is as follows: women with high A-trait drop their anxiety response such that they do not become over-reactive vis-à-vis the emotional information from baby; conversely, women with low A-trait increase their anxiety response to diminish avoidance of threat, thus increasing the probability of dealing with negative situations. Three studies in particular support this hypothesis. A critical review (Cisler, Bacon, Nathan & Williams, 2009) indicates that "only high trait anxious individuals exhibit attentional biases towards mildly threatening stimuli" (a bias that favours the processing). However, Mitte (2008) notes that when a threat stimulus is high enough, low-anxious persons, and not just high-anxious, allocate their resources towards it. Maner et al. (2007) provide evidence for the link between high anxiety and risk-avoidant decision-making on a behavioural decision-making task. Taken together, these reports lead me to believe that when stimuli from the baby are high enough both anxious and non-anxious mothers would be capable of detecting them. However, when stimuli are less clear, at least for primiparous women discovering signs of distress from their baby for the first time, anxiety could modulate attentional cueing by varying the current anxiety level from the A-trait. However, most authors in the cognitive field have studied the attentional bias for A-trait and rarely for A-state, citing Bar-Haim et al. (2007): "How state and trait anxiety contribute to threat-related attentional bias remains an unresolved issue"; and as far as I know the variation of A-state from A-trait has not been studied. Despite this, and in accordance with my hypothesis, Egloff and Hock (2001) revealed an interesting result showing that the interaction between the A-trait and A-state was the best predictor of attentional bias (in the Stroop task) compared to either A-trait or A-state alone. The positive correlation between trait and state anxiety in the high A-trait group indicates a "hypervigilant cognitive mode" for those who scored high state anxiety, but an "offset bias" for those with lower A-state, which concurs with my hypothesis. In contrast, the correlation was negative in the low A-trait group, which contradicts my hypothesis. Nonetheless, they did not assess defensiveness, and neither do I, while Eysenck (1997, cited by Ioannou, 2004) addressed the importance of classifying persons not only according to their anxiety scores but also according to their defensiveness. Indeed, Ioannou reported findings showing the effects of anxiety trait and defensiveness on bias vigilance for threat.

Overall, in light of these different studies, presumably regulating ones level of anxiety may be an important psychological adaptation to motherhood. The normalization of mood variation may therefore have a functional status. As such, this variation in anxiety (increase or decrease with respect to the A-trait) would contribute to the implementation of an optimal perception of the infant thus enabling responsiveness during interaction, care, and protection, as described by Winnicott (1958/1969) or Stern (1995/1997) as "motherhood constellation" or "maternal preoccupation" respectively. This self-regulation would enable women to attain an optimal level of anxiety and is congruent with the fact that too much or too little primary maternal preoccupation may be problematic (Winnicott).

A Renewed Approach to Maternal Anxiety

This chapter provides a clearer picture of perinatal anxiety in healthy population. It would appear that the intensity-alone approach, which prevails in anxiety literature, only provides a limited perspective of maternal anxiety. My results show differences within an individual as well as differences between individuals in the course of state anxiety, using the gap between assessment time points. Nevertheless, owing to aforementioned limitations, further studies are required to support the idea of the utility of distinguishing between level and direction of anxiety. Other advances in our understanding of anxiety patterns during peripartum period have been provided by the use of an alternative approach, measuring the gap between A-trait and A-state. The latter reveals that elevated A-State score does not necessarily reflect episodic perinatal anxiety or current symptoms. Thus, this gap indicates regulation and, more importantly, normalization of anxiety for women with an extreme A-trait. We can therefore assume that highly anxious women (high A-Trait) modulate their current level of anxiety in order to reduce attentional bias towards their baby, whereas women with low anxiety proneness (low A-trait) increase their current anxiety to improve their ability to process ill-being signals from the baby. The discrepancy between anxiety measures could be used as a complement to standard quantitative analysis by providing qualitative differences between subjects.

If the changes observed are confirmed, one could propose a plausible explanation for why there is so little evidence of improved outcomes for mothers within professional intervention groups and why it is difficult to detect anxious pregnant women (or mothers). Indeed, groups of women with high levels of anxiety (trait or state) may be heterogeneous, i.e. composed of women who experience normalization of their anxiety, and of women who suffer from occasional anxiety disorders. In the same vein, our findings could suggest why there are still inconsistent results regarding the effects of anxiety on both birth outcomes and child development that may be due in part to analytical methods that do not take the gap between anxiety measures into account, i.e. how mothers differ, over time, from themselves. Further research is needed to evaluate trait and state anxiety and the gap between them, thus enabling the differentiation between anxiety trait effects, anxiety state effects, and anxiety gap effects.

I hope these findings using novel composite measurements will provide new insights into perinatal anxiety. The notion of discrepancy between measurements provides an avenue for further work to understand the anxiety response, but would also have important practical implications for psychologists performing a consultative role with mothers. A dual interest could be envisaged: first of all, the discovery of self-regulation process will enable practitioners to improve the detection of women with anxiety disorders without confusing them with those who have both high anxiety *and* self-regulation, providing that they take into account the direction of change and not just intensity. Thus, if these findings are confirmed, they would be useful for the development and rapid implementation of targeted interventions. Second, the novel clue could be used to identify factors that promote the self-regulation of anxiety during the transition to motherhood. The patterning of state anxiety should differ as a function of inter-individual difference variables; research might focus on the individual difference variables, both personal and situational, that influence the gap. The new clues (DSS and DTS) may be viewed as a further level of maternal emotional appraisal. At a more fundamental level, although premature, one of many future avenues for research would be to determine whether there is a personal optimal anxiety zone during the transition to motherhood, or whether debilitative and facilitative anxieties exist in motherhood.

ACKNOWLEDGMENT

I would like to thank the midwives (especially C. Horbacz) who helped me to meet women as well as the association "Promotion de la Santé Psychique". I am grateful to the mothers who participated in this research. I would also like to thank those who helped me for the English rectifications: Fabien Bacro, Josephine Billet, Françoise Roland, Steven, and Isadora Vuong-Van.

REFERENCES

Altshuler, L.L. ,Hendrick, V., Cohen, L.S. (2000). An update on mood and anxiety disorders during pregnancy and the postpartum period. *Prim. Care Companion J. Clin. Psychiatry, 2*, 217–222.

Apter, M.J. (1989). Reversal theory: a new approach to motivation, emotion and personnality. *Anuario de psicologia, 42*(3), 17-29.

Apter, M.J. (1997). Reversal theory: what is it ? *The Psychologist, 10*(5), 217-220.

Apter, M. (Ed.) (2001). *Motivational styles in everyday life: A guide to reversal theory.* Washington, DC, US: American Psychological Association.

Apter, M. (2003). On a certain blindness in modern psychology. *The Psychologist, 16*(9), 474-475.

Apter, M.J., Mallows, R. & Williams, S. (1998). The development of the motivational style profile. *Person. Individ. Diff., 24*(1), 7-18.

Austin, M.P. (2004). Antenatal screening and early intervention for ''perinatal'' distress, depression and anxiety: where to from here ? *Archives of Women's Mental Health, 7*, 1-6. doi: 10.1007/s00737-003-0034-4.

Austin, M.-P., Frilingos, M., Lumley, J., Hadzi-Pavlovic, D., Roncolato W., Acland, S., Saint, K., Segal, N. & Parker, G. (2008). Brief antenatal cognitive behaviour therapy group intervention for the prevention of postnatal depression and anxiety: A randomised controlled trial. *Journal of Affective Disorders, 105*, 35–44. doi:10.1016/j.jad.2007.04.001.

Austin, M.P., Hadzi-Pavlovic, D., Leader, L. Saint, K. & Parker, G. (2005). Maternal trait anxiety, depression and life event stress in pregnancy: relationships with infant temperament. *Early human development, 81*, 183-190. doi:10.1016/j.earlhumdev.2004.07.001.

Austin, M.-P., Hadzi-Pavlovic, D., Priest, S.R., Reilly, N., Wilhelm, K., Saint, K. & Parker, G. (2010). Depressive and anxiety disorders in the postpartum period: how prevalent are they and can we improve their detection? *Arch Womens Ment Health, 13*, 395–401. doi: 10.1007/s00737-010-0153-7.

Ballard, C.G., Davis, R., Handy S. & Mohan, R.N.C. (1993). Postpartum anxiety in mothers and fathers. *The European Journal of Psychiatry, 7*(2), 117-121.

Banti, S., Borri, C., Camilleri, V., Cortopassi, C., Montagnani, M.S., Ramacciotti, D., Rambelli, C. & Mauri, M. (2009). Perinatal mood and anxiety disorders. Clinical assessment and management. A review of current literature. *Giorn Ital Psicopat, 15*, 351-366.

Barnett, B., & Parker, G. (1985). Professional and non-professional intervention for high anxious primiparous mothers. *British Journal of Psychiatry, 146*, 287-293.

Bar-Haim, Y., Lamy, D., Pergamin, L., Bakermans-Kranenburg, M. H., & van IJzendoorn, M. H. (2007). Threat-related attentional bias in anxious and non-anxious individuals: A meta-analytic study. *Psychological Bulletin, 133*, 1-24. doi: 10.1037/0033-2909.133.1.1.

Barnett, B., & Parker, G. (1986). Possible determinants, correlates and consequences of high levels of anxiety in primiparous mothers. *Psychological Medicine, 16*, 177-185.

Barnett, B., Schaafsma, M.F., Guzman, A.M., & Parker, G.B. (1991). Maternal anxiety: a 5 year review of an intervention study. *Journal of Child Psychology & Psychiatry and allied disciplines, 32*, 423-438.

Bhagwanani, S.G., Seagraves, K., Dierker, L.J., & Lax, M. (1997). Relationship between prenatal anxiety and perinatal outcome in nulliparous women: a prospective study. *Journal of the National Medical Association, 89,* 93-98.

Bourgeois M.-L., Sutter a.-L., Dubroca B., Benech-Plaire G., Dallay-Glatigny E., Oblet V., & Lagrange C. (1998). Le projet MATQUID de psychiatrie périnatale. Présentation et premiers résultats au 8ème mois de grossesse de l'enquête prospective d'une cohorte de 500 femmes. *Annales Médico-psychologiques, 156*(9), 577-587.

Breitkopf, C.R., Primeau, L.A., Levine, R.E., Olson, G.L., Wu, Z.H. & Berenson, A.B. (2006). Anxiety symptoms during pregnancy and postpartum. *J. Psychosom. Obstet. Gynaecol., 27*(3), 157–162. doi: 10.1080/01674820500523521.

Brockington, I.F., Macdonald, E., & Wainscott, G. (2006). Anxiety, obsessions and morbid preoccupations in pregnancy and the puerperium. *Archives of Women's Mental Health, 9,* 253-263. doi:10.1007/s00737-006-0134-z.

Brouwers, E.P.M., Van Baar, A.L., & Pop, V.J.M. (2001). Maternal anxiety during pregnancy and subsequent infant development. *Infant Behavior and Development, 24*, 95-106.

Bruchon-Schweitzer, M., & Paulhan, I. (1993). *Le Manuel du STAI-Y de C.D. Spielberger, french adaptation.* Paris : ECPA.

Capponi, I., & Horbacz, C. (2005). Evolution et déterminants éventuels de l'anxiété périnatale de primipares: du huitième mois de grossesse au troisième mois post-partum. *Devenir, 17,* 211-231.

Capponi, I., & Horbacz, C. (2007). A propos de l'invisibilité de l'anxiété périnatale. *Perspectives Psychiatriques, 46*(4), 362-367.

Capponi, I., & Horbacz, C. (2008). Le devenir mère : anxiété et temporalité de l'accompagnement. *Pratiques Psychologiques, 14* (3), 389-404. doi: 10.1016/j.prps.2008.05.001.

Catov, J.M., Abatemarco, D.J., Markovic, N. & Roberts, J.M. (2010). Anxiety and Optimism Associated with Gestational Age at Birth and Fetal Growth. *Matern Child Health J, 14*(5), 758–764. doi: 10.1007/s10995-009-0513-y.

Cisler, J.M., Bacon, A.K., Nathan L. & Williams, N.L. (2009). Phenomenological characteristics of attentional biases towards threat: A critical review. *Cogn Ther Res, 33*, 221–234. doi: 10.1007/s10608-007-9161-y.

Coates, A.O., Schaefer, C.A. & Alexander, J.L. (2004). Detection of Postpartum Depression and Anxiety in a Large Health Plan. *Journal of Behavioral Health Services & Research, 31*(2), 117-133.

Coplan, R.J., O'Neil, K., & Arbeau, K.A. (2005). Maternal anxiety during and after pregnancy and infant temperament at three month of age. *The International Journal of Prenatal and Perinatal Psychology and Health, 19,* 199-215.

Davis, E.P., Snidman, N, Wadhwa, P., Glynn, L.M., Dunkel-Schetter, C. & Sandman, C.A. (2004). Prenatal maternal anxiety and depression predict behavioral reactivity in infants. *Infancy, 6*(3), 319-331.

Dayan, J., Andro, G., & Dugnat, M. (1999). *Psychopathologie de la périnatalité*. Paris: Masson.

Delignières, D. (2008). *Psychologie du sport*. Paris : PUF.

Dollander, M. & de Tichey, C. (2002). Fragilité psychologique de l'enfant en devenir et période prénatale. *Evolution Psychiatrique, 67* (2), 290–311.

Dugnat, M., (2002). Santé mentale et psychiatrie périnatales : renouveler l'approche de la prévention. *Dialogue, 157*, 29–41.

Egloff, B. & Hock, M. (2001). Interactive effects of state anxiety and trait anxiety on emotional Stroop interference. *Personality and Individual Differences, 31*, 875-882.

Eysenck, M.W. (1984). *Handbook of Cognitive Psychology*. London: Psychology Press Ltd.

Faisal-Cury, A. & Rossi Menezes, P. (2007). Prevalence of anxiety and depression during pregnancy in a private setting sample. *Archives of Womens Mental Health, 10*, 25–32. doi: 10.1007/s00737-006-0164-6.

Fleming, A.S., Flett, G., Ruble, D.N., Van Wagner, V.(1990). Adjustment in first-time mothers: changes in mood and mood content during the early postpartum months. *Developmental Psychology, 26*(1), 137-143.

Glasheen, C., Richardson, G.A. & Fabio, A. (2010). A systematic review of the effects of postnatal maternal anxiety on children. *Archives of Women's Mental Health, 13*(1), 61-74. doi: 10.1007/s00737-009-0109-y.

Glazier, R.H., Elgar, F.J., Goel, V., & Holzapfel, S. (2004). Stress, social support, and emotional distress in a community sample of pregnant women. *Journal of Psychosomatic Obstetrics & Gynecololy, 25,* 247-255. doi: 10.1080/01674820400024406.

Glynn, L.M., Dunkel-Schetter, C., Hobel, C.J. & Sandman, C.A. (2008). Pattern of perceived stress and anxiety in pregnancy predicts preterm birth. *Health Psychology, 27*(1), 43-51. doi: 10.1037/0278-6133.27.1.43.

Goldstein, L.H., Diener, M.L. & Mangelsdorf, S.C. (1996). Maternal characteristics and social support across the transition to motherhood: associations with maternal behavior. *Journal of family Psychology, 10* (1), 60-71.

Goodman, J. & Tyer-Viola, L. (2010). Detection, treatment, and referral of perinatal depression and anxiety by obstetrical providers. *Journal of Women's Health, 19*(3), 477-490. doi:10.1089/jwh.2008.1352.

Grant, K.A., McMahon, C., & Austin, M.P. (2008). Maternal anxiety during the transition to parenthood: A prospective study. *Journal of Affective Disorders, 108,* 101-111. doi:10.1016/j.jad.2007.10.002.

Gunning, M.D., Denison, F.C., Stokley, C.J., Ho, S.P., Sandhu, H.K. & Reynolds, R.M. (2010). Assessing maternal anxiety in pregnancy with the State-Trait Anxiety Inventory (STAI): issues of validity, location and participation. *Journal of reproductive and infant psychology, 28*(3): 266-273. doi: 10.1080/02646830903487300.

Hart, R., & McMahon, C.A. (2006). Mood state and psychological adjustment to pregnancy. *Archives of Women's Mental Health, 9*, 329-337. doi: 10.1007/s00737-006-0141-0.

Heron, J., O'Connor, T.G., Evans, J., Golding, J., & Glover, J. (2004). The course of anxiety and depression through pregnancy and the postpartum in a community sample. *Journal of Affective Disorders, 80,* 65-73. doi:10.1016/j.jad.2003.08.004.

Hersen, M. (2004). *Comprehensive Handbook of Psychological Assessment: Personality assessment.* John Wiley & Sons.

Hosseini, SM, Biglan, MW, Larkby, C, Brooks, MM, Gorin, MB & Day, NL. (2009). Trait anxiety in pregnant women predicts offspring birth outcomes. *Paediatr Perinat Epidemiol., 23*(6), 557-66.

Howell, D.C., Rogier, M., Yzerbyt, V., & Bestgen, Y. (2007). *Méthodes statistiques en sciences humaines.* Bruxelles, De Boeck.

Hundley, V., Gurney, E., Graham, W., & Rennie, A.M. (1998). Can anxiety in pregnant women be measured using the State-Trait Anxiety Inventory. *Midwifery, 14,* 118-121.

Ioannou, M.C., Mogg, K. & Bradley, B.P. (2004). Vigilance for threat: effects of anxiety and defensiveness. *Personality and Individual Differences, 36*, 1879-1891. doi:10.1016/j.paid.2003.08.018.

Jomeen, J. (2004). The importance of assessing psychological status during pregnancy, childbirth and the postnatal period as a multidimensional construct: a literature review. *Clinical Effectiveness in Nursing, 8,* 143-155. doi: 10.1016/j.cein.2005.02.001.

Jones, G. (1995). More than just a game: Research developments and issues in competitive anxiety in sport. *British Journal of Psychology, 86*(4), 449-478.

Kaitz, M., & Maytal, H. (2005). Interaction between anxious mothers and their infants: an integration of theory and research findings. *Infant Mental Health Journal, 26,* 570-597.

Keeton, C.P., Perry-Jenkins, M. & Sayer, A.G. (2008). Sense of Control Predicts Depressive and Anxious Symptoms Across the Transition to Parenthood. *Journal of Family Psychology, 22*(2), 212–221. doi: 10.1037/0893-3200.22.2.212.

Knight, R.G., & Thirkettle, J.A. (1986). Anxiety and depression in the immediate post-partum period: a controlled investigation of a primiparous sample. *Australian and New Zealand Journal of Psychiatry, 20,* 430-436.

Lee, A.M., Chong, C.S.Y., Chiu, H.W., Lam, S.K., Fong, D.Y.T. (2007). Prevalence, course, and risk factors for antenatal anxiety and depression. *Obstetrics & Gynecology, 110*(5), 1102–1112.

Littleton, H.L., Breitkopf, R. C., Berenson, A.B. (2007). Correlates of anxiety symptoms during pregnancy and association with perinatal outcomes: A meta-analysis. American. *Journal of Obstetrics & Gynecology, 196*(5), 424-432. doi: 10.1016/j.ajog.2007.03.042.

Lonstein, J.S. (2007). Regulation of anxiety during the postpartum period. Frontiers in Neuroendocrinology, 28, 115–141. doi:10.1016/j.yfrne. 2007.05.002.

Maner, J.K., Richey, J.A., Cromer, K., Mallott, M., Lejuez, C.W., Joiner, T.E., & Schmidt, N.B. (2007). Dispositional anxiety and risk-avoidant decision-making. *Personality and Individual Differences, 42*, 665–675. doi:10.1016/j.paid.2006.08.016.

Matthey, S., Barnett, B., Howie, P., Kavanagh, D.J. (2003). Diagnosing postpartum depression in mothers and fathers: whatever happened to anxiety ? *Journal of Affective Disorders, 74,* 139–147. doi:10.1016/ S0165-0327(02)00012-5.

Macbeth, A.H. & Luine, V.N. (2010). Changes in anxiety and cognition due to reproductive experience: A review of data from rodent and human mothers. *Neuroscience and Biobehavioral Reviews, 34*(3), 452-467. doi:10.1016/j.neubiorev.2009.08.011.

Meades, R. & Ayers, S. (2010). Anxiety measures validated in perinatal populations: A systematic review. *J. Affect. Disord.* [in press]. doi:10.1016/j.jad.2010.10.009.

Mertesacker, B., Bade, U., Haverkock, A., & Pauli-Pott, U. (2004). Predicting maternal reactivity/sensitivity: the role of infant emotionality, maternal depressiveness/anxiety, and social support. *Infant Mental Health Journal, 25*(1), 47-61. doi: 10.1002/imhj.10085.

Mitte, K. (2008). Memory Bias for Threatening Information in Anxiety and Anxiety Disorders: A Meta-Analytic Review. *Psychological Bulletin, 134*(6), 886–911. doi: 10.1037/a0013343.

Mogg, K., & Bradley, B. P. (1998). A cognitive -motivational analysis of anxiety. *Behaviour Research & Therapy, 36*, 809-848.

Murgatroyd, S., Rushton, C., Apter, M.J. & Ray, C. (1978). The development of the Telic Dominance Scale. *Journal of personality assessment, 45*(5): 519-528.

Nicol-Harper, R., Harvey, H.G., & Stein, A. (2007). Interactions between mothers and infants: Impact of maternal anxiety. *Infant Behavior & Development, 30,* 161-167. doi: 10.1016/j.infbeh.2006.08.005.

Norbeck J.S., & Anderson N.J. (1989). Life stress, social support, and anxiety in mid- and late-pregnancy among low income women. *Research in nursing and health, 12*, 281-287.

O'Connor, T.G., Caprariello, P., Robertson Blackmore, E. et al. (2007). Prenatal mood disturbance predicts sleep problems in infancy and toddlerhood. *Early Human Development, 83,* 451-458. doi:10.1016/ j.earlhumdev.2006.08.006.

O'Connor T.G., Heron J., Golding J., Beveridge M. & Glover V. (2002). Maternal antenatal anxiety and children's behavioural/emotional problems at 4 years: report from the Avon Longitudinal Study of Parents and Children. *British journal of psychiatry, 180*, 502-508.

O'Connor, T.G., Heron, J., Golding, J., Glover, V. & the ALSPAC Study Team. (2003). Maternal antenatal anxiety and behavioral/emotional problems in children: a test of a programming hypothesis. *Journal of Child Psychology and Psychiatry and Allied Disciplines*, *44,* 1025-36.

Ouimet, A.J., Gawronski, B. & Dozois, D.J.A. (2009). Cognitive vulnerability to anxiety: A review and an integrative model. *Clinical psychology review, 29*, 459–470. doi: 10.1016/j.cpr.2009.05.004.

Orr, S.T., Reiter, J.P., Blazer, D.G., & Sherman, A, J. (2007). Maternal prenatal pregnancy-related anxiety and spontaneous preterm birth in Baltimore, Maryland. *Psychosomatic Medicine, 69*, 566–570.

Persson, E.K. & Dykes, A.-K. (2009). Important variables for parents' postnatal sense of security: evaluating a new swedish instrument (the PPSS instrument). *Midwifery, 25*(4), 449-460. doi: 10.1016/j.midw. 2007.08.001.

Poussin, G. (1993). *Psychologie de la fonction parentale*. Toulouse: Privat.

Robert, E., David, H., Reeves, N., Goron, S., & Delfosse, S. (2008). Adaptation à la maternité: évolution discontinue de l'anxiété en pré- et en post-partum et valeur prédictive des différents types d'anxiété. *Devenir, 20*(1), 151-171.

Ross, L.E., & McLean, L.M. (2006). Anxiety disorders during pregnancy and the postpartum period: a systematic review. *The journal of clinical psychiatry, 67,* 1285-1298.

Sarason, I.G., Levine, H.M., Basham, R.B., & Sarason, B.R. (1983). Assessing social support: the social support questionnaire. *Journal of Personality and social Psychology, 44*(1), 127-139.

Sayil, M., Güre, A., & Uçanok, Z. (2006). First time mothers' anxiety and depressive symptoms across to motherhood: associations with maternal and environmental characteristics. *Women & Health, 44*(3), 61-71. doi: 10.1300/J013v44n03_04.

Shaw, E., Levitt, C., Wong, S., & Kaczorowski, J. (2006). Systematic review of the literature on postpartum care: Effectiveness of postpartum support to improve maternal parenting, mental health, quality of life, and physical health. *Birth, 33*(3), 210-220.

Sjögren, B., Widström, A.M., Edman, G., & Uvnäs-Moberg, K. (2000). Changes in personality pattern during the first pregnancy and lactation. *J. Psychosom. Obstet. Gynaecol., 21*, 31–38.

Skari, H., Skreden, M., Malt, U.F., Dalholt, M., Ostensen, A.B., Egeland, T., & Emblem, R. (2002). Comparative levels of psychological distress, stress symptoms, depression and anxiety after childbirth - a prospective population- based study of mothers and fathers. *BJOG: an international Journal of Obstetrics and Gynaecology, 109*(10), 1154-1163.

Spielberger, C.D., Gorsuch, R.L., & Lushene, R.E., Vagg, P.R. & Jacobs, G.A. (1983). *Manual for the State-Trait Anxiety Inventory, STAI Form Y.* Palo Alto. CA: Consulting Psychologists Press.

Stern, D. (1997). *The motherhood constellation.* Mesnil sur l'Estrée, France: Calmann-Lévy. Original work published 1995.

Sutter, A.L., & Bourgeois, M. (1995). Grossesse, post-partum et troubles anxieux. *Confrontations Psychiatriques, 36*, 125–138.

Svebak, S. & Apter, M. (1997). The reversal process. In S. Svebak & M.J. Apter. *Stress and health. A reversal theory perspective.* Washington: Taylor & Francis.

Teixeira, C., Figueiredo, B., Conde, A., Pacheco, A. & Costa, R. (2009). Anxiety and depression during pregnancy in women and men. *Journal of Affective Disorders, 119*, 142–148. doi:10.1016/j.jad.2009.03.005.

Teixeira, J., Martin, D., Prendiville, O., & Glover, V. (2005). The effects of acute relaxation on indices of anxiety during pregnancy. *Journal of psychosomatic obstetrics & Gynecology, 26*(4): 271-276. doi: 10.1080/ 01674820500139922.

van Bussel, J.C.H., Spitz, B., Demyttenaere, K. (2008). Anxiety in pregnant and postpartum women. An exploratory study of the role of maternal orientations. *Journal of Affective Disorders* [in press]. doi: 10.1016/j.jad.2008.07.018.

Wenzel, A., Haugen, E.N., Jackson, L.C., & Brendle, J.R. (2005). Anxiety symptoms and disorders at eight weeks postpartum. *Journal of Anxiety Disorders, 19* (3), 295–311. doi:10.1016/j.janxdis.2004.04.001.

Wenzel, A., Haugen, E. N., Jackson, L. C., & Robinson, K. (2003). Prevalence of generalized anxiety at eight weeks postpartum. *Arch Womens Ment Health, 6,* 43–49. doi: 10.1007/s00737-002-0154-2.

Winnicott, D.W. (1969). *Through pediatrics to psycho-analysis*. Paris: Payot. Original work published 1958.

Zelkowitz, P., & Papageorgiou, A. (2005). Maternal anxiety: an emerging prognostic factor in neonatalogy. *Acta-paediatrica-Oslo, 94*(12), 1704-1705.

In: Trait Anxiety
Editor: Anna S. Morales
ISBN 978-1-61324-551-4

Chapter 3

TRAIT ANXIETY AND DENTAL ANXIETY

Lucía Lago-Méndez[1], Márcio Diniz Freitas[1], Carmen Senra-Rivera[2], Gloria Seoane-Pesqueira[2], and Abel García-García[1]

[1]Oral Surgery Department, School of Dentistry, University of Santiago de Compostela, Spain

[2]Department of Clinical Psychology and Psychobiology, University of Santiago de Compostela, Spain

ABSTRACT

The continual advances in dental treatment in recent years have not affected the fact that considerable numbers of patients undergo psychological discomfort, in the form of anxiety syndrome, in relation to such treatment. Dental anxiety may lead to negative effects on dental and also in general health or physical recovery after treatment, especially after surgical interventions. The possibility of successful treatment is reduced by insufficient knowledge, among dental clinicians, about dental anxiety, its presentation and evaluation, and the characteristics of the patients. Theories that link trait anxiety (the tendency for anxious people to perceive situations as potentially threatening) to dental anxiety suggest that identification of trait anxiety may be useful for predicting dental anxiety predisposition in patients. A prior awareness of the patient's predisposition to dental anxiety may thus be of value to the dentist, enabling him or her to take appropriate preventative and/or therapeutic measures. In accordance with this, in some situations it may be useful for the dentist to evaluate trait anxiety before interventions of this type, although bearing in mind that trait anxiety is only a partial predictor in the multifactorial etiology of dental anxiety. This chapter provides a theoretical introduction in which the conceptualization, etiology and manifestations of dental anxiety are considered, and some of the self-report measures most commonly used in this area are described. The results of different studies in which trait anxiety and different measures of dental anxiety have been explored in relation to surgical removal of the lower third molar, are then discussed. The effect of anxiety on both the duration of the intervention and the post-operative recovery of patients is also discussed. Finally, the relationship between trait anxiety and different aspects of dental anxiety is considered.

1. Dental Anxiety

1.1. Conceptual Delimitation: Anxiety, Fear and Phobia

In clinical terms, anxiety is usually defined as an emotional reaction characterized by feelings of apprehension, nervousness and worry, caused by anticipation of a close threat or danger, but which is intangible and diffuse, and is accompanied by activation of the autonomous nervous system [1,2,3,4,5,6]. As a concept, anxiety tends to be considered as an emotional state that appears as a multidimensional reaction characterized by different components or response systems: subjective (or cognitive), physiological (or somatic) and motor (or behavioral) [7]. The concept was formulated in 1963 by Lang and Lazovik [8], within the focus of the so-called "three-systems" model [9]. From this point of view, Miguel-Tobal [10] considered that anxiety includes unpleasant cognitive aspects, such as tension and apprehension; physiological aspects characterized by a high degree of activation of the autonomous nervous system, and motor aspects, which usually involve instrumental responses of escape and avoidance, as well as certain facial expressions and movements, and body postures. Several studies [11,12,13] on the triple response to anxiety coincide in indicating that the three components may be dissociated and will function with a certain degree of independence, giving rise to the phenomenon known as response fractionation, which in turn leads to different cognitive, physiological and/or behavioral profiles, depending on the predominance of each system.

The distinction between anxiety and fear has never been completely resolved, and nowadays it is accepted that both reactions take place when an individual perceives a situation to be dangerous or threatening. Traditionally, the terms fear and anxiety were differentiated because the first is an immediate emotional reaction to a real, identifiable danger, whereas the second is a more diffuse emotional state, with no recognizable external source of threat. However, this distinction is problematical because the stimuli that generate fear may exist, although they are not identifiable, and may also be internal and difficult to determine. Some authors have tried to resolve these problems by considering that fear is a primitive alarm that is set off in response to perception of the presence of a threat/danger, thus motivating escape behavior, whereas anxiety or anxious apprehension is an emotional state of unresolved fear or a state of activation that does not have a specific direction once a threat is perceived [14,15].

In fact, in general terms, fear and anxiety are used interchangeably, and fears and phobias are usually considered as anxiety-related problems or disorders.

However, it is also important to differentiate conceptually between fear and phobia because, although they are usually used interchangeably in the odontological literature, they are different constructs. The term phobia refers to intense, disproportionate, persistent and irrational fear directed at a specific object, situation or activity, which gives rise to an uncontrollable desire to avoid the source of fear [16]. Although in strict terms avoidance must occur for diagnosis of a phobia, clinically it is usually assumed sufficient that the person shows a strong desire to avoid the situation, or only tolerates the situation with a high degree of anxiety and discomfort. Phobia is therefore an anxiety-related disorder [17].

One important characteristic of anxiety is its anticipatory nature, i.e. the anxiety response anticipates danger or threat to a person. This confers anxiety an important functional role, with biological-adaptive value. However, this becomes a disadvantage when an unreal danger is anticipated. Thus anxiety does not always vary in direct proportion to a real (objective) danger, but is irrational and occurs in response to situations of low objective danger or situations that are not actually dangerous. Anxiety can therefore be understood either as a normal, necessary response, or as a disadvantageous response (pathological anxiety). Pathological anxiety is generally characterized by certain quantitative differences relative to normal anxiety, by e.g. taking the form of a phobia.

Anxiety has been widely associated with dental treatment. The dental situation is a special case, as certain odontological procedures may cause pain or other disagreeable experiences. The complex factors of anxiety influence the dental encounter and may give rise to a great variety of behavioral dysfunctions related to dental treatment [18].

In the dental situation fear and anxiety are almost indistinguishable [2,18]. The patient is confronted with "real" and "imaginary" threats, and reacts with different degrees of apprehension.

Some authors have used the terms "dental fear" to describe moderate apprehension that causes tension during treatment, but that allows the patient to receive dental care, "dental anxiety" to denote a more profound apprehension that interferes with routine treatment and that requires special attention, and the term "dental phobia" to refer to patients whose anxiety is so great that they avoid dental care, even to the point of negligence [3,4,6].

We consider the terms dental fear and dental anxiety as equivalent and will use them interchangeably throughout this chapter.

1.2. Manifestations of Dental Anxiety

The complexity of the phenomenon of anxiety may give rise to a large variety of dysfunctions related to dental treatment. As already mentioned, the construct of anxiety involves a variety of cognitive, physiological and behavioral responses.

Cognitive manifestations of dental anxiety [19] refer to the internal experience and may be manifested as changes in contents or patterns of thinking in patients. These include a wide range of variables related to the perception and subjective evaluation of stimuli and states associated with dental anxiety, as follows:

Anticipation: i.e. fear of losing teeth, fear of death, reflections about what is going to occur in the waiting room; hypersensitivity to dental stimuli and expectation of pain in response to these. The anxiety decreases the threshold of tolerance to pain, and increases the possibility that non-harmful stimuli will be interpreted as painful, especially in sensitive people [6,20,21].

Beliefs: this category includes patients' manifestations as regards their attitudes and those of other patients. Thus, a patient suffering from dental anxiety feels strange or weak in comparison with others, and believes that other people are not capable of understanding their anxiety. Some patients would even prefer to have all of their teeth extracted rather than have to attend the dentist regularly.

Negative feelings expressed as vulnerability and low self esteem.
Recall of traumatic dental experiences.

Physiological manifestations of dental anxiety [19], as commonly occur in response to fear. Most patients report physiological symptoms such as dry mouth, increased sweating, palpitations, tremors, etc. Such symptoms may appear on the same day as the dental appointment, or even earlier, e.g. the night before. These physiological responses often occur in the waiting room or during dental surgery, although they may also occur when the patient phones to make the dental appointment. Some patients experience great tiredness after the dental appointment, to the extent that their daily activities may be interrupted. Subjectively, these organic changes are usually perceived as annoying and disagreeable, which further reinforces the subjective state of anxiety.

Behavioral manifestations of dental anxiety [19]: the most common of these is avoidance of dental appointments, even when the patient is experiencing pain, with a visit to the dentist being the last resort. Surveys carried out in the USA have revealed that 5 - 6% of the adult population avoids dental treatment because of fear. In addition, it has been estimated that a much higher percentage of the population, up to 25%, avoids dental treatment except when they are suffering from some symptoms [22]. Alterations in eating habits may also be manifested. Thus many people with a high degree of dental anxiety modify their eating habits to avoid certain foods - because of difficulty in chewing -and cold drinks - to prevent the pain associated with sensitivity.

All of the above may have repercussions in terms of social interactions, health, and clinician-patient interactions. The social repercussions of dental anxiety may give rise to negative psychosocial consequences [23], which on occasions may affect a patient's work, as delays in visiting the dentist may lead to infection and oral pain that may prevent the patient from working. In addition, dental neglect may have a negative effect on the patient's perspectives of obtaining work or improving their work position. This may also have a negative effect on the development of interpersonal relationships, as patients with a high degree of dental anxiety are usually irritable and nervous prior to dental appointments.

As regards health, alterations in sleep patterns may occur (nightmares or insomnia the night before the dental appointment) or even worsening of oral health (delaying the visit to the dentist until the situation is unbearable).

However, dental anxiety is not only a serious problem for the sufferer, but also affects the dentist-patient relationship. The inability of the dentist to understand the problem causes many professional breakdowns and failures [24]. Anxious patients require 20% more time in the dentist's chair than relaxed patients [25], and dentists consider that anxious patients are one of the most annoying sources of professional stress [26,27], probably because the lack of cooperation by the patient makes dental procedures and treatment more difficult, which may give rise to unsatisfactory results [20,28]. A follow-up of the occupational illnesses of 56 dentists revealed that stress accounted for 42.1% of all such illnesses; in the under 45-year-old age group, the figure was 52.7% and in the over 45-year-old age group, the figure was 25% [24]. Howard, Cunningham and colleagues [29] have reported that dentists are abnormally subjected to the harmful effects of stress. They also reported that most dentists (80%) admitted becoming "anxious" themselves when attending patients suffering from dental anxiety [29].

In summary, the manifestations of dental anxiety present as a vicious cycle of anxiety and avoidance. Thus dental fear and anxiety lead to avoidance of dental appointments, and therefore dental neglect, which may involve real or perceived deterioration in oral health, which combined with the refusal by the patient to accept dental treatment, will eventually lead to feelings of embarrassment or inferiority, and in turn to low self-esteem. All of this may serve to increase the anxiety and reinforce the avoidance of dental care [23,30,31].

Ignoring the emotional conflicts of a person and their difficulties may lead to a traumatic experience [32]. The dentist must always be alert to the importance of treating the patient and not only the illness [24].

1.3. Prevalence of Dental Anxiety

There is general agreement as to the importance of dental anxiety, although it is difficult to evaluate the exact prevalence of the problem [18]. Proof of this is the wide range of values reported in different studies, possibly brought about by the different categorization of patients and by the different measuring instruments used. The first study [33] that provided data in this respect was published in 1958. Analysis of the prevalence of dental anxiety reported in studies between 1958 and 1984 reveals that the proportion of people with a high level of anxiety related to dental treatment ranged between

8 and 15%, and those with phobias, between 5 and 9%. Moderate anxiety appears at a rate of between 17 and 67% [34,35,36,37,38,39,40].

Studies carried out in the 1970s and 1980s in different parts of the USA reported a higher prevalence of dental fear than in the studies carried out in the late 1950s and early 1960s [18], which was then estimated at between 5 and 9% of the population. One study, carried out in Detroit in 2005 with a representative sample of adults between 18 and 69 years old, found that 12% presented high levels of dental anxiety [41]. A previous study, from 1998, in the same area had reported a prevalence of 10.2% [42]. In Canada, different epidemiological studies reported the prevalence of dental anxiety to be between 10.9% and 16.4% [43].

In Germany, in 1994, a media survey including the general question "What is your most common fear?", revealed that 36.1% of the population was above all, afraid of visiting the dentist [44]. More recent results, from 2006, have reported a prevalence of 11% for dental phobia in the general population, [45] and of 13.1% amongst army soldiers between 19 and 54 years old [46].

In Sweden, more than 9% of the adult population is thought to avoid dental care, and in England, of 419 people questioned, 15% reported being "very" or "extremely" anxious when subjected to preventative treatment, 30% were "very" or "extremely" anxious when they required treatment for dental caries, and 28% were "very" or "extremely" anxious in response to buccal injections; approximately 13% reported that they "always" or "almost always" postponed visits to the dentist because of anxiety [18]. However, another study carried out in the same year in Gothenburg reported a prevalence of 6.7% of people suffering from a high level of dental anxiety [47].

Epidemiological studies carried out in Norway between 1998 and 2003 reported figures of between 12 and 19% for the prevalence of dental anxiety interfering with good dental care [48,49], and of approximately 6.6% for dental phobia accompanied by frequent avoidance behavior.

The prevalence of dental anxiety in patients waiting for different types of buccal treatment was reported to be approximately 20% in the Netherlands in 1990 [50]. In Iceland, from a representative sample of 1548 people of between 25-74 years old, around 10 % admitted to suffering a considerable level of dental anxiety [51].

The problem of avoiding dental appointments is not specific to western cultures, and a report in 2005 indicated that approximately 9.9% of patients waiting for dental treatment in Istanbul displayed high levels of dental anxiety [52]. Studies carried out in Japan (1988) [53] with university students revealed that 31.5% of those interviewed admitted that they delayed making appointments to see the dentist because of fear of dental treatment. More than 80% reported "some degree of fear", whereas between 6 and 14% reported being "very fearful" or "terrified" about dental treatment; when the "very fearful" group was added to the latter two categories, the range increased from 21% to 33% of the students. Similar figures have been reported for populations in Indonesia, Taiwan and Singapore [54].

More recently, a study in Australia found that the prevalence of high dental fear ranged from 7.8% to 18.8%, and more incapacitating dental phobia from 0.9% to 5.4%, depending upon the scale, cut-point and specific criteria used. Also in 2010, the first study in Bulgaria on dental anxiety found that the percentage of people with high scores for dental anxiety (DAS 13-20) in this country (29.9%) is considerably higher than in some European and North American countries.

In Spain, a study on this topic [55], found that most people report often avoiding dental appointments because of fear, whereas cancellation of appointments was not as common.

As reported by various authors [56,57,58], dental anxiety is a disorder that has important negative repercussions for buccal health. It is estimated that 6-15% of the world's adult population avoids going to the dentist because of high levels of dental anxiety [18].

1.4. Etiology of Dental Anxiety

The origin of dental anxiety is multifactorial and involves physical, cognitive and learning-related aspects. Generally a combination of several factors leads to the development of dental anxiety [18]. Many elements have been implicated in the etiology and origin of dental fear in several studies, although most cite two type of acquisition: direct (prior experience) and indirect (transmission of information), with the approach used by Rachman in 1977 [59] being particularly noteworthy. Weiner and Sheehan [60] also classified patients with dental anxiety in terms of its etiology, differentiating between exogenous and endogenous etiology. With this system, in some individuals the development of dental fear is conditioned by specific adverse experiences (exogenous), whereas others appear to display constitutional vulnerability as regards developing anxiety disorders (panic disorder) that promote the susceptibility to developing dental anxiety (endogenous). Clinical observations led Milgrom, Weinstein, Kleinknecht and Getz [61] to develop an etiological categorization, known as the Seattle System, including four levels of dental anxiety (I: conditioned fear of specific stimuli; II: anxiety about reactions that may occur during treatment (dizziness, panic attacks); III: trait anxiety or multiphobia; IV: lack of confidence in dental personnel).

The importance of multifactorial etiology may be translated to different manifestations of and treatments for anxiety. Thus, Rachman [59] suggested that patients whose anxiety has developed directly, would display more physiological reactions that those who developed their anxiety through indirect routes (vicariously or via negative information). In a prior study [62] it was found that patients with traumatic etiology related more intense stories about avoiding dental treatment than those who had acquired their anxiety via cognitive learning. However, in 2002, de Jongh and colleagues [63] evaluated the consequences of trauma experienced by 56 highly anxious patients attending a dental fear clinic, and did not observe any differences between the scores for dental anxiety in relation to the etiology of the anxiety. They did not find any evidence suggesting that past traumatic events or the symptomology related to the trauma had a negative effect on the result of the treatment. Finally, the authors state that although knowledge of the origin of dental anxiety may be useful when providing the patient with information prior to treatment, it is not useful for treating the anxiety once established, as the treatments used have similar results in individuals suffering with anxiety of different etiology [63].

It can be seen that there are many causes of dental anxiety, described as follows:

Previous Traumatic Incidents or Adverse Experiences in the Dental Surgery

Traumatic or painful experiences during dental treatment appear to be the main cause of dental anxiety and fear [34,37,38,40,64,65,66,67,68,69]. Traumatic experiences may occur as a result of pain during treatment, non favorable attitudes of the dentist, or other disagreeable experiences during the consultation. Such experiences act as the initial stimulus that leads to the specific response patterns of fear or anxiety [30]. Most traumatic dental experiences occur during infancy or the schooling period [34,70], as reported by 85% of anxious patients [62].

Lautch [65] reported that although dental trauma is the most important etiological factor in the development of dental fear, at least two experiences of this nature are required before severe dental phobia develops. Öst and Hugdahl (1985) [71] found that 68.6% of dental phobias were due to traumatic events experienced directly by patients during dental treatment. Kleinknecht, Keplac and Alexander (1973) [66] identified the personal experiences associated with painful procedures as the main source of adverse reactions to odontological treatments and considered that in these cases, fear and avoidance are learned responses, and that traumatic experiences may be considered as classical conditioning factors. Thus, some dental stimuli that themselves do not cause fear or anxiety, but that occur during traumatic experiences, may become conditioned and acquire the capacity to provoke conditioned fear responses.

On some occasions the adverse experience may arise in the interpersonal relation between patient and dentist. The perception that the patient has about the doctor, in this case the dentist, is a significant factor as regards keeping future appointments and continuing with the treatment [72]. Johansson and colleagues [73] reported that dental anxiety is directly related to negative attitudes towards the dentist. In addition, other factors can be differentiated as regards the trauma caused by the dentist:

Causes of pain and errors made by the dentist, e.g. the dentist allowing the needle to slip, or refusing the use of anesthetic even when requested by the patient, beginning treatment before the anesthetic becomes effective, or treating the wrong tooth [66]. The two types of treatment in which these phenomena are most often observed are extraction (54%) and routine restoration (16%) [38]. According to Kleinknecht and colleagues [66] some 8.3% of participants related such errors. As a result, dental anxiety increases as the perception that the patient has of the dentist's competence decreases [74].

Criticism by the dentist about the patient's poor dental hygiene. Many patients fear that the dentist will comment on their poor dental hygiene or lack of cooperation during treatment [34,38,32,66,75]. In addition, anxious patients are much more susceptible to this type of comment that control patients [32]. A study carried out by Scott and colleagues [32] concluded that people suffering from a relatively high degree of dental anxiety are sensitive to any criticism in relation to their dental health. The criticism made by the dentist may significantly increase their discomfort, to the extent that they may change dentists or cease visiting the dentist.

Finally, another possible cause of dental fear is a disagreeable experience with another doctor. Scott and colleagues [32] reported that in comparison with control subjects, patients suffering from dental anxiety usually display more fear of injections at sites other than the mouth. Likewise, patients suffering from dental anxiety are those who most fear unpleasant medical treatments. However, as there were no differences between the groups in the number of personal and family traumas with other types of doctors, other medical treatments can be excluded as a factor causing dental fear.

Experiences Acquired through the Influence of Family Members and Close Friends

Fear and anxiety may be acquired not only by direct learning, but also by vicarious learning [66, 71]. The process of learning may be the result of observation, identification or indirect suggestion by role model, so that subjects do not have to suffer traumatic experiences directly in order to develop dental fear or avoidance behavior.

We learn about dental treatment not only from our personal experiences, by also by talking and observing others [34,38,32,64,65,66,67]. It is therefore possible to learn fear from others without being exposed to the object of fear. Social learning may generate a phobia, with parents being the best teachers. An anxious father or mother may subtly, or otherwise, communicate fear, thus interrupting the normal development of suitable resources for affronting situations in young patients [24]. For example, one explanation for dental anxiety in infancy is that the mother transmits her own anxiety to her child [76]. Patients suffering from dental anxiety recall that members of their family (or equivalent) influenced their fear and that they felt anxious when they heard anything about other people's dental treatment [66]. It has been found that the families of anxious patients, especially the mother and friends suffer a higher degree of anxiety than those of control patients [40]. Likewise, the parents of anxious patients are more permissive, and the mothers display lower levels of self-confidence and self- esteem [77]. Furthermore, these mothers only visited the dentist when suffering from a considerable degree of dental pain [70]. However, although the influence of the mother figure has been emphasized, some authors report that friends are most important, followed by brothers/sisters, the mother and finally the father [38]. Other authors not only minimize the importance of the mother figure in transmitting dental fear, but also consider that the importance of family members has been overestimated [34,78].

In addition, several variables affect or are related in some way to the anxiety and fear associated with dental treatment, as discussed in the following section.

1.5. Variables Related to Dental Anxiety

Previous publications reflect that there are factors that cannot be included among dental anxiety etiology but that are somehow involved in it:

Gender of the patients is one of the most studied variables in dental anxiety studies. Most authors agree that women show higher anxiety values than men [67,79,80]. However, not all studies find significant differences in dental anxiety between men and women [38,81]. In direct contradiction to the aforementioned results, Rome and Moore reported that men showed higher dental anxiety than women [82]. All of the above, can be modified depending on the frequency of visits to the dentist [33].

Some research studies suggest that differences in dental anxiety levels, in relation to gender, can be due to the different thresholds for pain in men and women [52]. It has also been argued that such differences could be due to the perception and meaning of painful experiences [80]. In a study on the characteristics of unpleasant dental experiences; the report stated that in high-anxiety groups men reach higher levels than women. This result suggests, according to these authors, that men require higher sensitivity than women for their anxiety expression to become dental fear [83]. In this regard, parental emotional references have been proven to be more frequent and diverse in daughters than in sons, this cut in emotional development can predispose differences in expression by gender. Thus, Adams et al. [84] highlighted that the fear level that children manifest is related to the role gender plays, but not biological sex, which illustrates the contribution of culture in the development and acquisition of phobias and fears. In any case, what does seem clear is that the gender of the stomatologists does not affect patients' fear and anxiety levels [85].

Age: The patient's age is also one of the factors involved, thus publications frequently show that dental anxiety levels are reduced as this variable increases [34,43,80,86,87]. Some papers [86] have explained this phenomenon by referring to the technological advances have taken place in dentistry over time; other argue the possibility of the patient becoming edentulous and thus their dental fear would disappear. Similarly, possible resignation or adaptation to the inevitable - related to the passage of time - was also analyzed. In any case, the ultimate cause of why many fears and phobias are reduced with age still remains unknown [88,89].

Contrary to the belief that dental phobia is acquired invariable during childhood, Locker et al. [90] stated that, although dental anxiety can begin during childhood (50% of cases), there is no typical age for its start. In this sense, other studies have reports that 15-30% of dental anxiety cases have their origin in adulthood and 15-20% during adolescence [47,91]. Without a doubt, age is a factor related to dental anxiety, given that the way this anxiety is acquired changes depending on the patient's age, since the nature of anxiety changes over the different periods in personal development [90,92,93]. According to the statement above, when the beginning of anxiety takes place during childhood it is more likely that this conditioning is due to traumatic experiences or vicarious learning; however, when it begins during adulthood there is usually certain vulnerability to anxiety disorders.

Ethnic and socio-demographic factors have also been said to be involved in dental anxiety. Schwarz and Birn [94] found differences in dental anxiety levels between Danish and Chinese populations. Although they found a significant relationship between dental anxiety and ethnic and socio-demographic variables, they only obtained small values, which led them to conclude that there should be other factors with a higher influence on anxiety. On the other hand, a study in Jerusalem on children showed no significant differences between dental anxiety and social class; as per ethnicity it was found to influence men [95].

For some authors, the socio-economic state and its relationship to cultural level can influence dental anxiety levels [33,96]. So, from a low socio-economic level one can expect lower cooperation and higher anxiety levels, since low cultural level impedes the functioning of adequate distraction and relaxation mechanisms during treatments [96]. However, other authors [47] report that there is no correlation between these variables and dental anxiety.

Components, characteristics and frequency of dental treatments can influence dental anxiety levels. Generally, patients with dental anxiety associate going to the dentist's office with experiences of great suffering; moreover, certain dental procedures generate more anxiety than others. Therefore, although patients are differentiated by in the values of their anxiety records, they report fear/anxiety when faced to the same situations [75]. Gale [75] in 1972, published a paper creating a dental fear hierarchy applicable to a great segment of the population, which agreed with previous studies [33]. This report indicated that the main reason for dental anxiety was fear of pain. The odontologist's attitude towards the patient and the generalized social attitude towards dental treatments and dentists also had a relevant place. Other factors implied in dental treatments were the characteristics of local anesthesia (needles, injections...) and the drill or high or low-speed turbine [4,40,65,67,97]. Extractions, which are a mutilation for patients, is - according to certain studies - one of the treatments causing greatest anxiety levels [34,38,67], although Mc Neil and Berryman (1989) [98] clarified that fear of mutilation was a significant component of dental anxiety only in women. Locker, Shapiro and Lidell [43] in 1997 concluded that fear of blood and injections has a little, yet significant, contribution to dental anxiety. Although, since the fourth edition of anxiety disorders, according to DSM-IV, dental phobia is classified under the same category as blood, injections, injuries [99].

Furthermore, the characteristics of each of the dental treatments can influence the anxiety level. In this regard, a relevant percentage of patients believe that dental pain cannot be cured spontaneously, requiring at least an emergency visit that, almost certainly, provides for further discomfort [100]. Additionally, patients are aware that they cannot interrupt a surgical treatment, whatever their degree of discomfort [21].

On the other hand, the frequency of the patients' visits influences their dental anxiety levels; thus, Kent [101] observed that patients who visited their dentists regularly showed less resentment and higher satisfaction than those who only visited them when they had a problem.

Certain personality traits and psychopathology. The relationship between dental fear and certain aspects or types of personality have been studied [2,66]. In general, most authors have not found a relationship between dental fear and personality traits, as Lautch stated in 1971 [65]. However, Berggren and Meynert (1984) [67], support that generalized anxiety, neuroticism and the tendency of phobic reactions could be causes for dental fear. Similarly, dental anxiety is positively related to a high frequency of negative thoughts [102]. Several authors

[40,65,103,104] have confirmed a positive correlation between generalized anxiety and dental anxiety.

Similarly, they have reported that they have lower tolerance to pain [65,104], therefore 47% of patients with dental anxiety are highly-sensitive to pain, when compared to 8% in control patients [40]. Anxiety disorders are frequent and some cases of schizoid personality and limit personality disorders have been detected [40,105]. Also, patients with addictions and social problems (in general) showed higher anxiety levels regarding dental treatments [20].

Some of the patient's systemic pathologies can influence their dental anxiety levels. Patients suffering from severe diseases show less anxiety in dental treatments, probably since their oral problem is secondary [100].

Association with other fears. Dental fear seems to be related to fear of pain [105]. Thus, dental pain can induce anxiety and, at the same time, anxiety can lead to overestimating pain [106]. Patients predisposed to answer with fear of pain usually fall into a vicious cycle of anxiety, fear of pain and avoidance of the dental treatment [107]. Considering that dental fear has been linked to poor oral health and avoidance of dental case, these findings suggest that a better understanding of fear of pain could improve our knowledge of dental fear.

1.6. Dental Anxiety in Minor Oral Surgery

Dental anxiety is manifested differently depending on the type of dental treatment the patient has to undergo. The degree of psychological distress, concomitant with a dental procedure is the result of adding two components: the difficulty of the procedure and the patient's perception as regards to its harmful nature [107]. This manifestation of anxiety, generated by the treatment, should be considered when evaluating its influence on the postoperative recovery and to establish necessary therapeutics to avoid it.

There are numerous investigations studying anxiety disorders of patients before surgery [108]. However, very few studies have been conducts to analyze the fears and anxiety produced by oral and maxillofacial surgery [109]. Extractions of the third molar likely the most frequent oral surgery, following simple extractions [110]. Third molar extraction is, in many cases, a surgical extraction and, as such, it may generate anxiety in the patient.

As we saw earlier, etiology of dental anxiety has multiple factors, so several factors can affect fear of oral surgery [111]. Therefore, a former experience can vary the level of anxiety of a patient - depending on its nature; thus, patients without previous experiences n oral surgery show higher anxiety levels than those who have undergone oral surgery before [79,112]. It has been proven that familiarity and routine dental treatment results in a reduction of anxiety [112], as long as a traumatic experience has not taken place. On the other hand, extraction of the third inferior molar has implicitly certain procedures that, frequently, are mentioned by patients as the main causes for their anxiety (fear of needles or the anesthetic injection) [75]. In this sense, it was observed that certain stimuli cause more anxiety, such as seeing and feeling the needle [113,114]; dental extractions [75]; the sound of the motor [75], since sometimes it is necessary to use the handpiece for ostectomies or tooth sections and, in general, fear of pain and postoperative complications [115]. It has also been noted that patient's anxiety traits can be a factor in dental anxiety related to extractions [108,116].

Anxiety in lower third molar extractions may occur at different times. It may appear before the surgery [79,110,116], due to etiologic factors as we have mentioned above, or they can appear postoperatively [109], as a consequence of the complications arising from the extraction. Both forms of anxiety can be interrelated [117], that is, if the patient present high preoperative anxiety, the time of the surgery may be longer [117], and in agreement with many studies [109,110] postoperative inflammation and pain increase thereby increasing postoperative anxiety. But preoperative anxiety may vary depending on the moment in which it is measured, thus, anxiety when making the appointment for the extraction would be lower than at the time of the surgery [109].

Often, surgeons treat patients with phobias that avoid dental case and only appear at the clinic when pain and swelling forces them [118]. Apprehensive patients see the surgeon ambivalently, as a feared and threatening person who should be avoided at all cost and as a person who has the skills and resources to alleviate their pain. Surgeons perceive phobic individuals as someone who can alter their daily practice. The role of the dental surgeon in the treatment of phobic patients poses many challenges. According to Trieger [118] it is advisable to refer the patient to a special clinic for dental phobias, for follow-up, once the acute pain, swelling or the traumatic lesion has been treated.

Taking into account all the above is useful when focusing on the treatment of anxiety generated by third molar extractions. As many studies have shown us preoperative and postoperative anxiety can be reduced by appropriately informing the patient about the different phases of their surgery [109,117].

1.7. Methods to Assess Dental ANXIETY and Fear

Behavioral assessment of anxiety is a complex process that involves collecting information regarding cognitive, physiological and motor responses, as well as a series of antecedent and consequent variables functionally related to the former. There are different behavioral assessment techniques, which are selected depending on different criteria, for example: the sample (children or adults); the type of response under evaluation (self-report, self-observation, external observation, psychophysical records - heart rate, electroheat response, electromyographic response, etc.); the time of evaluation (general or specific instruments); context (natural or artificial situations); the availability of assessors (self-reports, external observation); the goals (therapeutic or research goals); the cost-benefit relationship (self-reports, psychophysical records).

In this section we will solely refer to self-evaluation/self-report measures since these techniques are the most extended in the assessment of anxiety problems and because they were the type of instruments used by the research team.

Following the anxiety cognitive theory [119], that considers that the assessment of the cognitive component can only be done by asking the patient what they feel, which usually uses self-evaluation scales. The relevance of this sort of instruments comes from addressing the essential components of anxiety, because otherwise it would lack clinical value.

The instruments listed below can be classified as general or specific/situational, depending on whether they inquire on general anxiety manifestations or if they refer to specific aspects/situations relating to dental anxiety. The selection obeys, fundamentally, the frequency in which they are used during the research.

In the group of self-evaluation questionnaires that, although not specific to dental anxiety, we find: *"Spielberger's State-Trait Anxiety Inventory (STAI E-R)* [120]. This instrument tries to assess, by means of two separate self-evaluation scales, the levels of state anxiety and trait anxiety. State anxiety is conceptualized as a transitory emotional state or condition of the human organism characterized by subjective feelings, consciously perceived feelings of tension and apprehension, and heightened autonomic nervous system activity. It may fluctuate over time and vary in intensity. Trait anxiety refers to relatively stable individual differences in anxiety proneness in their trend to perceive situations as menacing, thus increasing their state anxiety levels. Both types of anxiety are assessed using a list of 40 items, 20 for each; with a 4 point scale, 0 (nothing) to 3 (much), for state anxiety; and 0 (seldom) to 3 (almost always) for trait anxiety. Total scores can range from 0 to 60 points. Direct and indirect questions are mixed to overcome the effect of acquiescence in the subject's responses. According to several studies [120,121] this instrument has shown good reliability and validity. STAI is recommended routinely for all dental patients, especially those requiring dental surgery [122].

Halfway between general and specific questionnaires we find *Endler's S-R Inventory* [123] that may be applied to dental situations. It is comprised of two parts: a anxiety stimulating situation, which may be modified by the researcher, and a list of 14 answers grading the anxious response. Pál-Hegedus, in 1989 [124], using the S-R Inventory as a model designed a questionnaire for situational anxiety that evaluates different anxious responses to a specific situation using a 5-point scale: "You are going to get an injection in your gums." This item was chosen because it was the most feared situation (41.3%) of a list of 3 dental fears in a previous research on 167 secondary school and college students of both genders. There were no differences in the total score related to the gender variable. There is no conclusive data on psychometric properties.

Similar in nature to the former is *Weiner´s fear questionnaire (FQ)* [125]. It was published in 1990 and is composed of two parts (A and B). Part A is formed by 16 questions studying general and dental fears. Part B is formed by 18 questions that inform about stress reactions, three of which are focused on panic attacks. This questionnaire provides information on general anxiety, dental anxiety and endogenous and exogenous anxiety symptoms. Therefore, in addition to self-assessment of cognitive aspects, it also studies the patient's physiological reactions to anxiety.

Geer Fear Scale (GFS) [126]

Was created by Geer in 1965, based on a research on a sample of college students who were asked to make a list of situations that made them anxious. He obtained 111 different fears, of which he selected the 51 that were repeated. In the questionnaire the items include situations or objects (their common denominator is that they are known to create fear) including some related to dental situation. Each item has seven degrees of fear that vary from 0 (no fear) to 6 (totally terrified)

Here follow some specific questionnaires for dental situations in adults, it is not a thorough review, but a representative one, of existing instruments.

Corah Dental Anxiety Scale (DAS) [87]

Is the most frequently used self-assessment instrument in dental anxiety research [127]. In 1969, Corah [87] developed this brief questionnaire (4 items) to evaluate the degree of anticipatory anxiety. It consists of four multiple-choice questions (having to choose one). The score can range from 4 (lack of anxiety) to 20 (maximum anxiety). Reliability and validity of this questionnaire has been contrasted by means of several studies [128,129]. The cutoff is set at 13, scores of 15 and above denote a high degree of anxiety. Variables, such as gender, age and presence or lack of orthodontia did not influence the total score of the test significantly. Although it is one-dimensional and only takes 5 minutes to complete, it competes with multidimensional measurements that usually require more application time and there is some doubt as to if they generate more information than DAS.

Among its limitations, it should be noted, as argued by Lindsay and Jackson [130], DAS can underestimate or overestimate patients' anxiety levels who do not respond physically to the treatment, since three of its items reflect feelings and physiological responses. Newton and Buck 131] recommended clinical use of DAS because it can provide a quick impression of the anxiety level and changes after treatment.

Dental Fear Survey (DFS) [66]

It initially consisted of 27 items which were later reduced to 20, by Kleinknecht et al. [66] in 1973. These 20 items are grouped into 3 assessed dimensions: avoidance of dental treatment, physiological reactions and subjective reactions to specific dental stimuli. Each of its items are assessed on a Liker-type scale ranging from 1 (no fear) to 5 (terrified). Total scores can range from 20 to 100 points. Some of its items are common to Gale's anxiety scale [75]. Several studies have shown that DFS has satisfactory psychometric properties [97,132,133].

Along with DAS it is one of the most commonly used instruments in research, but unlike the former it can detect what procedures generate more fear. However, it has been suggested that DFS could be improved with the inclusion of new items, for example, relating to extractions. Newton and Buck

[131] highlighted the research usefulness of DFS thanks to its great range of possible scores.

Stouthard's Dental Anxiety Inventory (DAI) [134]

This questionnaire was designed to overcome the limitations that the authors found in DAS and DFS. That is, to increase information offered by the first and add cognitive and affective reactions to the second. The purpose of DAI is not to identify extremely anxious dental patients, but to assess dental anxiety in "normal" dental patients and the prevalence of dental anxiety in the general population. It is formed by 36 items grouped in three dimensions or facets: time (in the chair, in the waiting room, etc.); situation (preliminary aspects of treatment, patient-dentist interaction, etc.) and reaction (physical, cognitive and affective). Each item is assessed on a 5-point Likert-type scale that goes from 1 (completely false) to 5 (completely true). Total scores can range from 36 (no dental anxiety) to 180 (extreme anxiety about dental treatment). Studies conducted by the authors have confirmed that DAI has adequate reliability and validity [133].

Gale´s Ranking Questionnaire (RQ) [75]

This scale consists of 29 questions. The first three items collect information about demographic variables (gender, age and number of visits to the dentist). The following question asks the patient to mark (on a 7 point scale - 1 being no fear to 7 being terror), the amount of fear they experiences in their visit to the dentist. The final 25 items use this same scale and ask the patient to respond "as if you were about to live the situation or if it were happening just now"; the patient then has to score a series of possible dental sequences. The two categories that produce most fear are those related to "current treatment" and the "dentist's comments" [75]. The questionnaire can be used to determine the amount of fear the patient has as an individual, but it does not classify patients according to their anxiety levels. There is no cutoff point, normative ranges have been considered, yet their usefulness has been considered limited [136].

Interval Scale of Anxiety Response (ISAR) [137]

This scale was developed to measure anxiety during dental processes, unlike other scales, it is not composed of multiple-choice questions. It consists of a vertical 90mm line with intervals marked by adjectives that describe the patient's psychological state. Patients are to mark with a horizontal line the point that best defines their anxiety state. Although ISAR is not as useful as

DAS in the clinical context, it can be a very valuable instrument when assessing the patient's reaction to treatment. Moreover, dentists may find it useful to verify the effectiveness in reducing patients' anxiety during treatment

Dental Belief Survey (DBS) [66]

This survey studies the patients' perception of how the dentist treats them, examining their relevant thoughts and attitudes as regards to the dental treatment. It is formed by 15 items, grouped in four dimensions: communication, control, contempt and confidence. Responses are measured on a Likert-type scale of 5 levels of agreement. Recently, in 2005, Coolidge et al. [138] conducted a studied to examine internal reliability of this scale, the conclusion was that DBS is adequate for use in clinical and non-clinical population in which it is desirable to have a valid measure of perceptions of the dental situation

Litt's Oral Surgery Confidence Questionnaire (OSCQ) [139]

It consists of five questions revolving around the confidence the patient believes to have to deal with oral surgery (keep the mouth open, remain relaxed, etc.) and six questions regarding the patient's expectations on their sensory (pain) and affective (nervousness) thresholds; including a question regarding the patient's confidence in enduring the treatment well. The score varies from 0 (no confidence in themselves) to 9 (complete confidence in themselves).

Dental Cognitions Questionnaire (DCQ) [140]

This questionnaire consists of a list of 38 negative cognitions (beliefs and self-statements) related to dental treatment. Fourteen of its items are related to negative beliefs related to dentistry in general (e.g.: dentists are careless) and patients (e.g.: I can't stand pain); the remaining 24 items are negative self-statements. Patients are asked about the presence and frequency of each negative cognition. The range of scores goes from 0 to 38. DCQ has adequate reliability and validity, according to its authors [139,141], and it is useful to monitor changes in the treatment of dental phobia with cognitive-behavioral therapy [142].

Iowa Dental Control Index (IDCI) [143]

For Logan et al. [142] the low control level perceived in a situation is not problematic if the subject does not wish to have a higher control level over that situation. Therefore, discrepancy between perceived and desired control (rather than absolute level of perceived control) is important to know the individual differences when faced with different stressors. IDCI is a self-report containing 4 items, 2 of which refer to the subject's desire for control (e.g.: "What level of control would you like to have over what happens in the dentist's chair?") and the other 2 refer to the control perceived during the dental treatment (e.g.: "How much control do you think you have on what happens on the dentist's chair?") These items are valued on a range that goes from 1 (none) to 5 (total). The total score is obtained from the difference between the sub-scales of Desired Control and Perceived Control. Greater discrepancy indicates a greater level of discomfort to the dental situation. Although, in general, reliability and validity of IDCI have been adequate [142,144], its authors - in an attempt to increase the internal consistency of the sub-scales - modified the instrument and changed its name to *Revised Iowa Dental Control Index (R-IDCI)* [145]. The changes in the new version consisted of an increase in the number of items and renaming the sub-scale of Perceived Control, which is now called Predictive Control. R-IDCI consists of 9 items, 5 for sub-scale of Desired Control and 4 for Predictive Control. The psychometric properties of the new instrument were satisfactory [144,146]. The new version was also useful in non-clinical contexts and in a 5 year follow-up study it proved to work adequately as a predictor of future dental anxiety [147].

2. Relationship between Dental Anxiety and Trait Anxiety

The existence of theories relating general levels of trait anxiety with specific dental anxiety [67] raises the possibility that trait anxiety may be a useful predictor of a patient's predisposition to dental anxiety.

A prior awareness of the patient's predisposition to dental anxiety may thus be of value to the dentist, enabling him or her to take appropriate preventative and/or therapeutic measures.

In a previous study [148], we found a strong association between measures of dental anxiety (DAS and DFS questionnaires) and trait anxiety. More especificly trait anxiety (STAI-T score) was a significant predictor of dental anxiety. When considering the different dimensions of the DFS separately, our results indicated that the dimensions showing the significant relationships with trait anxiety, state anxiety, and DAS were dimensions 2 and

3 (physiologic arousal and specific fear of dental procedures); by contrast, dimension 1 (anticipatory anxiety) showed a significant relationship only with DAS score. We also observed higher anxiety levels in female patients than in male patients, although the difference was only statistically significant in the case of trait anxiety. The results of our investigation suggest that a patient with high trait anxiety has a higher probability of showing dental anxiety. Similar correlations have been reported in previous studies [79,111] using different types of instruments for evaluating anxiety. Hakeberg et al. [149] found a significant positive relationship between trait anxiety and dental anxiety, using the DFS and DAS questionnaires (though, as noted, considering patients who had specifically consulted for dental anxiety). Likewise, Hägglin et al [150] found a significant relationship between trait anxiety and dental anxiety, although these authors used different instruments than those used in the present study.

According to these results, in some situations it may be useful for the dentist to evaluate trait anxiety before dental interventions; although bearing in mind a) that trait anxiety is only a partial predictor in the multifactorial etiology of dental anxiety, and b) that it evidently also makes sense for the dentist to evaluate state anxiety directly using a specifique questionnaire.

3. The Role of Trait Anxiety and Dental Anxiety in the Postoperative of Minor Oral Surgery

Anxiety not only produces emotional distress, but may also provoke patient behavior that hinders surgery, in some cases prolonging the intervention and complicating postoperative recovery. It has been shown that dental anxiety can exert influence on the perceived pain threshold, resulting in the patient experiencing more than the inevitable discomfort; this increase in pain sensitivity amplifies anxiety and so establishes a feedback cycle of anxiety and pain. [151] In addition, the fact that an apprehensive patient may be uncooperative during surgery may complicate the operation procedures.

Surgery and the subsequent recovery period can be a source of stress and physical trauma to patients. Psychological discomfort arises when patients anticipate the pain they may suffer during surgery. While there are few doubts that physical trauma can affect the postoperative period [152] little attention has been paid to the influence of psychological factors, despite their importance to recovery. It has been shown that psychological stress can have many physical effects ranging from increased sympathetic-adrenergic activity to illness susceptibility. [153] Stress may even adversely affect physical recovery after surgery. Several studies report a relationship between psychological factors and postsurgical recovery; however, the results are neither clear nor compelling. [154,155,155,156,157,158] Seymour et al. [159] stated that there is a significant variation in pain perception between patients, with painkiller requirements after surgery depending on various psychological factors. For this reason, we assessed to what extent anxiety could affect postoperative recovery of patients. We observed that patients with high compared to low trait anxiety reported more pain in all postoperative period (7 days), reaching significant levels in the last 2 postoperative days evaluated. Therefore, although the level of perceived pain during the first 5 days was higher in patients with high trait anxiety, the difference when compared to patients with low trait anxiety was not significant, since all patients experienced the inevitable consequence of the operation in that period. However, as postoperative time went on and the physiological discomfort lessened, patients with high trait anxiety not only continued to show pain but also a significantly more intense perception of pain. These findings are consistent with those obtained of George et al. [148] who concluded that high levels of trait anxiety were associated with a poorer recovery. Hoogenboom et al. [160] suggested that the use and effect of painkillers administered after third molar extraction depended on the level of anxiety. Taenzer et al. [161] subsequently confirmed that high levels of trait anxiety meant an increased perception of pain, as described for other types of surgeries. [154,162] Vallerand et al. [163] stated even that trait anxiety was an accurate predictor of postoperative pain and oral surgery recovery. Scott et al. [164] also showed that high preoperative anxiety was related to an increase in pain, although Johnston et al. [165] did not confirm this result. In 2005, Okawa et al [166] found that patients with higher trait anxiety tended to experience greater propensity to feel pain. Feinmann et al. [167] pointed out that although the influence of psychological variables on postoperative pain perception was obvious, it was not the same in the case of analgesic consumption. These authors also noted that trait anxiety predicted persistent postoperative pain and that this could be the cause of increased anxiety.

Vassend, [168] among other authors, has shown that anxiety as a consequence of pain expectation or dental procedures expected to be painful is a obstacle to seeking treatment. Following this line of reasoning, it is assumed that pain overestimation and a fear of pain is manifested by people with high dental anxiety [169]. However, we did not found significant relationships between specific measures of dental anxiety and pain, unlike trait anxiety and pain. [170]

Taenzer et al. [161] stated that state anxiety, unlike trait anxiety, was not significantly associated with most measures of pain and did not help predict pain levels. However, Vallerand et al [163] found the same behaviour patterns for both state and trait anxiety: both were accurate predictors of postoperative pain and oral surgery recovery. Scott et al. [32] also concluded that low state anxiety predicted a favourable result. Maggirias et al., [171] using 2 specific measures of dental anxiety (DFS and DAS) noted that anxiety related to dental treatment increased the probability of pain. More recently, Klages et al. [172] found that patients with high dental anxiety expected and experienced more pain than those with low anxiety.

Manso et al. [117] also assessed pain, inflammation and trismus after the removal of lower impacted third molars, finding more inflammation within the first 24 hours using the DFS as a measure of anxiety.

Manso et al. [117] showed that anxiety is not only directly associated with postoperative inflammation but also with operation duration. Filewich [173] demonstrated that anxious compared to calm patients required approximately 20% more time for routine canal obturation, due to breaks and additional explanations (since the time required to make the cavity was the same). According to Manso et al. [117] interruptions and/or explanations lead to greater inflammation within the first 24 hours. In a previous work, we demonstrated that average surgery time was always higher for the group of patients with high anxiety according to all the measures employed, although there were no significant differences when compared to the group with low anxiety. These results may not be statistically significant because, although the role of anxiety in surgery duration is important, other factors play a role, such as the difficulty of the intervention, the surgeon's experience, etc.

It seems reasonable to suppose that an increase in surgery duration may indirectly lead to an increase in perceptions of pain or in inflammation values. [170]

Conclusion

Unlike patients in general surgery, dental patients are active during surgery and recovery to a great extent depends on them. From a psychological point of view, it is important to give patients the tools that will help them deal with this type of surgery, especially when anxiety is involved, so that the intervention takes place with a minimum of discomfort and recovery is as fast and complete as possible. The postoperative course in oral surgeries can be potentially stressful for the patient due to pain, inflammation, limitation of mouth opening and other common sequelae, which can be minimized by providing information to improve the patient's global satisfaction. In this sense, some authors [108] stated that the increase of preparative information on the postoperative stage significantly increased pain relief that, in turn, mitigates the patient's anxious state, without having to increase analgesic dosage.

Throughout this chapter these issues have been addressed as regards to extractions of the inferior third molar, which is one of the most important contexts within dental practices, not only because of its frequency and the variety of presentations but also because of the pathology and the accidents it often triggers, which explains why its extraction is the most common surgery performed by dental and maxillofacial surgeons.

In summary, we have tried to stress the importance of psychological, factors to assess and foresee the postoperative course of inferior third molar extractions. We hope that our results prove useful for clinical odontology in general while helping improve the conditions for patients with dental anxiety.

References

[1] Miller AA. *Psychological considerations in dentistry*. JADA 1970; 81: 941-6.

[2] Luban-Plozza B, Pöldinger W. El enfermo psicosomático y el médico práctico. *Ed Roche. Basilea,* 1975; 105-14.

[3] Firestein SK. Patient anxiety and dental care practice. *JADA* 1976; 93: 1180-7.

[4] Messer JG. Stress in dental patients undergoing routine procedures. *J Dent Res* 1977; 56: 362-7.

[5] Le Gall A. La ansiedad y la angustia. Barcelona: Cipos-Tausa.; 1985.

[6] Sokol DJ, Sokol S, Sokol CK. A review of nonintrusive therapies used to deal with anxiety and pain in the dental office. *JADA* 1985; 110: 217-22.

[7] Rodriguez R, Cano-Vindel A. Relación entre adquisición y patrón de respuestas de ansiedad en la fobia dental. *Ansiedad y Estrés.* 1995; 1: 105-11.

[8] Lang PJ, Lazovik AD. Experimental desensization of a phobia. *J Abnorm Soc Psychol* 1963; 66: 519-25.

[9] Lang PJ. Fear reduction and fear behavior: problems in treating a construct. En: JM Shilen (Ed) *Research in psychotherapy: Vol III. American Psychological Association.* Washington DC; 1968.

[10] Miguel Tobal JJ. La ansiedad. In: J Mayor and JL Pinillos (Eds.) *Tratado de psicología general.* Motivación y Emoción. Madrid: Alambra Universidad; 1990.

[11] Carboles JA. Registros fisiológicos. In: Fernandez Ballesteros R and Carboles JA (Eds.) *Evaluación conductual: metodología y aplicaciones.* Madrid: Pirámide; 1981.

[12] Hugdall K. The three-system model of fear and emotion: a critical examination. *Behav Res Ther* 1981; 19: 75-85.

[13] Rachman S. The passing of the two stage theory of fear and avoidance: fresh possibilities. *Behav Res Ther* 1976; 14: 125-34.

[14] Barlow DH. *Anxiety and its disorders: the nature and treatment of anxiety and panic.* Nueva York: Guildford Press; 1988.

[15] Epstein S. The nature of anxiety with emphasis upon its relationship to expectancy. En: CD Spielberger (Ed.); *Anxiety: currents trends in theory and research.* Nueva York: Academic Press; 1972.

[16] Ganoug WF. *Review of Medical Psychology.* Los Altos, CA: Lange. 1985.

[17] Marks I. (1969). *Fears and phobias.* Nueva York: Academic Press.

[18] Eli LL. *Oral Psychophysiology. Stress, Pain and Behavior in Dental Care.* Boca Raton, Florida: CRC Press; 1992.

[19] Cohen SM, Fiske J, Newton T. The impact of dental anxiety on daily living. *Br Dent J* 2000; 189: 385-90.

[20] Pinkham JR, Schroeder CS. Dentist and psychologist: practical considerations for a team approach to the the intensely anxious dental patient. *JADA* 1975; 90: 1022-6.

[21] Wepman BJ. Psychological components of pain perception. *Dent Clin North Am* 1978; 22: 101-3.

[22] Corah NL. Dental anxiety. Assessment, reduction and increasing patient satisfaction. *Dent Clin North Am* 1988; 32: 779-90.

[23] Locker D. Psychosocial consequences of dental fear and anxiety. *Community Dent Oral Epidemiol* 2003; 31: 144-51.

[24] Rubin JG, Slovin M, Krochak M. The psychodynamics of dental anxiety and dental phobia. *Dent Clin North Am* 1988; 32: 647-56.

[25] Filewich RJ, Jackson E, Shore H. Effects of dental fear on efficiency of routine dental procedures. *J Dent Res* 1981; 60; 533 (Abstract).

[26] O´Shea RM, Corah NL, Ayer WA. Sources of dentist´s stress. *J Am Dent Assoc 1984*; 109: 48-51.

[27] Cooper Cl, Watts J, Kelly M. Job satisfaction, mental health and job stressors among general dental practitioners in the UK. *Br Dent J* 1987; 162: 77-81.

[28] Corah Nl, O´Shea RM, Ayer WA. Dentist´s management of patients´ fear and anxiety. *JADA* 1985; 110: 734-6.

[29] Howard JH, Cunningham DA, Rechnitzer P, Goode RC. Stress in the job and career of a dentist. *J Am Dent Assoc* 1976; 93: 630-6.

[30] Fernández C, Martín MD, Miguel F. Miedo, Ansiedad y Fobia Dental: Definiciones, Prevalencia y Antecedentes. *Ansiedad y Estrés* 1995; 1: 93-104.

[31] Abrahamsson KH, Bergrren U, Hakeberg M, Carlsson SG. Phobic avoidance and regular dental care in fearful dental patients. *Acta Odontol Scand* 2001; 59: 273-9.

[32] Scott DS, Hirschman R. Psychological aspects of dental anxiety in adults. *J Am Dent Assoc* 1982; 104: 27-31.

[33] Freidson E, FeldmanJJ. The public looks at dental care. *JADA* 1958; 57: 325-35.

[34] Molin C, Seeman K. Disproportionate dental anxiety. Clinical and nosological considerations. *Acta Odontol Scand* 1970; 28: 197-212.

[35] Steblay NM, Beeman AL. Reduction of fear during dental treatment through reattribution techniques. *JADA* 1982; 105: 1006-9.

[36] Lauder. A survey of attitudes toward dental treatment. Florida State University, 1983 (citado en Gatchel RJ, Ingersoll BD, Bowman L, Robertson C, Walker C. The prevalence of dental fear avoidance: a recent survey study. *JADA* 1983; 107: 18-27.

[37] Ayer AA, Domoto PK, Gale EN, Joy ED, Melamed BG. Overcoming dental fear: strategies for its prevention and management. *JADA* 1983; 107: 18-27.

[38] Rankin JA, Harris MB. Dental anxiety: the patient´s point of view. *JADA* 1984; 109: 43-7.

[39] Gatchel RJ, Ingersoll BD, Bowman L, Robertson C, Walker C. The prevalence of dental fear and avoidance: a recent survey study. *JADA* 1983; 107: 609-700.

[40] Scott DS, Hirschman R, Schroder K. Historical antecedents of dental anxiety. *JADA* 1984; 108: 42-5.

[41] Sohn W, Ismail AI. Regular dental visits and dental anxiety in an adult dentate population. *J Am Dent Assoc* 2005; 136: 58-66.

[42] Doer PA, Lang WP, Nyquist LV, Ronis DL. Factor associated with dental anxiety. *J Am Dent Assoc* 1998; 129: 1111-9.

[43] Locker D, Shapiro D, Liddel A. Who is dentally anxious? Concordance between measures of dental anxiety. *Community Dent Oral Epidemiol* 1996; 24: 346-50.

[44] Mayer R. Control del miedo y del dolor en el tratamiento estomatológico en la infancia mediante audioanalgesia. *Quintessence* 1994; 7: 188-91.

[45] Enkling N, Marwinski G, Jöhren P. Dental anxiety in a representative sample of residents of a large German city. *Clin Oral Investig* 2006; 10: 84-91.

[46] Eitner S, Wichmann M, Paulsen A, Holst S. Dental anxiety- an epidemiological study on its clinical correlation and effects on oral health. *J Oral Rehabil* 2006; 33: 588-93.

[47] Hakeberg M, Berggren U, Carlsson SG. Prevalence of dental anxiety in an adult population in a major urban area in Sweeden. *Community Dent Oral Epidemiol* 1992; 20: 97-101.

[48] Skaret E, Raadal M, Berg E, Kvale G. Dental anxiety among 18-yr-olds in Norway. Prevalence and related factors. *Eur J Oral Sci* 1998; 106: 835-43.

[49] Haugejorden O, Klock KS. Avoidance of dental visits: the predictive validity of three dental anxiety scales. *Acta Odontol Scand* 2000; 21: 329-39.

[50] Stouthard ME, Hoogstraten J. Prevalence of dental anxiety in The Netherlands. *Community Dent Oral Epidemiol* 1990; 18: 139-42.

[51] Ragnarsson E. Dental fear and anxiety in an adult Icelandic population. *Acta Odontol Scand* 1998; 56: 100-4.

[52] Llgüy D, Llgüy M, Dincer S, Bayirli G. Reliability and validity of the modified dental anxiety scale in Turkish patients. *J Int Med Res* 2005; 33: 252-9.

[53] Domoto PE, Weinstein P, Melnick S, OhmuraM, Hori M, Okazaki Y, Shimamoto T, Matsumura S, Shimoto T. Results of a dental fear survey in Japan: Implications for dental public health in Asia. *Community Dent Oral Epidemilol* 1988; 16: 199-201.

[54] Barberia B, Martín D, Tobal M, Fernández Frías C. Prevalencia, consecuencias y antecedentes de miedo, ansiedad y fobia dental. *Bol Asoc Odontol Argent P Niño*s 1997; 24: 3-10.

[55] Rodríguez G, Martínez MA, Caballero J. Reacciones de los pacientes a la experiencia odontológica. *Boletín informativo de la V Región* 1989; 3: 47-53.

[56] Johnsen B, Thayer J, Laberg J, Wormnes B, Raadal M, Skaret E, Kvale G, Berg E. Attentional and physiological characteristics of patients with dental anxiety. *J Anxiety Disorders* 2003; 17: 75-87.

[57] Schuuller AA, Willumsen T, Holst D. Are there differences in oral health and oral health behavior between individuals with high and low dental fear? *Community Dent Oral Epidemiol* 2003; 31: 116-21.

[58] Luciak-Donsberger C. Origins and benefits of dental hygiene practice in Europe. *Int J Dent Hyg* 2003; 1: 29-42.

[59] Rachman S. The conditioning theory of fear –acquisition: A critical examination. *Behav Res Ther* 1977. 15, 375-87.

[60] Weiner A, Sheehan DV. Etiology of dental anxiety: Psychological trauma or CNS chemical imbalance? *Gen Dent* 1990; 38: 39-43.

[61] Milgrom P, Weinstein P, Kleinecht R, Getz T. *Treating fearful dental patients: a clinical handbook.* Va: Reston; 1985.

[62] Berggren U, Carlsson SG, Hakeberg M, Hagglin C, Samsonowitz V. Assessment of patients with phobic dental anxiety. *Acta Odontol Scand* 1997; 55: 217-22.

[63] De Jongh A, van der Burg J, van Overmeir M, Aartman I, van Zuuren FJ. Trauma-related sequelae in individuals with a high level of dental anxiety. Does this interfere with treatment outcome? *Behav Res Ther* 2002; 40: 1017-29.

[64] Shoben SE, Borland L. An empirical study of the etiology of dental fears. *J Clin Psychol* 1954; 10: 171-4.

[65] Lautch H. Dental Phobia. *Br J Psychiatr* 1971, 119, 151-8.

[66] Kleinknecht RA, Keplac RK, Alexander LD. Origins and characteristic of fear of dentistry. *JADA* 1973; 36: 842-8.

[67] Berggren U, Meynert G. Dental fear and avoidance: causes, symptoms, and consequences. *JADA* 1984; 109: 247-51.

[68] Davey GCL. Dental phobias and anxieties: Evidence for conditioning processes in the acquisition and modulation of a learned fear. *Behav Res Ther* 1989; 27: 51-8.

[69] Rodolfa ER, Kraft W, Reilley ER. Etiology and treatment of dental anxiety and phobia. *Am J Clin Hypn* 1990 Jul; 33: 22-8.

[70] Cohen LA, Snyder TL, La Belle AD. Correlates of dental anxiety in a university population. *J Public Health Dentistry* 1982; 42: 228-35.

[71] Öst L, Hugdahl K. Acquisition of blood and dental phobia and anxiety in clinical patients: *Behav Res Ther* 1985; 23: 27-34.
[72] DiMatteo MR, Prince LM, Taranta A. Patient′s perceptions of physicians′ behaviour: Determinants of patient commitment to the therapeutic relationship. *J Community Health* 1980; 6: 18-34.
[73] Johansson P, Berggren U, Hakeberg M, Hirsch JM. Measures of dental beliefs and attitudes: their relationships with measures of fear. *Community Dent Health* 1993; 10: 31-9.
[74] Rouse RA, Hamilton MA. Dentist′s technical competence, communication, and personality as predictors of dental patient anxiety. *J Behav Med* 1990; 13: 307-19.
[75] Gale EN. Fears of dental situation. *J Dent Res* 1972; 51: 964-6.
[76] Bailey PM, Talbot A, Taylor PP. A comparison of maternal anxiety levels with anxiety levels manifested in the child dental patient. *ASDC J Dent Child* 1973; 40: 277-84.
[77] Venham L, Murray P, Gaulin-Kremer E. Child-rearing variables affecting the preschool child′s response to dental stress. *J Dent Res* 1979; 58: 2042-5.
[78] Klorman R, Michael R, Hilpert PL, Sveen OB. A further assessment of predictors of the childs behavior in dental treatment. *J Dent Res* 1979; 58: 2338-43.
[79] Frazer M, Hampson S. Some personality factors related to dental anxiety and fear of pain. *Br Dent J* 1988; 165; 436-9.
[80] Liddell A, Locker D. Gender and age differences in attitudes to dental pain and dental control. *Community Dent Oral Epidemiol* 1997; 25: 314-8.
[81] Economu GC. Dental Anxiety and Personality: Investigating the relationship between dental anxiety and self-consciousness. *J Dent Educ* 2003: 67; 970-80.
[82] Rome M, Moore T. Self-report measures of dental fear: gender differences. *Am J Health Behav* 1998: 22; 243-7.
[83] Liddell A, Gosse V. Characteristics of early unpleasant dental experiences. *J Behav Ther Exp Psychiatry* 1998; 29: 227-37.
[84] Adams S, Kubeli J, Boyle PA, Fivush R. Gender differences in parent-child conversations about past emotions: a longitudinal investigation. *Sex Roles* 1995; 33: 309-23.
[85] Douglas H, Reisine ST, Lipes MH. Characteristics and satisfaction of the patients, male versus female dentists. *JADA* 1985: 110; 926-9.

[86] Hägglin C, Berggren U, Hakeberg M, Hälström T, Bengtsson C. Variations in dental anxiety among middle-aged and elderly women in Sweden: A longitudinal Study between 1968 and 1996. *J Dent Res* 1999: 78; 1655-61.

[87] Corah NL. Development of a dental anxiety scale. J Dent Res 1969: 48; 596.

[88] Agras S, Silvestre D, Oliveau D. The epidemiology of common fears and phobia. *Compr Psychiatry* 1969; 10: 151-156.

[89] Liddell A, Locker D, Burman D. Self-reported fears (FSS-II) of subjects aged 50 years and over. *Behav Res Ther* 1991; 29: 105-12.

[90] Locker D, Thomson WM, Poulton R. Onset of and patterns of change in dental anxiety in adolescence and early adulthood: a birth cohort study. *Community Dent Health 2001*; 18: 99-104.

[91] Milgrom P, Fiset L, Melnick S, Weinstein P. The prevalence and practice management consequences of dental fear in a major US city. *J Am Dent Assoc* 1988; 116: 641-7.

[92] Marks I, Gelder D. Different ages of onset in varieties of phobia. *Am J Psychiat* 1966; 123: 218-21.

[93] Locker D, Liddell A, Dempster L, Shapiro D. Age of onset of dental anxiety. *J Dent Res* 1999; 78: 790-6.

[94] Schwarz E, Birn H. Dental anxiety in Danish and Chinese adults: a cross-cultural perspective. *Soc Sci Med* 1995; 41: 123-30.

[95] Fuks AB, Steinbock N, Zadik D. The influence of social and ethnic factors on dental care habits and dental anxiety: a study in Israel. *Int J Paediatr Dent* 1993; 3: 3-7.

[96] Rankin JA, Harris MB. Patient´s preferences for dentist´s behaviors. *JADA* 1985; 110: 323-7.

[97] Kleinknecht RA, Mc Glynn FD, Thorndike RM, Harkavy J. Factor analysis of the dental fear survey with cross-validation. *JADA* 1984; 108: 59-61.

[98] Mc Neil D, Berryman M. Components of dental fear in adults. *Behav Res Ther* 1989; 27: 233-6.

[99] American Psychiatric Association (APA). *Diagnostic and statistical manual of mental disorders.* (DSM-IV). 4th ed. Washington DC: APA; 1994.

[100] Calatayud J. Estudio de la ansiedad y el miedo en el paciente estomatológico. Tesis Doctoral. *Departamento de Estomatología Médica y Periodoncia.* Facultad de Medicina. Universidad Complutense de Madrid.1988.

[101] Kent G. Satisfaction with dental care. *Med Care* 1984; 22: 583-5.
[102] De Jongh A, Muris P, Ter Horst G, Van Zuuren FJ, De Wit CA. Cognitive correlates of dental anxiety. *J Dent Res* 1994; 73: 561-66.
[103] Forgione AG, Clark E. Comments on an empirical study of the causes of dental fears: *J Dent Res* 1974; 53: 496.
[104] Hall N, Edmondson HD. The aetiology and psychology of dental fear. A five-year study of the use of intravenous diazepam in its management. *Br Dent J* 1983; 154: 247-52.
[105] Mc Neil DW, Au AR, Zvolensky MJ, McKee DR, Klineberg IJ,Ho CKC. Fear of pain in orofacial pain patients. *Pain* 2001; 89: 245-52.
[106] Van Wijk J, Hoogstraten J. Experience with dental pain and fear of dental pain. *J Dent Res* 2005; 84; 947-50.
[107] Moore PA, Ramsay DS, Finder RL, Laverick W. Pharmacologic modalities in the management and treatment of dental anxiety. *Dent Clin North Am* 1988; 32: 803-16.
[108] Vallerand WP, Vallerand AH, Heft M. The effects of postoperative preparatory information on the clinical course following third molar extraction. *J Oral Maxillofac Surg* 1994; 52: 1165-70.
[109] Earl P. Patient´s anxieties with third molar surgery. *Br J Oral Maxillofac Surg* 1994; 32: 293-7.
[110] Ogden GR, Bissias E, Ruta DA, Ogston S. Quality of life following third molar removal: a patient versus professional perspective. *Br Dent J* 1998; 185: 407-10.
[111] Kaakko T, Murtomaa H. Factors predictive of anxiety before oral surgery: Efficacy of various subject screening measures. *Anesth Prog* 1999; 46: 3-9.
[112] Messer JG. Stress in dental patients undergoing routine procedures. *J Dent Res* 1977; 56: 362-7.
[113] Peretz B, Efrat J. Dental anxiety among young adolescent patients in Israel. *Int J Pediatr Dent* 2000; 10: 126-32.
[114] De Jongh A, Bongaarts G, Vermuele I, Visser K, De Voss P, Makkes P. Blood-injury-injection phobia and dental phobia. *Behav Res Ther* 1998; 36: 971-82.
[115] Garip H, Abali O, Göker K, Göktürk Ü, Garip Y. Anxiety and extraction of third molars in Turkish patients. *Br J Oral Maxillofac* Surg 2004; 42: 551-4.
[116] Ng SKS, Chau AWL, Leung WK. The effect of pre-operative information in relieving anxiety in oral surgery patients. *Community Dent Oral* Epidemiol 2004; 32: 227-35.

[117] Manso FJ, Calatayud J, Carrillo JS, Barbería E, Zaragoza JR. Anxiety, inflammation and intervation duration. Is there any interrelation?. *Av Odontoestomatol* 1989; 1: 31-3.

[118] Trieger N. An oral surgeon´s approach to the fearful patient. Intravenous sedation and general anesthesia. *Dent Clin North Am* 1988; 32: 817-22.

[119] Beck AT. *Anxiety disorders and phobias.* New York: Basic Books; 1985.

[120] Spielberger CD, Gorsuch RL, Lushene RE. *STAI. Cuestionario de Ansiedad Estado-Rasgo. Manual.* 4th ed. Madrid: TEA; 1970.

[121] Laux L, Glanzman P, Schaffner P, Spielberger CD. *Das State-Trait-Angst-Inventar.* Weinheim: Beltz;1981.

[122] Pál-Hegedus C, Baldioceda F. Evaluación conductual de los trastornos odontológicos. In: Buela-Casal G, Caballo V, Sierra C (Eds.). Manual *de evaluación en psicología clínica y de la salud* .Madrid: siglo XXI; 1996.

[123] Endler NS, Hunt J, Rosentein AJ. An S-R Inventory of Anxiousness. Psychol Monogr 1962; 76: 536.

[124] -Hegedús C. El cuestionario de ansiedad situacional de Endler y su aplicación a la acufobia. Manuscrito inédito, 1989 (cit. Por Pál-Hegedús C y Baldioceda F 1996. *Evaluación conductual de los trastornos odontológicos.* En G Buela-Casal, V Caballo y JC Sierra (Dirs.). Manual de evaluación en psicología clínica y de la salud. Madrid: Pirámide).

[125] Weiner A, Sheehan DV. Etiology of dental anxiety: Psychological trauma or CNS chemical imbalance? *Gen Dent* 1990; 38: 39-43.

[126] Geer JH. The development of a scale to measure fear. *Behav Res* Ther 1965; 3: 45-53.

[127] Sartory G, Heinen R, Pundt I, Jöhren P. Predictors of behavioural avoidance in dental phobia: the role of gender, dysfunctional cognitions and the need for control. *Anxiety, Stress and Coping* 2006; 19: 279-91.

[128] Corah N, Gale E, Illig SJ. Assessment of a dental anxiety scale. *J Am Dent Assoc* 1978; 97: 816-9.

[129] Pál-Hegedús C, Garnier L. La escala de ansiedad dental de Corah: una ayuda para los odontólogos. *Rev Mex Psicol.* 1991; 8: 33-6.

[130] Lindsay S, Jackson C. Fear of routine dental treatment in adults: its nature and management. *Psychol Health* 1993; 8: 135-54.

[131] Newton JT, Buck DJ. Anxiety and pain measures in dentistry: a guide to their quality and application. *JADA* 2000; 131; 1449-57.

[132] Milgrom P, Kleinknecht RA, Elliott HJ, Liu HH, Teo CS. A cross-cultural validation of the Dental Fear Survey in South East Asia. *Behav Res Ther* 1990; 28: 227-33.

[133] Kleinknecht RA, Berstein DA. The assessment of dental fear. *Behav Ther* 1978; 9: 626-34.
[134] Stouthard ME, Hoogstraten J, Mellenbergh GJ. A study on the convergent and discriminant validity of the dental anxiety inventory. *Behav Res Ther* 1995; 33: 589-95.
[135] Stouthard ME, Mellenberg GJ, Hoogstraten J. Assessment of dental anxiety: a facet approach. *Anxiety, Stress and Coping* 1993; 6: 89-105.
[136] Shuurs AHB, Hoogstraten J. Appraisal of dental anxiety and fear questionnaires: a review. *Community Dent Oral Epidemiol* 1993; 21: 329-39.
[137] Corah NL, Zielezny MA, O´Shea RM, Thines TJ, Mendola P: Development of an interval scale of anxiety response. *Anesth Prog* 1986; 33: 220-4.
[138] Coolidge T, Heima M, Coldwell SE, Weinstein P, Milgrom P. Psychometric properties of the Revised Dental Beliefs Survey. *Community Dent Oral Epidemiol* 2005; 33: 289-97.
[139] Litt MD, Nye C, Shafer D.Coping with oral surgery by self-efficacy enhancement and perceptions of control. *J Dent Res* 1993; 72: 1237-43.
[140] De Jong A, Muris P, Schoenmakers N, Ter Horst G. Negative cognitions of dental phobics: reliability and validity of the Dental Cognitions Questionnaire. *Behav Res Ther* 1995; 33: 507-15.
[141] De Jongh A, Muris P, Ter Horst G, Van Zuuren F, Schoenmakers N, Makkes P. One session cognitive treatment of dental phobia: preparing dental phobics for treatment by restructuring negative cognitions. *Behav Res Ther* 1995; 33: 947-54.
[142] Mansell W, Morris K. The dental cognitions questionnaire in CBT for dental phobia in an adolescent with multiple phobias. *J Behav Ther Exp Psychiatry* 2003; 34: 65-71.
[143] Logan HL, Baron RS, Keely K, Law A, Stein S. Desired control and felt control as mediators of stress in a dental setting. *Health Psychology* 1991; 10: 325-59.
[144] Baron RS, Logan HL, Hope S. Emotional and sensory focus as mediators of dental pain among patients diffcring in desired and felt dental control. *Health Psychol* 1993; 12: 381-9.
[145] Brunsman BA, Logan HL, Patil RR, Baron RS. The development and validation of the Revised Iowa Dental Control Index (IDCI). *Pers Individ Dif 2003*; 34: 1113-28.

[146] Coolidge T, Heima M, Coldwell SE, Weinstein P, Logan HL, Milgrom P. Reliability and validity of the Revised Iowa Dental Control Index in a non clinical sample. *Pers Individ Dif* 2005; 38: 773-83.

[147] Maggirias J, Locker D. Five-year incidence of dental anxiety in an adult population. *Community Dent Health* 2002; 19: 173-9.

[148] Lago-Méndez L, Diniz-Freitas M, Senra-Rivera C, Seoane-Pesqueira G, Gándara-Rey José Manuel, García-García A. Dental Anxiety Before Removal of a Third Molar and Association with General Trait Anxiety. *J Oral Maxillofac Surg* 2006; 64: 1404-1408.

[149] Hakeberg M, Hägglin C, Berggren U et al: Structural relationships of dental anxiety, mood and general anxiety. *Acta Odontol Scand* 2001; 59: 99.

[150] Hägglin C, Hakeberg M, Hällström T et al: Dental anxiety in relation to mental health and personality factors. A longitudinal study of middle-aged and elderly women. *Eur J Oral Sci* 2001; 109: 27.

[151] Cramer EH, Szmyd L. Identifying the overly anxious patient in impacted third molar surgery. *Tech Doc Rep SAMTDR USAF Aerosp Med* (SAM-TDR) 1962; 62-90: 1-5.

[152] George JM, Scoct DS, Turner SP, Gregg JM. The effects of psychological and physical trauma on recovery from oral surgery. *J Behav Med* 1980; 3: 291-310.

[153] Holmes TH, Masuda M. Life change and illness susceptibility. En: Dohrenwend BS y Dohrenwend BP. Stressful Life Events: *Their nature and effects,* John Wiley and Sons, New York, 1974.

[154] Johnson JE, Dabbs JM, Leventhal H. Psychosocial factors in the welfare of surgical patients. *Nursing Res* 1970; 19: 18-28.

[155] Wolfer JA, Davis CE. Assessment of surgical patients′ preoperative emotional condition and postoperative welfare. *Nursing Res* 1970; 19: 402-14.

[156] Auerbach SM. Trait-state anxiety and adjustment to surgery. *J Consult Clin Psychol* 1973; 40: 264-71.

[157] Cohen F, Lazarus RS. Active doping processes, doping dispositions and recovery from surgery. *Psychosom Med* 1973; 35: 375-89.

[158] Martinez-Urrutia A. Anxiety and pain in surgical patients. *J Consult Clin Psychol* 1975; 43: 437-42.

[159] Seymour R, Meechan JG, Blair GS. An investigation into post-operative pain after third molar surgery under local analgesia. *Br J Oral Maxillofac Surg* 1985; 23: 410-8.

[160] Hoogenboom LJ, Vielvoye-Kerkmeer APE. Relief of pain due to surgical extraction of the third molar. *Pain* 1984; 18: 109S.
[161] Taenzer P, Melzack R, Jeans ME. Influence of psychological factors on postoperative pain, mood and analgesic requirements. *Pain*1986; 24: 331-42.
[162] Chapman CR, Cox GB. Anxiety pain and depression surrounding elective surgery. A multivariate comparison of abdominal surgery patients with kidney donors and recipients. *Journal Psychosom Res* 1977; 21: 7-15.
[163] Vallerand WP, Vallerand AH, Heft M. The effects of postoperative preparatory information on the clinical course following third molar extraction. *J Oral Maxillofac Surg* 1994; 52: 1165-70
[164] Scott LE, Clum GA, Peoples JB. Preoperative predictors of postoperative pain. *Pain* 1983; 15: 283-93.
[165] Johnston M, Carpenter L. Relationship between preoperative anxiety and postoperative state. *Psychol Med* 1980; 10: 361-7.
[166] Okawa K, Ichinole T, Yuzuru K. Anxiety may enhance pain during dental treatment. *Bull Tokyo Dent Coll* 2005; 46: 51-8.
[167] Feinmann C, Ong M, Harvey W, Harris M. Psychological factors influencing post-operative pain and analgesic consumption. *Br J Oral Maxillofac Surg* 1987; 25: 285-92.
[168] Vassend O. Anxiety, Pain and Discomfort associated with dental treatment. *Behav Res Ther* 1993; 31: 659-66.
[169] Van Wijk J, Hoogstraten J. Experience with dental pain and fear of dental pain. *J Dent Res* 2005; 84; 947-50.
[170] Lago-Méndez L, Diniz-Freitas M, Senra-Rivera C, Gude-Sampedro F, Gándara-Rey JM, García-García A. Relationships between surgical difficulty and postoperative pain in lower third molar extractions. *J Oral Maxillofac Surg* 2007; 65: 979-83.
[171] Maggirias J, Locker D. Psychological factors and perceptions of pain associated with dental treatment. *Community Dent Oral Epidemiol* 2002; 30: 151-9.
[172] Klages U, Kianifard S, Ulusoy Ö, Wehrbein H. Anxiety sensitivity predictor of pain in patients undergoing restorative dental procedures. *Community Dent Oral Epidemiol* 2006; 34: 139-45.
[173] Filewich RJ, Jackson E, Shore H. Effects of dental fear on iency of routine dental procedures. *J Dent Res* 60 1981; 533 (Abstract).

In: Trait Anxiety
Editor: Anna S. Morales

ISBN 978-1-61324-551-4

Chapter 4

ANXIETY SENSITIVITY AFFECTS EARLY PROCESSING OF PHYSICAL THREAT WORDS: AN EVENT-RELATED POTENTIAL INVESTIGATION OF THE DOT-PROBE TASK

Isabel Taake, Fern Jaspers-Fayer and Mario Liotti
Laboratory for Affective and Developmental Neuroscience,
Department of Psychology, Simon Fraser University,
Burnaby, BC, Canada

ABSTRACT

The behavioral and electrophysiological correlates of attentional bias to physical threat words were investigated in healthy participants with high and low Anxiety Sensitivity using a word dot-probe task while recording high-density brain electrical activity.

Behaviorally, both groups displayed a small advantage in response time to targets in the location of a previous emotional word cue, independent of its emotional valence.

The event-related electrical response to threat-neutral word cue pairs showed enhanced occipital P1 amplitudes in the high relative to the low AS group. In contrast, low AS participants displayed greater P1 amplitude to positive-neutral word cue pairs compared to threat-neutral ones. Selective threat-related modulations also affected a later occipital P2, in response to the cued words, in the high AS group.

More importantly, the event-related response to targets following the emotional word cue pairs showed modulations as a function of trait-anxiety, spatial location, and emotion. In the high AS group, an occipital N1 wave was *increased* in response to probe targets in the same location as previous presented threat versus positive words. In contrast, in the low AS group, occipital N1 amplitudes were *decreased* in response to probe targets following threat word cues relative to neutral word cues, independent of validity. In addition, over parietal scalp, N1 amplitude to threat invalid trials was *increased* relative to threat valid trials.

Voltage of the later P3b wave also varied as a function of AS group, spatial location, and emotion. In the high AS group, P3b was *attenuated* for probe targets in the same location as previously presented threat words than to probe targets in the same location as positive words. In the low AS group, P3b to probes were reduced following positive relative to threat word cues, independent of validity. The present results in the dot-probe task are interpreted within a model in which early hypervigilance to threat in high trait anxiety leads to early enhancement of occipitally distributed sensory components (P1 to the threat pairs, N1 to following probe targets) and later attenuation of conscious top-down processing of threat stimuli (as indexed by the P3b). In contrast, low trait anxiety is accompanied by early attenuation of occipitally distributed sensory components (P1 to the threat cue pairs, N1 to following targets).

INTRODUCTION

One of the most important functions of the mechanisms underlying the fear system is rapid detection of threatening information in the environment, as it allows the organism to appropriately respond to potential danger, and therefore enhances survival. This early and rapid attention to threat is an adaptive response in healthy individuals (LeDoux, 1986; Öhmann, Flykt, & Esteves, 2001). However, in persons with clinical or sub-clinical levels of anxiety, this mechanism seems to be exaggerated and maladaptive. Specifically, anxious individuals seem to be distinctively sensitive to threatening information in the environment, and display a tendency to allocate attention preferentially to these stimuli (Williams, Mathews, & MacLeod, 1986; Taake, et al., 2009; Eysenck, Derakshan, Santos, & Calvo, 2007). This hypervigilance to threat takes the form of an attentional bias, and is thought to occur at early, automatic stages of processing, prior to conscious awareness. This increased processing of threatening information has been demonstrated in a variety of tasks in both clinically and non-clinically anxious individuals, appears to be largely content-specific to the particular symptoms of the various anxiety disorders, and is believed to play a role in the etiology and maintenance of clinical anxiety (e.g. Bar-Haim, Lamy, Pergamin, Bakermans-Kranenburg, & van Ijzendoorn, 2007; MacLeod, Matthews, & Tata, 1986; Mogg, Mathews, & Eysenck, 1992). Recently, attentional retraining has been used to modify attentional biases in Generalized Anxiety Disorder in order to reduce anxiety symptoms (Amir, Beard, Burns, & Bornyea, 2009).

A commonly used measure to study attentional biases in anxiety is the dot-probe paradigm (e.g. Frewen, Dozois, Joanisse, & Neufeld, 2008). This task involves the presentation of pairs of cues that vary in emotional significance (e.g. one threat, one neutral) followed by a dot probe target appearing in the location of one of the presented stimuli. Participants are required to respond as fast as possible to the appearance of the dot by pressing a key. It is thought that response latencies to the dot probe target can provide an index of attentional bias, that is, faster responses to a target indicate previous attention allocation to the cue that has just been replaced. Participants with clinical and non-clinical levels of anxiety have been shown to display faster reaction times to targets appearing at the location of a threat relative to a neutral stimulus, which is indicative of an attentional bias towards threat (e. g. Mueller et al., 2009; Bar-Haim et al., 2007). It has been recently argued that shorter response latencies in the dot-probe task can be produced by more than one mechanism. In particular, it is sometimes impossible to determine whether the threatening information draws, or holds attention of the participants. In the latter case, the attentional abnormality would express itself as a difficulty to disengage from threat, a phenomenon that has been investigated and reported in some studies (e.g. Fox, Russo, Bowles & Dutton, 2001). However, an attentional bias in the opposite direction has also been reported, with longer reaction times to probes replacing a threatening stimulus, a pattern, which indicates either *avoidance* of threat (Hunt, Keogh, & French, 2006), or when the response times are relative to positive stimuli, a bias towards positive information, i.e., an attentional positivity bias (Bradley et al., 1997; Keogh, Dillon, Georgiou, & Hunt, 2001) mostly in non-anxious control participants.

Neural mechanisms underlying attentional bias in a dot probe task can be studied with a high degree of temporal resolution by recording event-related potentials (ERPs) from the scalp, and such knowledge can provide unique information about the stage of information processing at which the attentional bias to emotional stimuli may affect information processing.

Only a few studies have been conducted using the dot-probe task in relation to anxiety. The majority of these studies have employed a modified dot-probe task using pairs of faces (one emotional – such as angry, fearful or happy, the other neutral).

In healthy participants unselected for anxiety status, RTs to a target following a fearful or angry face have been reported to be faster than those following a neutral face (Pourtois, Grandjean, Sander, & Vuilleumier, 2004; Santesso et al., 2008). Additionally, the corresponding evoked responses were found to show an enhanced occipital P1 component in this condition (Pourtois et al., 2004; Santesso et al., 2008). Both of these effects were not present in response to happy faces (but see Brosch, Sander, Pourtois, & Scherer, 2008, for an exception). A similar P1 enhancement was found in a further study employing pictures of threat stimuli (such as snakes or knives) paired to neutral stimuli (Brown et al., 2010).

In healthy participants with high trait anxiety status, two studies have employed the face dot-probe task to investigate attentional bias. Both studies reported faster RT to targets replacing angry faces than neutral faces in the high trait anxiety groups only. Furthermore, ERPs showed emotion modulation in response to the angry-neutral face pairs, in the form of an early posterior C1 effect (Elder, Yankelevitch, Lamy, & Bar-Haim, 2010), a posterior P1 effect (Helfinstein, White, Bar-Haim, & Fox, 2008) or a later posterior P2 effect (Elder et al., 2010; Helfinstein et al., 2008). No differences were found either in response to the following target.

A single study has employed the face dot-probe task (angry-neutral and happy-neutral) in a sample of patients with social anxiety disorder and matched controls. Behavioral results indicated that SAD patients had an attentional bias towards the location of angry faces. The SAD group displayed larger P1 amplitudes in response to the angry-neutral relative to happy-neutral faces. However, in response to the following targets, the SAD group had *smaller* P1 voltages to targets in the location of emotional relative to neutral faces, while the control group appeared to have the opposite bias.

Notably, no studies to date have investigated ERP correlates of the original dot-probe task, i.e., employing words. In addition, no studies have focused on anxiety sensitivity (AS), an important variety of trait anxiety. In AS, the individual's concerns are centred on the experience of the physical manifestations of anxiety. In other words, it describes the extent to which people fear a future situation in which they may experience symptoms of physical anxiety (e.g., palpitations, sweating, choking; McNally, 2002). AS has been recognized as a risk factor for the development of panic disorder, in which such symptoms are prevalent (Schmidt & Lerew, 1997).

Two behavioural studies have explored attentional bias as it relates to AS status. Keogh et al. (2001) employed pairs of physical threat-neutral, social threat-neutral, and positive-neutral words as cues. Those high in AS showed an attentional bias towards the location of the physical threat cues, compared to the neutral cues. In the low AS group, the opposite effect, an *avoidance bias*, occurred where there was an attential bias away from the location of the physical threat cues. Furthermore, the high AS group displayed an avoidance of the positive words, while the low AS group had a bias towards them. In a follow-up study by the same group, Hunt et al. (2006) presented the same word pairs in masked and unmasked conditions. High AS participants exhibited a bias towards the physical threat words in both masked and unmasked conditions, while they displayed an avoidance bias to positive words only in the masked condition.

The aim of the present study was to address the above limitations of the existing literature by exploring the electrophysiological correlates of attentional bias to physical threat words in healthy individuals with high and low AS using the original, word-based, dot-probe task..

The following hypotheses were formulated. Behaviourally, we expected an attentional facilitation of responses to targets presented in the previous location of physical threat words, in the high AS group only. Our first ERP hypothesis was that threat-neutral conditions would elicit greater P1 activity in the high AS group, while no such modulation would be present for positive-neutral conditions. Our second ERP hypothesis concerned the modulation of the evoked response to the targets. Since previous ERP studies have reported effects of spatial attention on both the occipital P1 and N1 waves (see a review in Luck, 1995) we predicted that P1 and/or N1 waves to the target would be modulated by location of the target in relation to the preceding threat cue.

METHODS

Screening Session

933 undergraduate students took part in a screening session in which they completed the Anxiety Sensitivity Inventory (ASI) and a demographic questionnaire. The ASI is a 16-item scale used to reveal the fear of anxiety related sensations (Reiss, Peterson, Gursky & McNally, 1986). Scores were distributed as such: Mean = 21.3 ± 9.6, Range 2 – 53. Cut-off points were made at ± 1 standard deviation; those with ASI scores ≥ 30 were classified as

high AS, while those with ASI scores ≤ 11 were labeled as low AS. Subjects in the two subgroups, who also reported in the demographic questionnaire being native English speakers, were contacted by email and invited to participate in the second study session.

Experimental Session

A total of 34 participants agreed to take part in the experimental study session (17 low AS and 17 high AS) in exchange of course credits or monetary compensation. On the day of the EEG session, they first completed three additional questionnaires, a medical screening form, the Spielberger State Inventory (STAI-S; Spielberger, Gorsuch, & Lushene, 1983), and two Likert scales assessing subjective ratings of current anxiety and sadness, (scale 0-10). All participants reported normal color vision, normal or corrected-to-normal visual acuity, and claimed to be free of current and previous neurological and psychiatric disorders, and current use of psychotropic medication (as determined through the self-administered medical questionnaire). Participants were then tested in a sound-attenuated room facing a computer monitor, and electrical brain activity was recorded while they performed the dot-probe task. Finally, they filled out two more questionnaires, the Beck Depression Inventory, version 2 (BDI-II; Beck, Steer, & Carbin, 1988), and the Spielberger Trait Inventory (STAI-T; Spielberger et al., 1983).

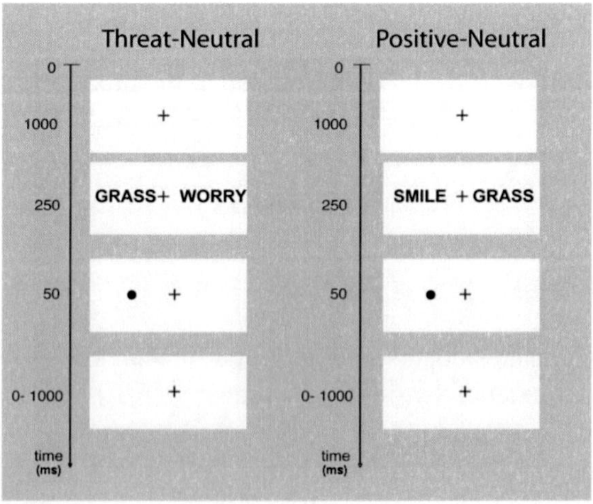

Figure 1. Trial sequence for Threat-Neutral and Positive-Neutral Blocks.

Behavioral Task

A modified version of a visual dot-probe task was employed (see Figure 1). The participants sat in front of a computer monitor, with their eyes 60 cm from a central fixation cross. A total of 180 words, generated from 3 distinct word types (60 physical threat, 60 positive and 60 neutral), were selected (See Appendix 1). Words were matched for word length and frequency of use (Kucera & Francis, 1967). Stimuli were presented in two blocks: Threat-neutral (60 word pairs), and positive-neutral (60 word pairs). Within each block, the target dot appeared randomly and with equal probability either at the location corresponding to the center of the preceding emotional word (threat or positive), or at the location corresponding to the center of the preceding neutral word. Order of presentation of the blocks was varied across subjects and groups according to a Latin square design. Each trial began with the presentation of the fixation point (1000 ms), followed by a word pair (duration: 250 ms). After that, the dot appeared for 50 ms replacing the word to the left or right of the fixation cross. The trial ended with a randomly jittered interstimulus interval of 0-1000 ms (average 500 ms). Participants were instructed to maintain their eyes on the central fixation, and to respond as quickly as possible to the appearance of the dot, by pressing one of two keys on a game-pad controller with the index finger of the hand on the same side as the presented dot (left visual field-left hand and right visual field-right hand). Subjects were informed that word pairs were flashed on the screen, but the task would be to respond as fast and accurately as possible to the location of the dot immediately following each word pair. A short practice block (using different words) preceded the actual experiment, to familiarize the subjects with the task and make sure they would comply with the instruction of keeping their eyes on the central fixation. Mean reaction times were calculated for each condition. Only correct hits were used in the averaged RTs. The visual dot-probe task took approximately 25 minutes to complete.

ERP Measures

Participants' electrical brain activity was recorded from 63 tin electrodes positioned at FP1, FPz, FP2, AF3, AF4, F7, F5, F3, F1, Fz, F2, F4, F6, F8, FC5, FC3 FC1, FCz, FC2, FC4, FC6, T7, C5, C3, C1, Cz, C2, C4, C6, T8, CP5, CP3, CP1, CPz, CP2, CP4, CP6, P9, P7, P5, P3, P1, Pz, P2, P4, P6, P8, P10, PO7, PO3, POz, PO4, PO8, O1, Oz, O2, Iz, and M1 (American

Electroencephalographic Society, 1994) and five non-standard sites inferior to the standard occipital locations. All EEG signals were references to the right-mastoid during recording. Electrode impedances were kept below 10 kΩ. The horizontal electrooculogram (HEOG) was recorded bipolarly using two electrodes positioned lateral to the external canthi. All signals were acquired with a bandpass of 0.1–100 Hz (-3 dB point; -12 dB per octave). EEG data were digitized at a sampling rate of 500 Hz and a gain of 20,000 (amplifier: SA Instrumentation, San Diego, CA). Horizontal eye movements were detected on the HEOG channel, and blinks were detected at FP1. Artifact rejection was performed to remove epochs that contained horizontal eye movements, blinks, and amplifier blocking. A total of six subjects (three for each group) were excluded for either excessive blinking or technical difficulties while recording behavioral performance, leaving a total of 14 high AS and 14 low AS participants for further analysis.

Behavioral Data Analysis

Mixed design ANOVAs were employed on the mean correct RT (RTs <150 ms or >1500 ms were excluded). The between group factor was AS status (high vs. low). Within group factors were emotional block (threat versus positive), and validity (probe in the same location as the emotional stimulus or in the opposite location).

ERP Data Analysis

For each participant two sets of ERP averages were obtained. For the cue analysis, two averages were calculated for word pairs in the Threat blocks and the Positive Blocks, time-locked to word onset. For the Target analysis, four distinct ERP averages were obtained: For the Threat blocks, targets in same location as previous threat word (threat valid) or in the opposite location as the preceding threat word (threat invalid); for the Positive blocks, targets in same location as previous positive word (positive valid) or in the opposite location as the preceding positive word (positive invalid).

Only ERPs to correct RT responses (hits, 150-1500 ms range) were included. All channels were re-referenced to the average of the two mastoid electrodes, and smoothed twice with a 7-point running average filter. ERP amplitudes were aligned to a 200 msec prestimulus baseline period. For each

AS group, corresponding grandaverages were created for each trial type for both cues (emotional words) and target (probes). To help isolating effects of interest, difference waves were calculated both within and between groups. To facilitate visualization, scalp voltage topographic distributions were obtained using spherical spline interpolation. After inspection of grand-average waveforms and scalp topography distributions for each stimulus type and corresponding difference waves, several effects of interest were identified.

For the cue analysis, two posterior components (P1 and P2) appeared to vary across emotional blocks and AS groups. For the P1 effect (75-115 msec), an occipital lateral region of interest (ROI) was selected, by averaging together two neighbor electrode sites for each hemisphere (sites O1, PO7, and O2, PO8). Similarly, for the posterior P2 effect (150-200 msec), an occipital lateral region of interest (ROI) was selected, by averaging together three neighbor electrode sites for each hemisphere (sites O1, PO7 and PO3, and O2, PO8 and PO4, respectively).

For the target analysis, visual inspection of the data revealed modulations of the N1 component and the later P3 wave, while no clear P1 waves or P1 modulations were observed. For the N1 effect (80-150 msec), an occipital lateral region of interest (ROI) was selected, by averaging together two neighbor electrode sites where the voltage difference was maximal (sites O1 and Oz). In addition, N1 amplitudes in the low AS group appeared to differ between threat valid and threat invalid trials, suggesting avoidance of threat in this group. The effect appeared to have a different scalp distribution, with a parietal focus. Therefore, in this group, an additional analysis was carried out on two parietal regions of interest, averaging together sites P1, P3, P5 and P2, P4, P6. For the P3 analysis (300-400 msec), a lateral parietal region of interest (ROI) was selected, by averaging together four neighbor electrode sites for each hemisphere (sites O1, PO3, P1, CP3, and O2, PO4, P2 and CP2, respectively).

For analyses of the ERP data to the cues, mixed design ANOVAs were used, with between-factor being group (high vs. low anxiety), and within factor being emotional block (threat versus positive), and hemisphere (left versus right ROI). For analyses of the ERP data to the targets, the factor validity (same or opposite location as previous emotional word) was added. Global analyses were followed by more restricted ANOVAs and t-tests upon significance of interactions, or when *apriori* hypotheses for group differences were present. For all analyses, the critical p-value was set at .05, and degrees of freedom were corrected with the Greenhouse-Geisser epsilon method to correct for sphericity (Greenhouse & Geisser, 1954).

Table 1. Summary of socio-demographic and self-report measures of mood and symptom severity for participants with high anxiety sensitivityand healthy controls

	High ASI participants (n = 14)	Low ASI participants (n = 14)	t or χ^2 value	p value
Age (years)	19.1 (1.64)	23.1 (4.7)	$t(26) = 2.99$	$p = .006$
Men/Women	3/11	5/9	$\chi^2(1) = 5.14$	$p = .023$
Education in years [a]	13.9 (1.6)	15.6 (2.1)	$t(21) = 2.14$	$p = .044$
Anxiety Sensitivity Score	35.7 (5.9)	9.9 (6.2)	$t(26) = -11.34$	$p = .000$
Beck Depression Inventory -II	13.3 (12.8)	3.1 (2.3)	$t(26) = -2.93$	$p = .007$
State-Trait Anxiety Inventory - State	40.0 (6.5)	28.4 (7.3)	$t(26) = -4.44$	$p = .000$
State-Trait Anxiety Inventory - Trait	46.4 (9.1)	32.1 (7.4)	$t(26) = -4.52$	$p = .000$
Anxious VAS	2.86 (1.99)	1.57 (1.72)	$t(26) = -1.82$	$p = .081$
Sad VAS	1.86 (2.12)	1.14 (2.38)	$t(26) = -.84$	$p = .41$

Values given as means (standard deviations).

[a] Degrees of freedom (df) = 21 because of missing values of five participants.

RESULTS

Demographic Variables

Demographic characteristics of the participant groups are summarized in Table 1. The high and low AS participants differed on age, [$t(1, 26) = 2.99$, $p = .006$], and Education, [$t(1, 21) = 2.14$, $p = .044$], with the high ASI participants being on average 4 years younger. Furthermore, there was a greater number of women overall, $\chi 2$ (1) = 5.14, p = .023, as well as within the high AS group, $\chi 2$ (1) = 4.57, p = .033, but not within the low AS group, $\chi 2$ (1) = 1.14, p = .26. High AS participants also reported significantly higher scores on the BDI, [t(1, 26) = -2.93, p = .007], the STAI-S, [t(1, 26) = -4.44, p = .000], the STAI-T, [t(1, 26) = -4.52, p = .000], but did not differ on the Anxious VAS, [t(1, 26) = -1.82, p = .081], or the Sad VAS, [t(1, 26) = -.84, p = .41].

RT Effects

In the mixed design ANOVA, there was a significant main effect of validity [F(1, 26)= 4.26 p = .049], with overall faster reaction times to probes replacing a previous emotional word compared to probes in the location of a neutral word (valid = 369.3 ± 4.45 ms, invalid = 372.52 ± 4.80 ms). However, there was no hint of significant interactions involving validity and emotional block or AS group (for all p > .20). Therefore, there was no evidence of a selective validity effect to threat words in the high AS group. An illustration of such results is presented in Figure 2.

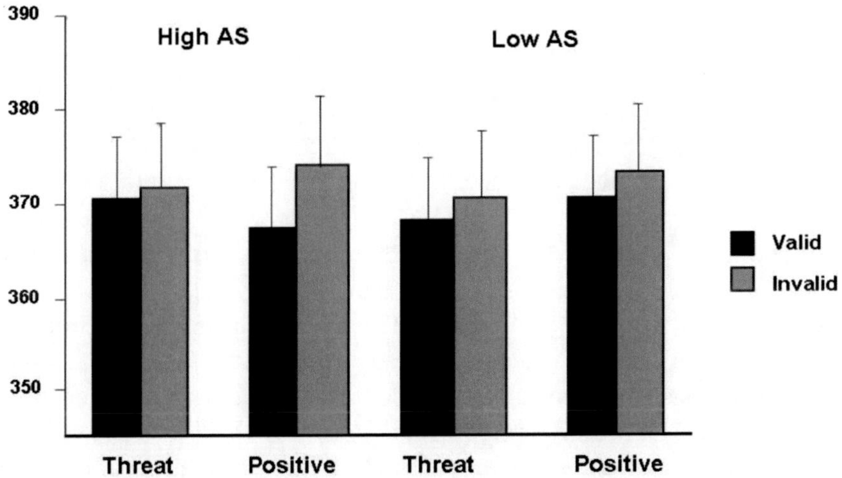

Figure 2. Mean RT in ms as a function of Group, Emotion and Cue Validity.

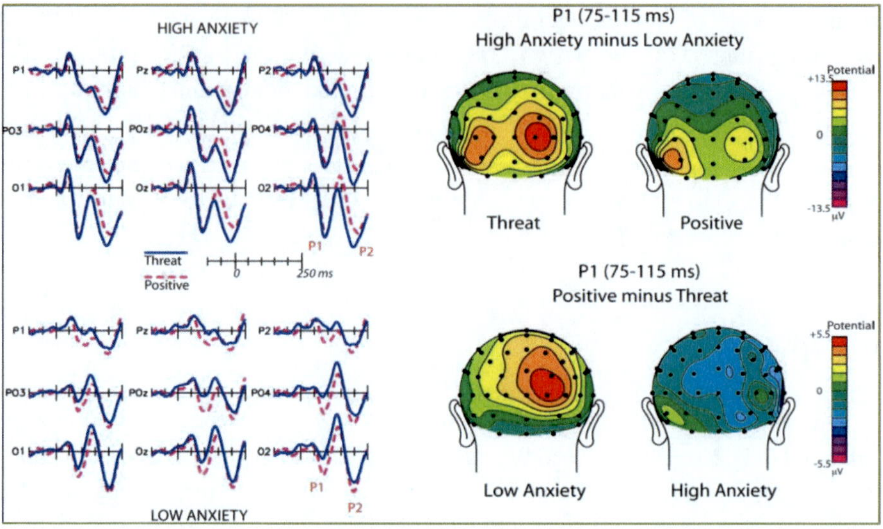

Figure 3. P1 Effect to the Cues. Representative waveforms and topographic maps.

ERP Results

ERPs to Cues

P1 (75 – 125 ms)

P1 effects are illustrated in Figure 3. In the global ANOVA, there was a significant main effect of emotional block [$F(1, 26)= 5.35$ $p = .029$], indicating that amplitudes were overall greater in the positive than threat blocks (threat = 3.36 ± 1.34 µV, positive = 5.08 ± 1.12 µV). There was also a main effect of group [$F(1, 26) = 5.04$ $p = .033$], with the high ASI participants displaying greater ERP amplitudes than the low ASI participant overall (High ASI = 8.86 ± 1.66 µV, Low ASI = 1.58 ±1.66 µV). The interactions involving Group and Emotional Block failed to reach significance ($p > .10$). However, given our apriori hypothesis of P1 enhancement for threat blocks as a function of AS status, we proceeded with restricted within group ANOVAs as well as planned t-tests. In the high AS group, there was no significant main effect of emotional block ($p > .10$). In contrast, in the low AS group, there was a significant main effect of emotional block [$F(1, 13) = 6.94$, $p = .021$], indicating that amplitudes were greater in the positive relative to the threat blocks for these participants (threat = .15 ± 1.45 µV, positive = 3.02 ± 1.54 µV). Furthermore, two apriori planned t-tests indicated that the high ASI [AS?] participants had greater P1 amplitude for threat blocks relative to the low AS participants [$t(1, 26) = -2.36$, $p = .025$), (high AS = .145 ± 1.90 μV, low AS = 6.58 ± 1.90 μV)], while the two groups did not differ for positive blocks[$t(1, 26) = -1.86$, p = .075].

P2 (150 – 200 ms)

P2 effects are illustrated In Figure 3. In the global ANOVA, there was a significant interaction of emotional block x group [$F(1, 26) = 7.95$ $p = .009$]. In the high AS group, threat blocks elicited greater mean P2 amplitude than positive blocks [(threat = 14.06 ± 2.27 μV, positive = 8.67 ± 1.82 μV), $t(1, 26) = 2.55$, $p = .024$)]. In contrast, in the low AS group, mean P2 voltage did not differ as a function of emotional block [(threat = 7.20 ± 2.27 μV, positive = 8.39 ± 1.82 μV), $t(1, 26) = -1.21$, $p = 0.25$)]. Furthermore, planned independent-samples t-tests indicated that the high AS participants had greater mean P2 amplitude for threat blocks relative to the low AS participants [(high AS = 14.06 ± 10.81 μV, low AS = 7.12 ± 5.28 μV), $t(1, 26) = -2.14$, $p = .042$], while the corresponding comparison for positive blocks did not approach significance, [$t(1, 26) = -.11$, p = .91].

ERPs to Probes

Occipital N1 (80-150 ms)

N1 effects are illustrated in Figure 4. In the global ANOVA, there was a significant interaction of emotional block x group [$F(1, 26) = 6.65$, $p = .016$]. This effect was further qualified by a significant three-way interaction of emotional block x validity x group [$F(1, 26) = 4.79$, $p = .038$]. To help interpreting these interactions, restricted ANOVAs were performed within each AS group separately. For the High AS Group, there was a significant emotional block x validity interaction [$F(1, 13) = 5.27$, $p = .039$]. This was explained by a significant N1 relative *enhancement* for Threat Valid relative to Positive Valid trials [(threat valid = -6.15 ± 3.25 μV, positive valid = -2.33 ± 2.07 μV); t(13) = -2.31, p = .049]. In spite of greater mean N1 voltages for Threat Valid than Threat Invalid trials, the contrast did not approach significance [(threat valid = -6.15 ± 3.25 μV; threat invalid = -3.50 ± 1.94 μV); t(13) = -.155, p = .15]. All other comparisons were far from significant.

In contrast in the low AS group, there was a significant main effect of emotional block [$F(1, 13) = 5.93$, $p = .030$], due to a relative N1 *decrement* for threat relative to positive blocks [threat trials = -3.25 ± 1.66 μV; positive trials

= -4.90 ± 1.45 μV]. There was no hint of a significant interaction involving emotional block and validity [$F(1, 13) = 0.74$, $p = .41$].

Parietal N1 (80-150 ms)

Unlike the occipital N1 in the threat blocks of the low AS group, there was a significant main effect of validity, $F(1, 13) = 5.88$, p = .031, which was not affected by hemisphere (validity x hemisphere: $F(1, 13) = 2.81$, p = .12). Mean N1 amplitudes to Threat Invalid trials were greater than to Threat Valid trials (Threat Invalid = -5.21 ± 1.40 μV, Threat Valid = -3.85 ± 1.46 μV).

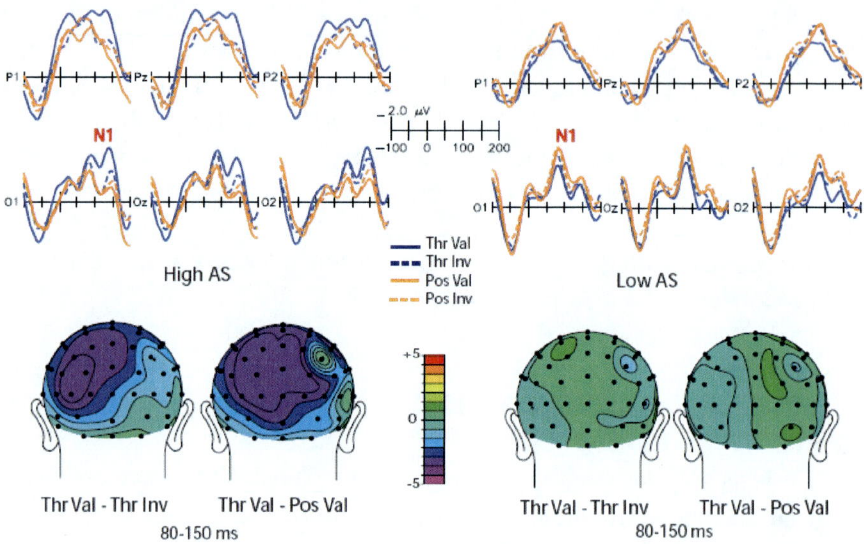

Figure 4. N1 Effect to Probes. Representative scalp sites and topographic maps.

P3b (300-400ms)

P3b effects are illustrated in Figure 5. In the global ANOVA, there was **a** significant interaction of emotional block x group [$F(1, 26) = 8.17$, p =.008]. This was qualified by a significant three-way interaction of emotional block x validity x Group [$F(1, 26) = 5.02$, $p = .034$]. To help interpret these effects, restricted ANOVAs were carried out within each AS group. In the High AS group, there was a significant emotional block X validity interaction [$F(1, 13)$ = 8.41, p = .012]. This was due to a significant P3 amplitude *decrease* ["decreament" is an awkward word to use here] for Threat Valid relative to Positive Valid trials [Threat Valid = 7.03 ± 3.2 μV; Positive Valid = 10.90 ±

3.0 μV, *t*(12) = -2.53, p = .025], which was absent for the correspondent contrast of Threat Invalid vs. Positive Invalid trials [Threat Invalid = 9.29 ± 2.5 μV; Positive Invalid = 9.48 ± 2.5 μV, *t*(12) = -.26]. No validity effects within blocks approached significance.

In the Low Group, there was a marginally significant main effect of emotional block, with an overall P3 amplitude increase for Threat than Positive blocks [Threat trials = 12.43 ± 2.2 μV; Positive trials = 10.91 ± 1.9 μV; *F*(1, 13) = 4.60, p = .051]. However, there was no hint of a significant interaction of emotional block and validity, *F*(1, 13) = .089, p = .77.

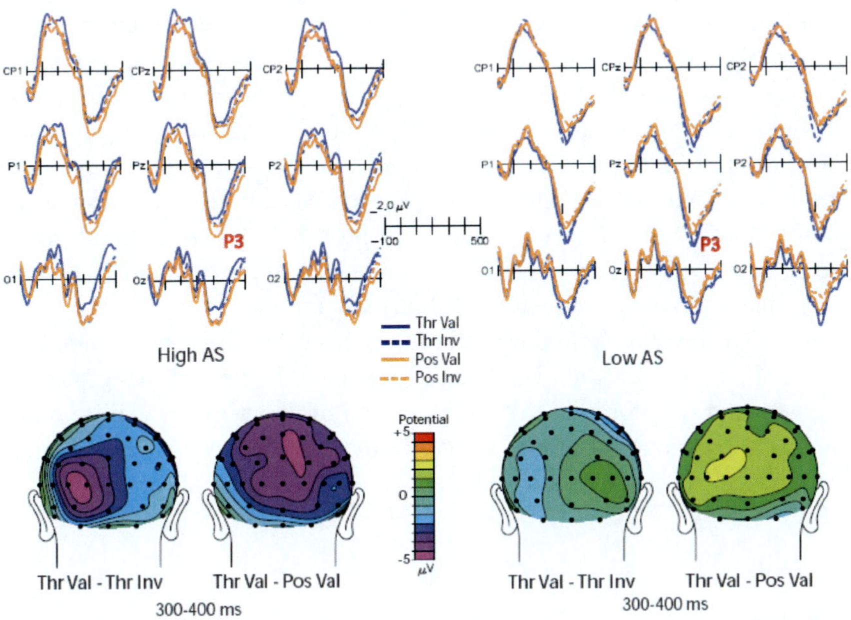

Figure 5. P3 Effect to Probes. Representative scalp sites and topographic maps.

CONCLUSION

The present study explored the behavioral and electrophysiological correlates of attentional biases in a non-clinical sample of young adults varying in levels of trait anxiety for physical symptoms (Anxiety Sensitivity) using a visual dot-probe task.

Our behavioral hypothesis, of a selective attentional bias to threat words in the high AS group, was not supported. Rather, both groups displayed a small advantage to respond to probes in a valid location following emotional words independent of their threat or positive content.

A number of threat-specific ERP effects were found. First, consistent with our first ERP hypothesis, the evoked response to threat-neutral cues showed enhanced occipital P1 amplitudes in the high relative to the low AS group. Furthermore, low AS participants were characterized by greater P1 amplitudes to positive-neutral word pairs compared to threat-neutral ones. While no specific predictions were made, selective threat-related modulations also affected a later occipital P2 component, with greater voltage in response to threat blocks than positive blocks in the high AS participants.

the second ERP hypothesis, event-related responses to targets did show modulations as a function of trait-anxiety, validity, and emotion. In the high AS group, an occipital N1 wave (80-150 ms) was *enhanced* in response to probes presented in the same location as previous threat words, compared to probes presented in the same location as previous positive words. In contrast, in the low AS group, occipital N1 amplitudes were *reduced* in response to probes following threat words relative to probes following neutral words, independent of validity. In addition, over parietal scalp, N1 amplitude to threat invalid trials was *enhanced* relative to threat valid trials.

While no specific predictions were made, later P3b waves also varied as a function of AS group, validity and emotional block. In the high AS group, P3b was *attenuated* for probes in the same location of threat words than to probes in the same location of positive words. In the low AS group, P3b to probes were reduced following positive relative to threat stimuli independent of validity.

RT Effects

No selective RT bias to respond more quickly to targets in the location of a threat word was found in the high anxiety group. In both groups, targets in the location of previous emotional words were slightly faster than in the opposite location, independent of valence. Electrophysiological effects in absence of significant behavioral differences have been repeatedly reported before. This has been interpreted as being due to greater sensitivity of brain activity than behavioral measures in the detection of differences in attentional bias (e.g., Brown et al., 2010; Li, Zinbarg & Paller, 2007; Taake et al., 2009; Thomas, Johnstone, & Gonsalvez, 2007).

ERP Cue Effects

P1 (75-125 ms)

P1 amplitude modulations have been previously reported to a variety of emotional relative to neutral stimuli (e.g., Smith et al., 2003; Li et al., 2007; Taake et al., 2009). A more pronounced and earlier occipital P1 modulation, starting as early as 50 ms, has been reported in high trait-anxiety individuals (Bar-Haim et al., 2005; Li et al., 2007). These P1 effects have been typically interpreted as attentional enhancements through early sensory gain in visual extrastriate cortex (e.g. Woldorff et al., 2002) for *blocks* of stimuli of greater salience. It has been argued that very early modulations of visual cortex activity originate in the magnocellular pathways, rely on coarse spatial information, and are being modulated in the amygdala. P1 effects to threat have been shown to be absent in patients with amygdala damage (Rotshtein et al., 2010), or when low spatial frequency information was filtered out of the presented threat stimuli (Pourtois, Dan, Grandjean, Sander, Vuilleumier, 2005). Our results therefore are in agreement with the existing literature.

P2 (150-200 ms)

While not as often reported before, our finding of increased posterior P2 amplitude to threat stimuli is consistent with recent findings in the emotion literature. Eldar et al. (2010) employed a face dot probe in healthy participants with high and low trait anxiety. They reported increased occipital P2 voltage (195-250 ms) in response to all faces (angry-neutral, happy-neutral, neutral-neutral) in the high vs. low trait-anxiety group contrast. None of the ERP analyses associated with target processing were significant. Bar-Haim et al. (2005) used a face dot-probe task in high and low trait anxiety participants. They found increased central P2 amplitudes for high relative to low anxiety group, particularly for angry faces, and no differences to targets. Thomas et al. (2007) employed an emotional Stroop task and found increased parietal P2 amplitudes (150-210 ms) for threat relative to neutral words under both covert (color processing) and overt (emotion processing) conditions. Therefore our results of increased P2 waves to threat words in the high AS group are consistent with the existing, albeit limited, literature.

ERP Target Effects

N1 (80-150 ms) and Threat Signals

Our finding of increased occipital N1 amplitude to targets in the location of threat words in the high AS group points to an early modulation of threat signals in visual areas in these individuals. This result is consistent with a recent paper by Shackman, Maxwell, McMenamin, Greischar, and Davidson (2011), who presented lateralized visual targets in a threat condition (anticipation of painful shocks) or in a neutral 'safety' condition (no shocks). They reported that occipital N1 voltage was greater in the threat condition, and speculated that stress may affect processing of incoming visual stimuli by increasing the gain in early visual areas, possibly through top-down influences from structures such amygdala and prefrontal cortex. A body of ERP studies shows that attentional orienting to a given spatial location gives rise to a contralateral N1 enhancement (Luck et al., 1990; Yagamuchi, Tsuchiya, & Kobayashi, 1995; Luck, 1995). It has been proposed that posterior N1 modulation indexes *exogenous* orienting of attention in response to relevant events occurring at random lateralized locations, while P1 attention effects may reflect a preset bias consequent to sustained gating of input at an attended or pre-specified location, *after* attention has been allocated to that location (Mangun and Hillyard, 1991; Natale, Marzi, Girelli, Pavone, & Pollmann, 2006). In relationship to our findings, we propose that the N1 increase to probes in the location of a previous threat word in the high AS individuals reflects greater attentional orienting to the spatial location of emotionally relevant event. Although not predicted, N1 findings in the low AS group were also noteworthy. Over occipital sites, N1 was reduced in threat relative to positive blocks, suggesting an opposite tendency to down-regulate early sensory processing of threat stimuli in low anxiety individuals. Furthermore, over parietal scalp, N1 amplitude was greater to the target in the *opposite* relative to the same location to the preceding threat stimulus, suggesting that our low-anxiety participants preferentially oriented attention to the location opposite to where a threat stimulus had just occurred. This is consistent with previous behavioral findings in the dot-probe task in non-anxious groups displaying a similar pattern to avoid threat stimuli (Hunt et al., 2006; Bradley et al., 1997; Keough et al., 2001). The parietal distribution (with a right-sided maximum) may suggest the intervening influence of an N1 sub-generator engaged during online spatial attentional shifts (Fichtenholz, Hopfinger, Graham, Detwiler, & LaBar, 2007; Corbetta, Patel, & Shulman, 2008).

P3b (300-400 ms) and Threat Processing

Consistent with the literature on later processing positivities and emotion (LPP, for a recent review see Hajcak, MacNamara , & Olvet, 2010), the low AS group displayed an enhanced P3b amplitude to targets in the threat blocks. The unanticipated finding in the High AS group of a reduction of P3b amplitude to visual stimuli in the threat blocks requires an additional explanation. Such results fit nicely with Shackman et al.'s findings of similarly attenuated visual P3b responses in the stress blocks. They speculate that stress-induced P3b reduction stems from disruption of top-down regulatory mechanisms, not unlike the effect of a resource-demanding secondary task (Shackman et al., 2011).

In line with these authors, we also interpret our combined findings in the high AS group – a reduced P3b amplitude in association with enhanced N1 voltage- as the consequence of a processing bias whereby early hypervigilance to threat at more automatic stages of stimulus selection (reflected by the N1) may be followed by attenuated processing at later stages of conscious evaluation of the threat stimulus (indexed by the P3b).

Time Course of Emotion Regulation of Threat Stimuli in Trait-anxiety

The present ERP results allow to formulate a model in which processing of physical threat words is modulated in two ways by anxiety sensitivity status. In high anxious subjects early hypervigilance leads to enhancement of occipitally distributed sensory components (P1 to the threat pairs, N1 to following targets) and later attenuation of conscious top-down processing of threat (as indexed by the P3b/LPP).

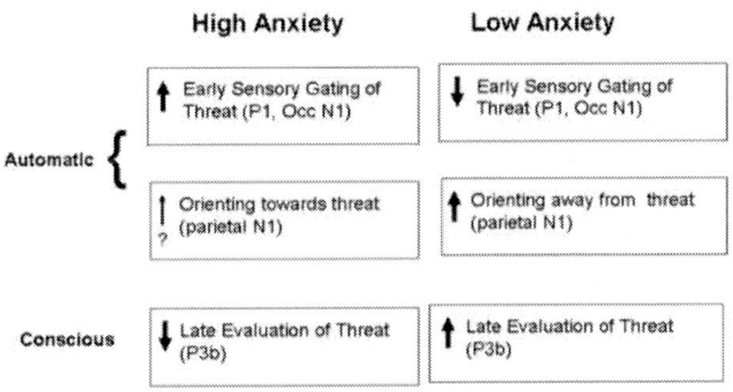

Figure 6. Model of Emotion Regulation as a function of High or Low AS status.

In contrast, low anxious subjects would take consciously note of the salience of the threat stimulus (with a relatively increased P3b) and show an opposite trend towards early down-regulation of threat information, accompanied by orienting of attention away from the location of a threat word. A schematic illustration of the model is proposed in Figure 6.

Final Remarks and Caveats

A first limitation of the present study is the small sample size. Giving the paucity of available studies of the dot-probe, and the often contradictory findings, the present results should be replicated in larger samples of high and low AS participants. Such a study may also address the role of gender, given the high number of women in both groups in the present study. Second, no source localization of the present ERP effects was carried out, limiting our ability to relate the results to underlying brain structures and to existing neuroimaging studies.

These limitations notwithstanding, this is the first study to report electrophysiological correlates of attentional bias in individuals with high AS using the dot-probe task. Future directions of the present study could address whether the reported findings can generalize to other forms of trait-anxiety or to the various clinical disorders. In particular, given the proposed role of anxiety sensitivity as a predictor of future panic disorder, it would be interesting to carry out a similar study in such disease state.

APPENDIX 1

	Threat	Positive	Neutral
01	Funeral	Harmony	Charter
02	Exhaustion	Fairy-tale	Fahrenheit
03	Breathless	Peacefully	Measurable
04	Cancer	Fortune	Saddle
05	Insane	Loving	Sealed
06	Death	Money	Field
07	Injury	Virtue	Mirror
08	Headache	Comedian	Diplomat
09	Nervous	Amazing	Founded
10	Bruise	Hurrah	Magnet

Threat		Positive	Neutral
11	Hospital	Security	Language
12	Tired	Proud	Latin
13	Wound	Laugh	Verse
14	Harm	Star	Pile
15	Fever	Angel	Boots
16	Sweat	Glory	Clock
17	Blind	Funny	Urban
18	Ambulance	Amusement	Fishermen
19	Stress	Engergy	Season
20	Panic	Honey	Slope
21	Fatal	Lucky	Valid
22	Pain	Rose	Bank
23	Needle	Reward	Shower
24	Sniffle	Empower	Inhabit
25	Virus	Haven	Thumb
26	Danger	Beauty	Object
27	Drowsy	Joyful	Edible
28	Collapse	Fairness	Township
29	Disorder	Blessing	Antelope
30	Stroke	Flower	String
31	Worry	Smile	Grass
32	Ulcer	Shine	Olive
33	Asthma	Humour	Helmet
34	Bacteria	Sunshine	Wardrobe
35	Allergy	Dolphin	Fishery
36	Arthritis	Gentility	Itinerary
37	Surgery	Glamour	Feather
38	Blood	Faith	Hotel
39	Cast	Luck	Wood
40	Sick	Holy	Pink
41	Lesion	Honour	Washer
42	Fracture	Altruism	Windmill
43	Sneezing	Cheering	Analogue
44	Parasite	Goodwill	Nutshell
45	Choke	Unite	Stamp
46	Anxiety	Comfort	Journal
47	Seizure	Ecstasy	Cyclist
48	Chronic	Elegant	Nominal

APPENDIX 1 (CONTINUED)

	Threat	Positive	Neutral
49	Ache	Swan	Tack
50	Vaccine	Empathy	Boatmen
51	Dizzy	Super	Tenth
52	Cough	Cheer	Elect
53	Fatigue	Reunion	Calcium
54	Surgeon	Leisure	Nucleus
55	Spit	Grin	Curb
56	Suffering	Desirable	Automatic
57	Emergency	Discovery	Furniture
58	Pharmacy	Kindness	Mustache
59	Therapy	Mastery	Sweater
60	Trembling	Impressed	Partially

REFERENCES

Amir, N., Beard, C., Burns, M. & Bornyea, J. (2009). Attential modification program in individuals with generalized anxiety disorder. *Journal of Abnormal Psychology, 118*, 28-33.

Bar-Haim, Y., Lamy, D., Glickman, S. (2005). Attentional bias in anxiety: A behavioural and ERP study. *Brain and Cognition*, *59*, 11–22.

Bar-Haim, Y., Lamy, D., Pergamin, L., Bakermans-Kranenburg, M. J., & van Ijzendoorn, M. H. (2007). Threat-related attentional bias in anxious and nonanxious individuals: A meta-analytic study. *Psychological Bulletin, 133*, 1-24.

Beck, A. T., Steer, R. A., & Carbin, M. G., 1988. Psychometric properties of the Beck Depression Inventory: Twenty-five years of evaluation. *Clinical Psychology Review, 8*, 77-100.

Bradley, B. P., Mogg, K., Milar, N., Bonham-Carter, C., Fergusson, E., Jenkins, J. &

Parr, M. (1997). Attentional biases for emotional faces. *Cognition and Emotion, 11*, (1), 25-42.

Brosch, T., Sander, D., Pourtois, G., & Scherer, K. R. (2008). Beyond Fear. Rapid spatial orienting toward positive emotional stimuli. *Psychological Science, 19*(4), 362-370.

Brown, C., El-Deredy, W., & Blanchette, I. (2010). Attentional modulation of visual-evoked potentials by threat: Investigating the effect of evolutionary relevance. *Brain and Cognition, 74*, 281-287.

Clark, V. P., & Hillyard, S. A. (1996). Spatial selective attention affects early extrastriate but not striate components of the visual evoked potential. *Journal of Cognitive Neuroscience, 8*, 387-402.

Corbetta, M., Patel, G., Shulman, G.L. (2008) The reorienting system of the human brain: From environment to theory of mind. *Neuron, 58*,306 –324.

Eldar, S. & Bar-Haim, Y. (2010). Neural plasticity in response to attention training in anxiety. *Psychological Medicine, 40*, 667-677.

Eldar, S., Yankelevitch, R., Lamy, D., & Bar-Haim, Y. (2010). Enhanced neural reactivity and selective attention to threat in anxiety. *Biological Psychology, 85*, 252-257.

Eysenck, M. W., Derakshan, N., Santos, R., & Calvo, M. (2007). Anxiety and cognitive performance: The attentional control theory. *Emotion, 7*(2), 336-353.

Fichtenholz, H. M., Hopfinger, J. B., Graham, R., Detwiler, J. M., & LaBar, K. S. (2007). Happy and fearful emotions in cues and targets modulate event-related potential indices of gaze-directed attentional orienting. *Social Cognitive and Affective Neuroscience, 2*(4), 323-333.

Fox, E., Russo, R., Bowles, R., & Dutton, K. (2001). Do threatening stimuli draw or hold visual attention in subclinical anxiety? *Journal of Experimental Psychology: General, 130*(4), 681-700.

Frewen, P.A., Dozois, D. J. A., Joanisse, M. F., & Neufeld, R. W. J. (2008). Selective attention to threat *versus* reward: Meta-analysis and neural network modeling of the dot-probe task. *Clinical Psychology Review, 28*, 307-337.

Greenhouse, S., & Geisser, S., 1954. On methods in the analysis of profile data.*Psychometrika, 24*, 95-112.

Hajcak, G., MacNamara, A., & Olvet, D. M. (2010). Event-related potentials, emotion, and emotion regulation: An integrative review. *Developmental Neuropsychology, 35*(2), 129-155.

Helfinstein, S. M., White, L. K., Bar-Haim, Y., & Fox, N. A. (2008). Affective primes suppress attention bias to threat in socially anxious individuals. *Behaviour Research and Therapy, 46*, 799-810.

Hunt, C., Keogh, E., & French, C. C. (2006). Anxiety sensitivity: The role of conscious awareness and selective attentional bias to physical threat. *Emotion, 6*(3), 418-428.

Keogh, E., Dillon, C., Georgiou, G., & Hunt, C. (2001). Selective attentional biases for physical threat in physical anxiety sensitivity. *Journal of Anxiety Disorders, 15*, 299-315.

Kucera, H. & Francis, N., 1967. Computational analysis of present-day American English Index. Providence, RI: Brown University Press.

LeDoux, J. E. (1986). The Emotional Brain: The mysterious underpinnings of emotional life. New York: Simon and Schuster.

Li, W., Zinbarg, R. E., & Paller, K. A. (2007). Trait anxiety modulates supraliminal and subliminal threat: Brain potential evidence for early and late processing influences. *Cognitive, Affective, & Behavioural Neuroscience, 7*(1), 25-36.

Lindstroem, K., Guyer, A. E., Mogg, K., Bradley, B. P., Fox, N. A., Ernst, M., Nelson, E. E., Leibenluft, E., Britton, J. C., Monk, C. S., Pine, d. S., & Bar-Haim, Y. (2009). Normative data on development of neural and behavioural mechanisms underlying attention orienting toward social-emotional stimuli: An exploratory study. *Brain Research, 1292*, 61-70.

Luck, S.J. (1995). Multiple mechanisms of visual-spatial attention: Recent evidence from human electrophysiology. *Behav. Brain Res., 71*,113–123.

Luck, S.J., Heinze, H.J., Mangun, G.R. and Hillyard, S.A. (1990). Visual event-related potentials index focused attention within bilateral stimulus arrays. 2. Functional dissociation of P1 and N1 components. *Electroen. Clin. Neuro., 75*, 528–542.

MacLeod, C., Mathews, A., & Tata, P. (1986). Attentional bias in emotional disorder. *Journal of Abnormal Psychology, 95*, 15-20.

McNally, R.J. (2002). Anxiety sensitivity and panic disorder. *Biological Psychiatry 52*(10), 938–946.

Mangun, G.R., & Hillyard, S.A. (1991). Modulations of sensory-evoked brain potentials indicate changes in perceptual processing during visual-spatial priming. *J Exp Psychol Hum Percept Perform, 17*, 1057–1074.

Mogg, K., Mathews, G., & Eysenck, M. (1992). Attentional bias in clinical anxiety states. *Cognition and Emotion, 6*, 149-159.

Monk, C. S., Telzer, E. H., Mogg, K., Bradley, B. P., Mai, X., Louro, H. M. C., Chen, G., McClure-Tone, E. B., Ernst, M., & Pine, D. S. (2008). Amygdala and ventrolateral prefrontal cortex activation to masked angry faces in children and adolescents with generalized anxiety disorder. *Arch Gen Psychiatry, 65*(5), 568-576.

Mueller, E. M., Hofmann, S. G., Santesso, D. L., Meuret, A. E., Bitran, S., and Pizzagalli, D. A. (2009). Electrophysiological evidence of attentional biases in social anxiety disorder. *Psychological Medicine, 39*, 1141-1152.

Natale, E., Marzi, C. A., Girelli, M., Pavone, E. F., & Pollmann, S. (2006). ERP and fMRI correlates of endogenous and exogenous focusing of visual-spatial attention. *European Journal of Neuroscience, 23*, 2511-2521.

Öhmann, A., Flykt, A., & Esteves, F. (2001). Emotion drives attention: Detecting the snake in the grass. *Journal of Experimental Psychology: General, 130*, 466-478.

Pourtois, G., Dan, E. S., Grandjean, D., Sander, D., & Vuilleumier, P. (2005). Enhanced extrastriate visual response to bandpass spatial frequency filtered fearful faces: Time course and topographic evoked-potentials mapping. *Human Brain Mapping, 26*, 65–79.

Pourtois, G., Delplanque, S., Michel, C., & Vuilleumier, P. (2008). Beyond conventional event-related brain potential (ERP): Exploring the time course of visual emotion processing using topographic and principal component analysis. *Brain topography, 20*, 265-277.

Pourtois, G., Grandjean, D., Sander, D., & Vuilleumier, P. (2004). Electrophysiological correlates of rapid spatial orienting towards fearful faces. *Cerebral Cortex, 14*, 619-633.

Pourtois, G. & Vuilleumier, P. (2006). Dynamics of emotional effects on spatial attention in the human visual cortex. Anders, Ende, Junghoefer, Kissler & Wildgruber (Eds). Progress in Brain Research, Vol 156.

Reiss, S., Peterson, R. A., Gursky, D. M., & McNally, R. J. (1986). Anxiety sensitivity, anxiety frequency, and the prediction of fearfulness. *Behaviour Research and Therapy, 24*, 1-8.

Rotshtein, P., Richardson, M. P., Winston, J. S., Kiebel, S. J., Vuilleumier, P., Eimer, M. et al. (2010). Amygdala damage affects event-related potentials for fearful faces at specific time windows. *Human Brain Mapping, 31*, 1089–1105.

Santesso, D. L., Meuret, A. E., Hofmann, S. G., Mueller, E. M., Ratner, K. G., Roesch, E. B., & Pizzagalli, D. A. (2008). Electrophysiological correlates of spatial orienting towards angry faces: A source localization study. *Neuropsychologia, 46*(5), 1338-1348.

Shackman, A. J., Maxwell, J. S., McMenamin, B. W., Greischar, L. L., & Davidson, R. J. (2011). Stress potentiates early and attenuates late stages of visual processing. *The Journal of Neuroscience, 31*(3), 1156-1161.

Schmidt, N. B. & Lerew, D. R. (1997). The role of anxiety sensitivity in the pathogenesis of panic: Prospective evaluation of spontaneous panic attacks during acute stress. *Journal of Abnormal Psychology, 106*(3), 355-364.

Smith, N.K., Cacioppo, J.T., Larsen, J.T., & Chartrand, T.L., (2003). May I have your attention, please: Electrocortical response to positive and negative stimuli.*Neuropsychologia 41*, 171–183.

Spielberger, C. D., Gorsuch, R. L., & Lushene, R. E., 1983. STAI manual for the State-Trait Anxiety Inventory. Palo Alto, California: Consulting Psychologists Press.

Stolarova, M., Keil, A. & Moratti, S. (2006). Modulation of the C1 visual event-related component by conditioned stimuli: Evidence for sensory plasticity in early affective perception. *Cerebral Cortex, 16*, 876-887.

Taake, I., Jaspers-Fayer, F., & Liotti, M. (2008). Early frontal responses elicited by physical threat words in an Emotional Stroop Task: Modulation by anxiety sensitivity. *Biological Psychology, 81*, 48-57.

Telzer, E. H., Mogg, K., Bradley, B. P., Mai, X., Ernst, M., Pine, D. S., & Monk, C. S. (2008). Relationship between trait anxiety, prefrontal cortex, and attention bias to angry faces in children and adolescents. *Biological Psychology, 79*(2), 216-222.

Thomas, S. J., Johnstone, S. J., & Gonsalvez, C. J. (2007). Event-related potentials during an emotional Stroop task. *International Journal of Psychophysiology, 63*, 221-231.

Williams, J. M. G., Mathews, A., & MacLeod, C. (1986). The emotional Stroop task and psychopathology. *Psychological Bulletin, 120*(1), 3-24.

Woldorff, M.G., Liotti, M., Seabolt, M., Busse, L., Lancaster, J.L., Fox, P.T. (2002). The temporal dynamics of the effects in occipital cortex of visual-spatial selective attention. *Cognitive. Brain Research 15* (1), 1–15.

Yamaguchi, S., Tsuchiya, H., & Kobayashi, S. (1995). Electrophysiologic correlates of visuo-spatial attention shift. *Electroencephalogr. Clin. Neurophysiol., 94*, 450-461.

In: Trait Anxiety
Editor: Anna S. Morales
ISBN 978-1-61324-551-4

Chapter 5

IS IT ME? FEARS OF CAUSING DISCOMFORT TO OTHERS AND OF NEGATIVE EVALUATION AS PREDICTORS OF SOCIAL ANXIETY IN MEN AND WOMEN FROM A COMMUNITY SAMPLE OF MEXICO

R. Robles-García[a,b], F. Páez[b], A. Fresán[a,*], J. Tejero[b], M. Lomelí[c] and A. C. Padilla[c]

[a]Instituto Nacional de Psiquiatría *Ramón de la Fuente Muñíz*, Secretaría de Salud. Mexico City, Mexico

[b]Instituto para el Fortalecimiento de Capacidades en Salud: FOCUS Salud México S.C. Mexico City, Mexico

[c]Universidad Iberoamericana. Campus Santa Fé. Mexico City, Mexico

ABSTRACT

A persistent fear of social or performance situations in which embarrassment may occur is the essential feature for social anxiety. Cognitive theories of social anxiety emphasize the role of negative self-

---

* Ana Fresán, PsyD, PhD. and Rebeca Robles-García MPsych, PhD. Instituto Nacional de Psiquiatría Ramón de la Fuente, Calz. México-Xochimilco 101, Mexico City, 14370 Mexico, Telephone: (5255) 41605069 Fax Number: (5255) 55133722. E-mail: a_fresan@yahoo.com.mx; reberobles@imp.edu.mx

appraisals and the anticipation of negative consequences for oneself. Nevertheless, other cognitive constructs have a significant role in the maintenance of social anxiety; specifically, the tendency to see oneself as overly responsible for other people's discomfort and the distress arising from concerns of being negatively judged by others. The interest in the assessment of these fears in patients with social anxiety is increasing, but research is also required to determine their impact in the development of social anxiety in non-clinical samples and the extent to which gender differences may arise in a specific cultural setting.

Objective

To determine if the fear of causing discomfort to others and the fear of negative evaluation are predictors of social anxiety in men and women. We hypothesized that fear of causing discomfort to others will be more related to social anxiety in women while the fear of negative evaluation will be more related to anxiety in men. Additionally, psychometric properties of the *Social Anxiety–Discomfort to Others Scale (SADOS)* and the *Brief Fear of Negative Evaluation Scale–Revised (BFNE-II)* in Mexican population were obtained.

Method

Recruitment was performed by a convenience sampling approach with subjects who agreed to participate in the study. A total of 500 volunteers were included. For the assessment of fear and avoidance in situations of performance and social interaction, the *Liebowitz Social Anxiety Scale–Self Report (LSAS-SR)* was used. A cutoff point of 30 in the total score of the *LSAS-SR* was employed to identify subjects with social anxiety and non-anxious subjects. The *SADOS* was applied to evaluate the fear of causing discomfort to others in social anxiety. Finally, the apprehension and distress arising from concerns about being judged disparagingly or hostile by others was assessed with the *BFNE-I)*.

Results

The *SADOS* and the *BFNE-II* showed excellent alpha values (>0.85). Principal component analyses were performed to determine the factor structure of the *SADOS* and the *BFNE-II;* three factors were identified for the *SADOS* and a unitary factor was obtained for the BFNE-II. Women exhibit higher scores in the fear subscale of the *LSAS-SR* and in the *BFNE-II* total score when compared to men. No differences by gender emerged in the *LSAS-SR* avoidance subscale, in the *SADOS* score or using the cut-off point of the *LSAS-SR*. Both cognitive constructs were predictors of social anxiety in women, while in men the only predictor of social anxiety was the fear of negative evaluation.

Conclusions

The reliability and validity information in Mexican population presented support the utility of the *SADOS* and the *BFNE-II* as adequate tools for the assessment of cognitive constructs related to social anxiety and could be useful in aiding mental health professionals in the recognition and management of this phenomenon. Our results highlights the importance of considering gender differences in the experience of social anxiety as women may express it in a more severe form as result of a higher fear and concern of not acting cooperatively and creating discomfort to other people.

Keywords: Social anxiety, cognition, fear of negative evaluation, fear of causing discomfort to others, gender

Introduction

Fear is defined as a normal reaction to a real or imagined threat and is considered to be an integral and adaptive feature related to the primary function of survival (Gullone 2000). Most people experience fear or discomfort in social situations involving being under the gaze of familiar or unfamiliar persons, although this experience is considered as normal and transient.

Some people experience more intense and frequent fear in these situations. This persistent fear of social or performance situations where embarrassment may occur is one of the core features of social anxiety (American Psychiatric Association 2000). Social anxiety interferes significantly with everyday routine and activities, or there is marked distress about having it; people may exhibit avoiding behaviors to feared social settings (den Boer 1997) and report general social impairment and weak social support (Letamendi et al. 2009; Lipsitz and Schneier 2000).

Cognitive theories of social anxiety emphasize the role of negative self-appraisals and the anticipation of negative consequences for oneself in the maintenance of the anxiety (Alden 2001; Heimberg and Becker 2002; Rector et al. 2006). In this way, there is a consensus that the fear of negative evaluation is the central cognitive content in social anxiety (Rector et al. 2006). The fear of negative evaluation refers to apprehension and distress arising from concerns about being judged disparagingly or hostile by others (Carleton et al. 2006). Nevertheless, other cognitive constructs have a significant role in the maintenance of anxiety, specifically, the fear of causing discomfort to others. This construct which refers to the perceived affective and behavioral consequences of their own anxiety or embarrassment, for instance, the tendency to see oneself as overly responsible for other people's discomfort (Rector et al. 2006). Fear of causing discomfort to others impacts on the cognitive processing of some individuals with social anxiety, which may serve to increase anticipated threats in social situations and worries about symptoms during social encounters.

Some authors consider that fears related to the consequences of anxiety to others may be connected to the same beliefs related to the perceived inadequacy that give rise to fear of negative evaluation (Wells 1997). Nonetheless, meaningful differences exist between them as individuals with social anxiety tend to allocate their attentional resources not only in external sources of threat (as the fear of negative evaluation), but also in internal sources of threat (fear of causing discomfort to others) (Singh and Hope 2009). In this way, the first one, is focused on the anticipated consequences of anxiety for oneself while the second is focused on the anticipated consequences of anxiety for others (Rector et al. 2006).

When talking about fears, females have been placed as more fearful than men (Brook and Schmidt 2008) and according to this conception several studies report that females have higher rates of social anxiety disorder than males by a ratio approximately of 3:2 (Hidalgo et al. 2001; Rapee and Spence 2004). Some authors proposed a gender role theory to explain gender differences in anxiety symptoms. Gender role is defined as the degree to which a person demonstrates traits, behaviors and attitudes consistent with stereotypical female o male roles (Brook and Schmidt 2008) according to specific cultural patterns of behavior. Although this theory potentially can explain why it is expected that women are generally more fearful than men, few research evaluating specific fears related to social anxiety have been performed. It is possible that internal and external sources of fear perceived by men and women may have a different impact in the manifestation of social anxiety.

The interest in the assessment of the fear of negative evaluation and of causing discomfort to others in patients with social phobia is increasing, but research is also required to determine their impact in the development of social anxiety in non-clinical samples and the extent to which gender differences may arise in a specific cultural setting.

Our study had two main purposes. First, to determine if the fear of causing discomfort to others and the fear of negative evaluation are predictors of social anxiety. Second, assuming successful prediction in the general sample, we wanted to determine if these two cognitive constructs predict social anxiety differently in men and women.

We hypothesized that fear of causing discomfort to others will be more related to social anxiety in women while the fear of negative evaluation will be more related to anxiety in men. Additionally, we also obtain psychometric properties of the *Social Anxiety – Discomfort to Others Scale (SADOS)* and the *Brief Fear of Negative Evaluation Scale – Revised (BFNE-II)* in Mexican population.

METHODS

Subjects

Recruitment was performed by a convenience sampling approach with subjects who agreed to participate in the study. A total of 500 volunteers were included. The sample comprised 334 (66.8%) women and 166 (33.2%) men, with a mean age of 26.8 ± 12.6 years (range from 16 – 77 years). More than half of the subjects were students at the time of the study (undergraduate n=196, 39.2%; college n=116, 23.2%), while 21.6% (n=108) were professional workers and 16.0% (n=80) were non-professional employees.

All subjects gave verbal informed consent after receiving a comprehensive explanation of the nature and objectives of the study.

Assessment Procedures

Liebowitz Social Anxiety Scale – Self Report (LSAS-SR)

The LSAS-SR is a self-report version of the Liebowitz Social Anxiety Scale (LSAS) (Liebowitz 1987) and requires subjects to answer questions in a paper-pencil format. As the LSAS, it consists of 24-items that assess fear and avoidance in situations of performance and social interaction. The items of both subscales – fear and avoidance - have a scoring range from 0 to 3, where "0" denotes the less severe form of fear or avoidance, and "3" the most severe form. A total score is calculated by summing all of the fear and avoidance items (score range from 0 to 144 points). It has shown adequate psychometric properties (Baker et al. 2002; Fresco et al. 2001; Levin et al. 2002; Oakman et al 2003). Although cut-off points have been suggested for the total score of the LSAS in Spanish-speaking populations (Bobes et al. 1999), there are no studies addressing the use of these cutoff points with the use of the LSAS-SR. In this way, we decide to use the cutoff point of 30 points proposed by Rytwinski et al. (2009) which provided the best balance between sensitivity and specificity and correctly identified subjects with social anxiety and non-anxious subjects.

Social Anxiety – Discomfort to others Scale (SADOS)

The SADOS was designed to evaluate the fear of causing discomfort to others in social anxiety. Also, it has shown adequate convergence with measures of interpersonal fears related to negative evaluation. It is a single-dimensional self-report scale with 12 items rated on a Likert scale ranging from 1 *(strongly disagree)* to 5 *(strongly agree)*. The alpha reliability of the SADOS was of 0.89 in a sample of patients with social phobia and of 0.84 in a student sample, with significant differences in mean scores between these groups (Rector et al. 2006).

Brief Fear of Negative Evaluation Scale – Revised (BFNE-II)

The BFNE-II is a measure designed to assess fear of negative evaluation which refers to the apprehension and distress arising from concerns about being judged disparagingly or hostile by others (Carleton et al. 2006). The original BFNE (Leary 1983) includes 8 straightforwardly-worded and 4 reverse-worded items, while in the BFNE-II these 4 reverse-items were reworded to be straightforward (Carleton et al. 2007; Carleton et al. 2006). This modification has shown strong relationship with theoretically related measures (Rodebaugh et al. 2004) and an excellent internal consistency (α=0.95) (Carleton et al. 2006).

Statistical Analysis

All analyses were carried out with version 17.0 of the SPSS statistical software. First, internal consistency of the SADOS and BFNE-II was estimated with the Cronbach´s alpha coefficient and two exploratory principal-components analysis with Varimax rotations were performed for each instrument. Second, descriptive statistics (mean scores and standard deviation) of the measurements for the whole sample were determined and compared by gender with independent sample *t*-tests. Third, Pearson correlation coefficients were used to estimate the linear association between the total scores of the LSAS-SR, SADOS and BFNE-II in men and women. Finally, logistic regression analyses were performed in the whole sample and in men and women with the backward-conditional stepwise selection method including fear of causing discomfort to others and the fear of negative evaluation as explanatory variables while the presence or absence of social anxiety was included as the outcome variables. The significance level for tests was established at $p \leq 0.05$ (2-tailed).

RESULTS

Psychometric Properties of the SADOS and BFNE-II Scales in Mexican Subjects

Internal consistency of all the scales used in the study was obtained with the Cronbach´s alpha coefficient. The LSAS-SR showed excellent alpha values for the total score (α=0.93) and very good values for the fear and avoidance subscales (α=0.88, respectively). Also, internal consistency was adequate for the SADOS (α=0.86) but excellent for the BFNE-II (α=0.92). The correlation matrix and individual item removal did not affect the SADOS or the BFNE-II internal consistency (lowest alpha value of 0.85 for the SADOS and of 0.92 for the BFNE-II).

Principal component analyses were performed to determine the factor structure of the SADOS and the BFNE-II in a Mexican sample. For the analyses, eigenvalues greater-than-one were fixed as criterion for factor extraction and items were retained and allocated in factors if their communality was greater than 0.40. Three factors were identified for the SADOS accounting for 57.51% of the variance (Table 1). Descriptive names were assigned to each factor: 1) *emotion reflection*, 2) *environment control* and

3) *anger and avoidant reactions*. A unitary factor was obtained for the BFNE-II scale which accounts for the 56.37% of the variance (Table 2).

Table 1. Factor loadings of the SADOS items – Varimax

	Item	Factors		
		1	2	3
4.	I often think if I could just be less anxious, others would have a better time.	0.922		
10.	If I just knew people were relaxed with me it would be so much easier.	0.510		
12.	I've often noticed that once I've made one person feel uncomfortable, everybody becomes uncomfortable.	0.591		
13.	I've often noticed that if I'm feeling anxious, others become impatient.	0.549		
14.	I often think that if I feel awkward, I must be making others feel awkward.	0.922		
6.	When interacting with others, I've noticed that what I say or do can "make" or "break" the way things go.		0.467	
7.	I often think that if I don't create a comfortable environment for others, then I am to blame.		0.459	
8.	When I'm with other people, I find it hard to relax unless everything is going perfectly.		0.957	
9.	I often think that people expect me to act in a certain way.		0.957	
1.	I often think people avoid me because I make them feel on edge.			0.636
2.	I've often noticed that when I'm feeling anxious, others appear distracted.			0.649
3.	I often think if I'm anxious, others appear distracted.			0.619
5.	Being anxious can spoil the fun for everyone.			.0447
11.	I've noticed that if I feel anxious, others become agitated.			0.477
	Eigenvalue	**5.31**	**1.63**	**1.10**
	Variance (%)	**37.95**	**11.64**	**7.92**

Table 2. Factor loadings of the BFNE-II items – Varimax

	Item	Factor
1.	Sometimes, I think I am too concerned with what other people think of me.	0.712
2.	I worry about what kind of impression I make on people.	0.772
3.	I am afraid that other people will find fault with me	0.776
4.	I am concerned about other people's opinions of me.	0.809
5.	When I am talking to someone, I worry about what they may be thinking about me.	0.791
6.	I am afraid that others will not approve of me.	0.753
7.	I am usually worried about what kind of impression I make.	0.740
8.	I am frequently afraid of other people noticing my shortcomings.	0.756
9.	I worry about what other people will think of me even when I know it doesn't make any difference.	0.744
10.	It bothers me when people form an unfavorable impression of me.	0.733
11	I often worry that I will say or do wrong things.	0.744
12	If I know someone is judging me, it tends to bother me	0.670
	Eigenvalue	**6.76**
	Variance (%)	**56.37**

Comparison of Social anxiety and Fears by Gender

The mean score of the LSAS-SR for the total sample was of 35.4 ± 21.0 points. The fear subscale had a scoring of 17.7 ± 10.8 points and the avoidance subscale of 17.7 ± 11.4 points. The SADOS and the BFNE-II scores were of 28.6 ± 11.2 points and 15.9 ± 9.8 points, respectively. Women exhibit higher scores in the fear subscale of the LSAS-SR and in the BFNE-II total score when compared to men. No differences emerged in the LSAS-SR avoidance subscale nor in the SADOS score (Table 3). Also, when using a cutoff point of 30 in the LSAS-SR total score, no differences by gender were observed in the percentage of subjects with probable social anxiety (men: n=87, 52.4%; women: n=192, 57.5%; χ^2=1.15, df 1, p=0.28).

Table 3. Social anxiety and fears between men and women

	Men n=166		Women n=334		Statistics
	Mean	S.D.	Mean	S.D.	
LSAS-SR					
Fear score	16.0	10.5	18.5	10.9	t=-2.50, 498
Avoidance score	17.4	11.8	17.8	11.2	df, p=0.01
Total	33.4	21.3	36.4	20.9	t=-0.32, 498
					df, p=0.74
					t=-1.46, 498
					df, p=0.14
SADOS total score	28.5	11.3	28.7	11.2	t=-0.13, 498
					df, p=0.89
BFNE-II total score	14.5	9.13	16.6	10.0	t=-2.30, 498
					df, p=0.02

Fear of Causing Discomfort to others and Fear of Negative Evaluation as Predictors of Social Anxiety in Men and Women

The results of the Pearson correlation coefficient show that the fear of causing discomfort and the fear of negative evaluation as cognitive constructs are related to the presence of social anxiety. It seems that men and women who exhibit these fears will also exhibit higher social anxiety (Table 4).

Beside the differences found between men and women and correlations among social anxiety and fears, we performed logistic regression models for the whole sample and for men and women to determine if these fears will be significant predictors of social anxiety. The logistic regression model for the whole sample was capable of correctly classifying just 69.8% of the participants (non-anxious 65.6% vs social anxiety 73.1%). Subjects with fear of causing discomfort were 1.03 more likely to show social anxiety (B=0.03±0.01, CI $95\%^{ExpB}$=1.01–1.06, p<0.001), while fear of negative evaluation conferred a risk 1.09 higher for social anxiety (B=0.09±0.01, CI $95\%^{ExpB}$=1.06–1.12, p<0.001). Similar results were obtained for women for the prediction of social anxiety by fear of causing discomfort (B=0.04±0.01, ExpB=1.0, CI $95\%^{ExpB}$=1.02–1.07, p<0.001) and fear of negative evaluation (B=0.09±0.01, ExpB=1.1, CI $95\%^{ExpB}$=1.07–1.17, p<0.001) (p<0.001). Nevertheless, fear of negative evaluation was the only predictor for social anxiety in men. Men with this fear are 1.08 times more prone to display social anxiety (B=0.08±0.02, CI $95\%^{ExpB}$=1.04–1.13, p<0.001).

Discussion

The aim of the present study was to determine if the fear of causing discomfort to others and the fear of negative evaluation are predictors of social anxiety in men and women. We think that fear of causing discomfort to others will be more related to social anxiety in women while the fear of negative evaluation will be more related to anxiety in men. Additionally, psychometric properties of the *Social Anxiety–Discomfort to Others Scale (SADOS)* and the *Brief Fear of Negative Evaluation Scale–Revised (BFNE-II)* in Mexican population were obtained.

Our results support the utility of the *SADOS* and the *BFNE-II* as adequate tools for the assessment of cognitive constructs related to social anxiety. Both instruments, as well as the LSAS-SR displayed high internal consistencies which make them reliable for its use in Mexican population. Although it has been proposed a single dimension for the SADOS, our results show three main dimensions based on the principal component analysis. The first dimension, named *emotion reflection*, includes 5 items of the scale and refers to self negative emotions and sensations that are also perceived in others. This dimension appears to be prominent in its contribution (37.9% of variance) to the presentation of fear of causing discomfort to others. The *environment control* dimension was second in order of relative importance, and is defined as the capacity of modifying social environment according to the way the person think or behave. Finally, the dimension named *anger and avoidant reactions* reflects the responses to the person's anxiety. On the other hand, a coherent unidimensional scale was derived from the BFNE II which supports the results observed by other researchers (Carleton et al. 2007; Leary 1983; Stopa and Clark 2001; Turner et al. 1987).

The different domains derived from the SADOS and the BFNE II bring the possibility to focus widely on several markers or processes that could be used to increase the understanding of social anxiety as both cognitive constructs assessed by these instruments were significant predictors of social anxiety. Additionally, the evaluation of these cognitive constructs can help mental health professionals for the recognition and management of this phenomenon.

Table 4. Lineal associations of the LSAS-SR with the SADOS and the BFNE-II in men and women

		LSAS-SR	SADOS	BFNE-II	
MEN	**LSAS-SR**		0.42 (0.001)	0.48 (0.001)	WOMEN
	SADOS	0.37 (0.001)		0.45 (0.001)	
	BFNE-II	0.41 (0.001)	0.43 (0.001)		

r (p).

In line with this, our results highlight the importance of considering gender differences in the experience of social anxiety. No gender differences were found in terms of presence of social anxiety according to the cut-off point of 30 in the LSAS-SR total score. It is possible to assume that this ratio of social anxiety is equal between men and women due to the methodology used. The LSAS-SR was used as a screening tool for the detection of social anxiety and not as an instrument to obtain an accurate diagnosis of social anxiety disorder (SAD), which depends on careful attention of the subject's history and confirmation of DSM criteria. In this way, our result show that social anxiety is common in the general population (den Boer 1997). Future studies should address the prevalence of social anxiety disorder in general population as it may be an underreport diagnosis. It has been reported that the chronic course of the disorder increases the risk of comorbid conditions which may mask the SAD; the resulting disability of this condition placed a burden on the individual and the society (den Boer 1997).

Men and women are argued to be different, each one with dominant characteristics which are promoted or inhibited by sociocultural patterns of behavior. As proposed by the gender role theory, society socializes men and women differently to display specific roles (Brook and Schmidt 2008). Our results of higher scores in the fear subscale of the LSAS-SR and in the BFNE-II in women may support this previous assumption. Several research groups have found a higher proportion of anxiety symptoms associated with feminine traits and general stereotypical roles of accepted feminine behaviours include the expression of fearfulness and anxiety (Brook and Schmidt 2008; Ginsburg and Silverman 2000; Muris et al. 2005; Palapattu et al. 2006).

In addition, fear of negative evaluation and fear of causing discomfort to others were predictors of social anxiety in women while fear of negative evaluation was the only predictor for men. Not only the sociocultural meaning of being a man or a woman have an influence on the way these fears promote social anxiety, the individual significance of each role and the way the person responds to the environment have to be consider. In this way, it is possible that both fears predict social anxiety in women due to particular individual features. Women have been described to be more sympathetic, sentimental, and understanding; as more empathetic, compassionate, and supportive as well as more unpretentious, selfless, and spiritual compared to men (Miettunen et al. 2007). All these features can make women more prone to express these fears in a more severe form as result of a higher concern of being criticized and of not acting cooperatively creating discomfort to other people while for men the concern of being negatively judged by others is the fundamental fear related to the expression of social anxiety.

The question whether social anxiety is expressed differently in men and women by means of the fears of negative evaluation and causing discomfort to others merits further investigation of the gender role theory. Despite the study limitations related to the cross-sectional nature of the study, our findings reflect the need to direct efforts for the design and implementation of specific gender interventions for the management of fears pertaining negative evaluation and of causing discomfort to others. Recognizing gender differences is the first step to promote the targeting of these fears in an evidence-based and gender sensitive way in the detection and treatment of social anxiety.

REFERENCES

Alden L (2001): Interpersonal perspectives on social phobia. In: Crozier W, Alden L editors. *International handbook of social anxiety: Concepts, research and interventions relating to the self and shyness*. New York: John Wiley & Sons, pp 381-404.

American Psychiatric Association (2000): *Diagnostic and statistical manual of mental disorders (4th ed.,text revision)*. Washington, DC.

Baker S, Heinrichs N, Kim H, Hofmann S (2002): The Liebowitz Social Anxiety Scale as a self-report instrument: a preliminary psychometric analysis. *Behav Res Ther* 40:701-715.

Bobes J, Badía X, Luque A, García M, González M, Dal-Ré R, et al (1999): Validación de las versiones en español de los cuestionarios Liebowitz Social Anxiety Scale, Social Anxiety and Distress Scale y Sheenan Disability Inventory para la evaluación de la fobia social. *Medical Clinical* 112:530-538.

Brook C, Schmidt L (2008): Social anxiety disorder: A review of environmental risk factors. *Neuropsychiatr Dis Treat* 4:123-143.

Carleton R, Collimore K, Asmundson G (2007): Social anxiety and fear of negative evaluation: construct validity of the BFNE-II. *J Anxiety Disord* 21:131-141.

Carleton R, McCreary D, Norton P, Asmundson G (2006): Brief fear of negative evaluation scale-revised. *Depress Anxiety* 23:297-303.

den Boer J (1997): Social phobia: epidemiology, recognition, and treatment. *BMJ* 315:796-800.

Fresco D, Coles M, Heimberg R, Liebowitz M, Hami S, Stein M, et al (2001): The Liebowitz Social Anxiety Scale: a comparison of the psychometric properties of self-report and clinician-administered formats. *Psychol Med* 31:1025-1035.

Ginsburg G, Silverman W (2000): Gender role orientation and fearfulness in children with anxiety disorders. *J Anxiety Disord* 14:57-67.

Gullone E (2000): The development of normal fear: a century of research. *Clin Psychol Review* 20:429-451.

Heimberg R, Becker R (2002): *Cognitive-behavioural group therapy for social phobia: Basic mechanisms and clinical strategies*. New York: Guilford.

Hidalgo R, Barnett S, Davidson J (2001): Social anxiety disorder in review: two decades of progress. *International Journal of Neuropsychopharmacology* 4:279-298.

Leary M (1983): A brief version of the Fear of Negative Evaluation Scale. *Pers Soc Psychol Bull* 9:371-375.

Letamendi A, Chavira D, Stein M (2009): Issues in the assessment of social phobia: a review. *Isr J Psychiatry Relat Sci* 46:13-24.

Levin J, Marom S, Gur S, Wechter D, Hermesh H (2002): Psychometric properties and three proposed subscales of a selfreport version of the Liebowitz Social Anxiety Scale translated into Hebrew. . *Depress Anxiety* 16:143-151.

Liebowitz M (1987): Social phobia. *Modern Problems in Pharmacopsychiatry* 22:141-173.

Lipsitz J, Schneier F (2000): Social phobia. Epidemiology and cost of illness. *Pharmacoeconomics* 18:23.32.

Miettunen J, Veijola J, Lauronen E, Kantojärvi L, Joukamaa M (2007): Sex differences in Cloninger's temperament dimensions--a meta-analysis. *Comprehensive Psychiatry* 48:161-169.

Muris P, Meesters C, Knoops M (2005): The relation between gender role orientation and fear and anxiety in nonclinic-referred children. *J Clin Child Adolesc Psychol* 34:326-332.

Oakman J, Van Ameringen M, Mancini C, Farvolden P (2003): A confirmatory factor analysis of a self-report version of the Liebowitz Social Anxiety Scale. . *J Clin Psychol* 59:149-161.

Palapattu A, Kingery J, Ginsburg G (2006): Gender role orientation and anxiety symptoms among African american adolescents. *J Abnorm Child Psychol* 34:441-449.

Rapee R, Spence S (2004): The etiology of social phobia: empirical evidence and an initial model. *Clinical Psychology Review* 24:737-767.

Rector N, Kocovski N, Ryder A (2006): Social anxiety and the fear of causing discomfort to others. *Cogn Ther Res* 30:279-296.

Rodebaugh T, Woods C, Thissen D, Heimberg R, Chambless D, Rapee R (2004): More information from fewer questions: the factor structure and item properties of the original and brief fear of negative evaluation scale. *Psychol Assess* 16:169-181.

Rytwinski N, Fresco D, Heimberg R, Coles M, Liebowitz M, Cissell S, et al (2009): Screening for social anxiety disorder with the self-report version of the Liebowitz Social Anxiety Scale. *Depress Anxiety* 26:34-38.

Singh J, Hope D (2009): Cognitive-behavioral approaches to the treatment of social anxiety disorder. *Isr J Psychiatry Relat Sci* 46:62-69.

Stopa L, Clark D (2001): Social phobia: comments on the viability and validity of an analogue research strategy and British norms for the fear of negative evaluation questionnaire. *Behav Cogn Psychother* 29:423-430.

Turner S, McCanna M, Beidel D (1987): Validity of the Social Avoidance and Distress and Fear of Negative Evaluation scales. *Behav Res Ther* 25:113-115.

Wells A (1997): *Cognitive therapy of anxiety disorders: A practice manual and conceptual guide*. Chichester, UK: John Wiley & Sons.

In: Trait Anxiety
Editor: Anna S. Morales
ISBN 978-1-61324-551-4

Chapter 6

The Association between Sociodemographic Factors and Anxiety of Infertile Women Undergoing Fertility Treatment

***Kleanthi Gourounti*[1] *and Katerina Lykeridou*[2]**
[1]Elena Benizelou Hospital, Clinical Collaborator in Department of Midwifery, Technological Educational Institution of Athens, Greece
[2]Department of Midwifery, Technological Educational Institution of Athens, Greece

Abstract

Infertility is defined as the lack of conception after 12 months of unprotected intercourse and is perceived as a problem in all cultures and societies. It is estimated that between 16 and 26% of European women trying to have children face infertility. From recent studies, it appears that a common reaction during fertility treatment is anxiety, while after an unsuccessful IVF, feelings of sadness, depression and anger may appear. A range of psychosocial variables (personality traits, coping strategies, social support) may influence infertile women's anxiety and stress during infertility treatment. The objective of the present chapter was to review studies describing specifically the impact of sociodemographic factors on anxiety experienced by infertile women undergoing fertility treatment. The sociodemographic background information includes variables concerning age, educational level, annual income and occupational social position. Sociodemographic factors are known to influence a wide range of issues, opinions, beliefs and feelings. According to Waser and Isenberg, reproductive suppression should vary according to the economic and social resources available to the individual because, humans as a species are social, and these resources are fundamental tools in the defence against stressful life events. Individuals with more resources have stronger defences and are better able to withstand the effects of stress than those with fewer resources. Therefore, it is expected and hypothesized that sociodemographic factors may influence levels of anxiety and stress during fertility treatment and that women of lower educational level, lower income and lower social class will experience a higher level of anxiety because they lack environmental 'buffers' against psychosocial stress. A systematic search of the psychological and medical electronic databases (Medline, PsycINFO, CINAHL, EMBASE and Scopus) was performed. Finally, thirteen studies that were relevant to the objective of the review chapter were included. The majority of the included studies failed to find a significant association between female age and levels of anxiety during fertility treatment. The majority of the included studies found that educational level and annual income level are statistically associated with levels of anxiety during fertility treatment. Nevertheless, the association between occupational social class and levels of anxiety is not significant. Thus, this chapter suggests that certain sociodemographic factors might make particular infertile individuals more vulnerable to anxiety. Low educational level and low income could be considered as risk factors for increased anxiety in infertile individuals undergoing infertility treatment. By assessing these factors, medical professionals who work in infertility clinics, may be able to identify individuals who are at greater risk of adjustment difficulties. Health care professionals should provide counselling which is tailored to the educational and social needs of the women.

INTRODUCTION

Infertility, the failure for a woman to become pregnant after one year of regular sexual relationships without contraceptives, is perceived as a problem across virtually all cultures and societies. In industrialized countries 16-26% of women trying to have children face infertility (Malin et al. 2001, Schmidt et al. 2003). At the same time, the use of assisted reproduction technology (ART) methods, such as in vitro fertilization, becomes more evident as time passes (Nyboe-Andersen et al. 2006). What is also important to note is that infertility has been found to be the fourth most dramatic life event in a lifetime of a woman, compared with the death of parents and the unfaithfulness of the partner (Oddens et al., 1999, Matsubayashi et al., 2004). As a life crisis, infertility is conceptualised as a currently unsolvable problem that threatens important life goals and taxes personal resources (Stanton and Dunkel-Schetter, 1991). Women who undergo fertility treatment have to deal with two types of stressors. The chronic stressor, that results from the threat of definite infertility and the loss of hope of parenthood, and the acute stressor, that results from the fertility treatment (Verhaak et al. 2001). Threatening situations with much uncertainty about the fertility treatment can evoke anxiety, while a sense of loss and loss of control can evoke feelings of depression and hopelessness (Verhaak et al. 2001, Lazarus, 1999). Clinicians and researchers consistently report that infertile women view infertility and its treatment as extremely stressful (Chen et al. 2004, Dyer et al. 2005, Ozkan and Baysal 2006, Wang et al. 2007). From recent studies, it appears that a common reaction during fertility treatment is anxiety, while after an unsuccessful IVF, feelings of sadness, depression and anger may appear (Eugster and Vingerhoets, 1999, Matsubayashi et al. 2001). In addition, many previous studies report that IVF patients report a higher prevalence of anxiety and depression than controls (Matsubayashi et al. 2001, Cwikel et al. 2004, Dyer et al. 2005, Ozkan et al. 2006, Wang et al. 2007).

Stress is very frequently defined as the troubled reaction to stressful stimuli, which is a response definition of stress (Lazarus, 1999). According to Lazarus and Folkman (1984) stress is defined as a transaction between the person and the environment that is appraised by the person as taxing or exceeding his or her resources and endangering his or her well being. This definition is appropriate in explaining individual variability in response to infertility. The stressor of infertility problems comprises various elements that individuals are most likely to appraise as stressful (Lazarus and Folkman, 1984): unpredictability, negativity, uncontrollability and ambiguity. Distress, anxiety, depression, sadness, disturbance, and pressure are what stress means in emotional response terms (Lazarus, 1999). It should be obvious that certain emotions, for example, anger, envy, anxiety, distress, sadness-depression, could be called stress emotions, because they usually arise from stressful conditions. In fact, most IVF patients state that IVF treatment is primarily a psychological stressor rather than a physical stressor (Eugster and Vingerhoets, 1999).

Individual differences in psychological stress independent of health status suggest that various psychological processes mediate or moderate the relationship between stressors and the psychological reaction to a chronic disease (Lazarus and Folkman 1984). It is therefore, increasingly important to understand both the magnitude of the stress and personal coping resources of infertile women, as they try to adapt to the problems of infertility and its treatment. A range of psychosocial and medical variables may influence infertile women's stress during infertility treatment. Psychosocial variables such as coping skills and medical variables such as infertility duration, infertility aetiology and number of fertility treatments may be considered determinants of emotional stress. These factors may be also considered as either risk or protective factors to explain individual differences in emotional stress due to infertility. Many previous studies have explored the association between specific biomedical variables and the level of anxiety during fertility treatment. The evidence regarding the impact of women's age, infertility duration, infertility aetiology and number of previous fertility treatments on anxiety of infertile women is contradictory. The majority of studies have concluded that there is no significant association between women's age and anxiety (van Balen and Trimbos-Kemper, 1994, Matsubayashi et al. 2001, Chen et al. 2004, Ramezanzadeh et al. 2004, Boivin et al. 2006, Lykeridou et al. 2008) and between infertility duration and anxiety (van Balen and Trimbos-Kemper, 1994, Matsubayashi et al. 2001, Chen et al. 2004). Nevertheless, some studies have suggested that there is a statistical and positive association between age and anxiety (Uokong et al. 2006, Wang et al. 2007, Gourounti et al. 2010), between duration of infertility and anxiety (Ramezanzadeh et al. 2004, Donkor and Sandall, 2007, Wang et al. 2007) and between history of previous fertility treatments and anxiety (Wang et al. 2007). In addition, a couple of studies have suggested that there is a significant association between male factor infertility and women's anxiety during fertility treatment (Lee et al. 2001, Lykeridou et al. 2008). In addition, previous studies have shown that there is a significant negative association between the frequent use of coping strategies such as, escape/avoidance, self-blame coping and accepting-responsibility coping and increased level of anxiety during fertility treatment or after a failed treatment (Stanton, 1991, Litt et al. 1992, Stanton et al. 1992, Morrow et al. 1995, Berghuis et al. 2002, Mindes et al. 2003, Peterson et al. 2006, Lechner et al. 2007, Bayley et al. 2009). It has also been found that there is a consistent positive effect of active/ problem-focused coping, positive re-appraisal coping and social support seeking coping on anxiety during fertility treatment. It has been also found that demographic variables, such as educational level, income level and social class may influence infertile women's stress during infertility treatment.

experienced high anxiety levels. However, two studies suggested that there is no significant association between income and anxiety levels during fertility treatment (Chen et al. 2004, Gourounti et al. 2010). In addition, four of the included studies revealed that there is no significant relationship between social class and anxiety level during or after fertility treatment (van Balen and Trimbos-Kemper, 1994, Matsubayashi et al. 2001, Boivin et al. 2006, Lykeridou et al. 2008). Nevertheless, three studies showed that there is a significant negative relationship between social class and anxiety related to infertility treatment (Ramezanzadeh et al. 2004, Donkor and Sandall, 2007, Lykeridou et al. 2010).

Conclusion

This chapter suggests that certain sociodemographic factors might make particular infertile individuals more vulnerable to anxiety. Low educational level and low income could be considered as risk factors for increased anxiety in infertile individuals undergoing infertility treatment.

Kristenson and colleagues (2004) found that sustained stress hormone activation (e.g. higher cortisol levels) and altered responsivity to stressful situations are more common in people from low educational and socioeconomic backgrounds. Thus, it could be hypothesized that infertile women of lower educational and social level would experience a higher level of anxiety because they lack environmental 'buffers' against psychosocial stress. Second, a high educational level is often associated with a greater capacity of for handling crises and a higher level of well-being (van Balen and Trimbos-Kemper, 1994). However, it has been argued that infertility and involuntarily childlessness is such a meaningful event that the socio-educational level is a factor that does not matter in this situation (van Balen and Trimbos-Kemper, 1994, Boivin et al. 2006).

Another possible explanation of the significant relationship between socio-educational and anxiety levels is that educational level and socio-economic level might associate with psychological adjustment indirectly through the maladaptive coping strategies that individuals use under stress. Few studies have focused on the relationship between social status and coping strategies (Thoits, 1995, Taylor and Seeman, 1999, Schmidt et al. 2005). Taylor and Seeman (1999) found that, when socio-economic status decreased, avoidant coping was more prevalent. Ross and Mirowsky (1989) found that highly educated people were more likely to use active problem solving, and

Grossi (1999) also reported that problem-focused coping was less frequent among participants with a low education coupled with low financial strain. Billings and Moss (1981) found that better educated respondents were more likely to rely on problem-focused coping strategies and less likely to use avoidance coping. Holahan and Moss (1987) found that sociodemographic variables of education and income made a significant incremental contribution to predicting active and avoidance coping. In addition, findings of the study conducted by Donkor and Sandall (2007) suggested that infertile women of low occupational social class experienced a higher level of infertility-related stress while women of high occupational social class experienced the least infertility-related stress. Possibly, individuals of higher social class are more likely to use approach coping and less likely to use avoidance coping. However, Schmidt and colleagues (2005) and Lykeridou and colleagues, (2010) showed that infertile women from lower social classes used significantly more active-confronting coping.

Implications for Practice

Initially, the psychological status and specifically the distress levels of infertility patients should be assessed, ideally through structured interviews with a mental health professional and at a minimum through the use of valid questionnaires (Cousineau and Domar, 2007). A state and trait anxiety questionnaire could produce reasonable acceptable data to decide whether to initiate stress reduction intervention and to measure its efficacy, on the condition that the questionnaire is applied as early as possible and preferably before the treatment initiation (Campagne, 2006). As the level of stress is always subjective and personal, initial thresholds are indicative only and serve as a screening method for further selection (Campagne, 2006). Patients who score above the norm on measures of psychological distress (anxiety and/ or depression) should be assessed and referred for mental health counseling (Cousineau and Domar, 2007). The objectives of counselling to highly distressed patients are to enable the expression of their emotions, to identify the causes of distress and to provide interventions to minimize distress and help patients better manage distress (Boivin, 2001). Furthermore, the goal of psychological interventions should be the minimization of identified risk factors for infertility-related distress and the strengthening of protective factors.

Medical professionals, who work in infertility clinics, should be aware regarding the impact of socio-demographic factors on women's psychological status. Medical professionals should be prepared that infertile women with low educational and economical level may experience high levels of anxiety during fertility treatment or after a failed fertility treatment. Health care professionals should provide counselling which is tailored to the educational and social needs of the women. In addition, staff of the fertility clinics should provide counseling after taking into consideration the lay people's perceptions and concerns (e.g. taboos) on the subject of infertility and its treatment (Adashi et al., 2000).

In conclusion, the current chapter represents an attempt to understand how certain socio-demographic factors make infertile women undergoing fertility treatment more vulnerable to stress. This chapter also contributes to the broader literature examining the relationships between socio-demographic variables and fertility related anxiety. It is hoped that information acquired from this review will help to identify women at risk of experiencing high anxiety and will enhance the implementation of treatment and support services for infertile women undergoing fertility treatment.

REFERENCES

Adashi, E., J. Cohen, L. Hamberger, H. Jones, D. de Kretse, B Lunenfeld, Z. Rosenwaks, and A. Van Steirteghem. 2000. Public perception on infertility and its treatment: an international survey. *Hum Reprod* 15(2): 330-334.

Bayley, T., Slade, P., Lashen H. Relationships between attachment, appraisal, coping and adjustment in men and women experiencing infertility concerns. *Hum Reprod* 2009; 24(11), 2827-2837.

Berghuis J, Stanton A. Adjustment to a dyadic stressor: a longitudinal study of coping and depressive symptoms in infertile couples over an insemination attempt. *J Consult Clin Psychol,* 2002; 70(2): 433-438.

Billings A. and Moos R. The role of coping responses and social resources in attenuating the stress of life events. *Journal of Behavioral Medicine,* 1981; 4: 157-189.

Boivin J, Sanders K, Schmidt L. Age and social position moderate the effect of stress on fertility. *Evolution and Human Behavior* 2006; 27, 345-356.

Boivin, J., Appleton, T.C., Baetens, P., et al. Guidelines for counseling in infertility: outline version. Human Reproduction 2001; 16 (6), 1301-1304

Campagne D. Should fertilization treatment start with reducing stress? *Human Reproduction* 2006; 21(7): 1651-1658

Chen TH, Chang SP, Tsai CF, Juang KD. Prevalence of depressive and anxiety disorders in an assisted reproductive technique clinic. *Human Reproduction* 2004; 19 (10), 2313-2318.

Cousineau T. and Domar A. Psychological impact of infertility. *Best Practice and Research Clin Obst Gynaecol* 2007; 21(2): 293-308

Cwikel J, Gidron Y, Sheiner. Psychological interactions with infertility among women. *Eur J Obstet Gynecol Reprod Biol* 2004; 117: 126-131.

Donkor E and Sandall J. The impact of perceived stigma and mediating social factors on infertility-related stress among women seeking infertility treatment in Southern Ghana. *Social Sciences and Medicine* 2007; 6: 1683-1694.

Dyer J, Abrahams N, Mokoena N, Lombard C, van der Spuy Z. Psychological distress among women suffering from couple infertility in South Africa: a quantitative assessment *Hum Reprod* 2005; 20 (7) :1938–1943.

Eugster A, Vingerhoets A. Psychological aspects of in vitro fertilization: a review. *Soc Sci Med,* 1999; 48: 525-589.

Gourounti K., Anagnostopoulos F., Vaslamatzis G. Psychometric properties and factor structure of the Fertility Problem Inventory (FPI) in a sample of infertile women undergoing fertility treatment. *Midwifery* 2010 (doi:10.1016/j.midw.2010.02.007).

Grossi G. Coping and emotional distress in a sample of Swedish unemployed. *Scandinavian Journal of Psychology* 1999; 40, 157–165.

Holahan C. and Moos R. Personal and contextual determinants of coping strategies. *Journal of Personality and Social Psychology* 1987; 52: 946-955.

Kristenson M, Eriksen H, Sluiter J, Starke D, Ursin H. Psychobiological mechanisms of socioeconomic differences in health. *Social Sciences and Medicine* 2004; 58: 1511-1522.

Lazarus R. Stress and emotion. In Lazarus R ed. *Stress and Emotion, A new synthesis.* New York: Springer 1999; 49-85.

Lazarus R, Folkman S. *Stress, appraisal and coping*. New York: Springer 1984.

Lechner L, Bolman C, Van Dalen A. Definite involuntary childlessness: associations between coping, social support and psychological distress. *Hum Reprod,* 2007; 22 (1): 288-294.

Lee, T.Y., Sun, G.H. & Chao, S.C. (2001). The effect of an infertility diagnosis on the distress, marital and sexual satisfaction between husbands and wives in Taiwan. *Human Reproduction,* 16, 1762-1767.

Litt M, Tennen H, Affleck G, et al. Coping and cognitive factors in adaptation to in vitro fertilization. *J Behav Med,* 1992; 15(2): 171.

Lykeridou, K., K. Gourounti, A. Deltsidou, D. Loutradis, and G. Vaslamatzis. The impact of infertility diagnosis on psychological status of women undergoing fertility treatment. *J Reprod Infant Psychol* 2008; 27(3):223-237.

Lykeridou K., Gourounti K., Sarantaki A., Loutradis D., Baslamatzis G., Deltsidou A. Occupational social class, coping responses, and infertility-related stress of women undergoing infertility treatment. *Journal of Clinical Nursing 2010* (doi: 10.1111/j.1365-2702.2011. 03696.x).

Malin M, Hemmink E, Räikkönen O, et al. What do women want? Women's experiences of infertility treatment. *Soc Sci & Med* 2001; 53: 123–133.

Matsabayashi H., Hosaka T., Izumi S., Suzuki T., Kondo A., Makino T. Increased depression and anxiety in infertile Japanese women resulting from lack of husband's support and feelings of stress. *General Hospital Psychiatry* 2004; 26: 398-404.

Matsubayashi H, Hosaka T, Izumi S, Suzuki T and Makino T. Emotional distress of infertile women in Japan. *Hum Reprod* 2001; 16: 966–969.

Mindes E, Ingrama K, Kliewera W, et al. Longitudinal analyses of the relationship between unsupportive social interactions and psychological adjustment among women with fertility problems. *Soc Sci. Med.,* 2003; 56: 2165–2180.

Morrow K, Thoreson R, Penney L. Predictors of psychological distress among infertility clinic patients. *J Consult Clinic Psychol.* 1995; 63(1): 163-167.

Mussani F. Investigating the effect of socio-economic status on perceived infertility related stress in women. *University Toronto Medical Journal* 2009; 87(1): 53-56.

Schmidt L, Holstein B, Boivin J, et al. Patients' attitudes to medical and psychosocial aspects of care in fertility clinics: findings from the Copenhagen Multi-centre Psychosocial Infertility (COMPI) Research Programme. *Hum Reprod* 2003; 18: 628-637.

Newton, C., W. Sherrard, and I. Glavac. The Infertility Problem Inventory: measuring perceived infertility- related stress. *Fertil Steril* 1999; 72: 54-62.

Nyboe Andersen A, Gianaroli L, Felberbaum R, et al. Assisted reproductive technology in Europe. Results generated from European registers by ESHRE. *Hum Reprod* 2006; 21 (7): 1680–1697

Oddens, B.J., Den Tonkelaar, I. and Nieuwenhuyse, H. Psychological experiences in women facing fertility problems. *Human Reproduction,* 1999; 14, 255-261.

Ozkan M, Baysal B. Emotional distress of infertile women in Turkey. *Clin Exp Obstet Gynaecol* 2006; 33(1): 44-6.

Peterson B, Newton C, Rosen K, et al. The relationship between coping and depression in men and women referred for in vitro fertilization. *Fertil Steril,* 2006; 85(3): 802-804.

Ramezanzadeh F., Aghssa M., Abedinia N., Zayeri F., Khanafshar N., Shariat M., Jafarabadi M. A survey of relationship between anxiety, depression and duration of infertility. *BMC Womens Health.* 2004; 6,4(1):9.

Ross CE & Mirowsky J. Explaining the social patterns of depression: control and problem solving—or support and talking? *Journal of Health and Social* Behavior 1989; 30, 206–219.

Schmidt L, Christensen U & Holstein BE. The social epidemiology of coping with infertility. *Human Reproduction* 2005; 20, 1044–1052.

Stanton AL, Tennen H, Affleck G, et al. Coping and adjustment to infertility. *J Soc Clin Psychol,* 1992; 11: 1-13.

Stanton A. and Dunkel-Schetter C. Psychological adjustment to infertility: an overview of conceptual approaches. In Stanton AL, Dunkel-Schetter C, eds. *Infertility: Perspectives from stress and coping research.* New York: Plenum Press 1991: 3-13

Stanton AL. Cognitive appraisals, coping processes and adjustment. In Stanton AL, Dunkel-Schetter C, eds. *Infertility: Perspectives from stress and coping research.* New York: Plenum Press 1991: 87-108.

Taylor SE & Seeman TE. Psychosocial resources and the SES-health relationship. In *Socioeconomic Status and Health in Industrialised Nations* (Adler NE, Marmot M, McEwen BS & Stewart J eds), New York Academy of Sciences, New York, USA, 1999: 210–225.

Thoits P. Stress, coping and social support processes: where we are? What next? *Journal of Health and Social Behavioral* (Extra Issue), 1995; 53-79.

Van Balen F. and Trimbos-Kemper T. Factors influencing the well-being of long –term infertile couples. *Journal of Psychosomatic in Obstetrics and Gyneacology, 1994*; 15: 157-164.

Verhaak C, Smeenk J, Eugster A, et al. Stress and marital satisfaction among women before and after their first cycle of in vitro fertilization and intracytoplasmic sperm injection. *Fertil Steril* 2001; 76(3): 525-531.

Wang K, Li J., Zhang J, Zhang L, Yu J, Jiang P. Psychological characteristics and marital quality of infertile women registrered for in vitro fertilization - intracytoplasmatic sperm injection in China. *Fertil Steril* 2007; 87(4): 792-798.

Waser S and Isenberg D. Reproductive failure among women: Pathology or adaptation? *Journal of Psychosomatic Obstetrics Gynecology* 1986; 5, 153-175.

In: Trait Anxiety
Editor: Anna S. Morales

ISBN 978-1-61324-551-4

Chapter 7

STATE/TRAIT ANXIETY, AVIATION, AND THE FRONTAL LOBE

F. R. Ferraro**, *M. Butler and J. Reckow
University of North Dakota, US

ABSTRACT

Thirty-four students with extensive aviation experience (A+) and 35 students without such experience (A-) completed tests designed to tap into the impact of frontal lobe function (Executive Function Index; Spinella, 2005) and State/Trait anxiety performance (Speilberger et al, 1980). Experienced Aviation students showed worsening executive function performance (motivation/drive, organization) with increases in State, but not Trait, anxiety. (rs > -.34, ps < .05). Inexperienced aviation students showed the exact opposite; worsening executive function (motivation/drive, organization) with increases in Trait, but not State, anxiety (rs = -.41, ps < .05). Implications for the impact of anxiety in an applied setting will be discussed.

Keywords: Anxiety, Aviation, Executive Function

* **Address all correspondence to:** F. Richard Ferraro, Ph.D. Professor of Psychology; Chester Fritz Distinguished Professor, Director, General/Experimental Ph.D. Program Fellow, National Academy of Neuropsychology, Dept. Psychology - University of North Dakota, Corwin-Larimore Rm. 215, 319 Harvard Street Stop 8380, Grand Forks, ND 58202-8380; 701-777-2414 (O); 701-777-3454 (Fax); f.ferraro@und.nodak.edu

State/Trait Anxiety, Aviation, and Frontal Lobe

The majority of aviation accidents are attributed to human error. (Mcfadden & Towell, 1999). In fact, a recent study found that over 50% of aviation mishaps involved crewmembers making active failures, which includes judgment and decision-making errors (Tvaryanas & Thompson, 2008). Both judgment and decision making can be affected by anxiety during a dangerous situation (Paul et al., 2011). How affected a pilot is by anxiety may influence their potential to engage in hazardous activity. Two types of anxiety, state and trait, may affect a pilot's potential for engaging in dangerous or risky behavior.

State anxiety refers to a transient emotional condition characterized by activation of the autonomic nervous system and feelings of worry, tension and apprehension (Spielberger, 1963). The effect of anxiety on performance has been studied in a variety of contexts (Spielberger, 1963). Research often indicates an inverse relationship between high anxiety and performance. However, instances exist where high and low anxious groups perform at equal levels (Eyesenck, Derakshan, Santos, & Calvo, 2007). The Attentional Control Theory (Eyesenck et al. 2007) proposes reasons how anxiety can effect performance through attention processes. The Attentional Control Theory posits high levels of anxiety negatively affect processing efficiency, but not necessarily processing effectiveness. High anxious individuals have more difficulty inhibiting irrelevant stimuli and shifting attention to task-relevant stimuli, both of which are exacerbated by a task's demand on working memory (Eyesenck et al. 2007).

Trait anxiety refers to the level of proneness individuals are to experience anxiety (Spielberger, 1963). High Trait Anxiety (HTA) individuals perceive events as more threatening and are more likely to respond with increased state anxiety (Spielberger, 1963). The effect of state and trait anxiety on cognitive performance has shown a complex relationship. During heightened state anxiety from an examination, HTA individuals showed an attentional bias toward threatening words while low trait anxiety (LTA) individuals showed an attentional bias away from threatening words (Mogg, Bradley & Hallowell, 1994). When the HTA and LTA groups had lab induced state anxiety the group differences for attentional biases no longer existed (Mogg, et al. 1994).

Negative emotions, such as anxiety, appear to be controlled in part by the frontal lobe (Lyvers, Thorberg, Ellul, Turner, & Bahr, 2010). Even though it remains unclear how anxiety is regulated specifically, the frontal lobe has been implicated in controlling anxiety through both suppression and maintenance of negative emotions (Phan et al. 2005). In addition, a positive correlation has been seen between frontal lobe dysfunction and the state of negative emotions, including anxiety (Spinella, 2005). This relationship suggests that the frontal lobe plays a key role in regulating the suppression of anxiety. The frontal lobe is also attributed as the region where executive functions, such as decision making and reasoning, are stored and performed (Spinella, 2005).

Decision-making and reasoning varies between individuals and can be influenced by personality traits (Bensi, Giusberti, Nori, & Gambetti, 2010).Bensi *et al.* investigated how state and trait anxiety affect the amount of information gathered prior to decision-making in probabilistic decisions. Results showed state and trait anxiety had negative relationships with amount of information collected. However, after accounting for state anxiety the relationship between trait anxiety and information gathered was negligible. Trait anxiety does not account for differences in the amount of information gathered in a probabilistic decision-making task (Bensi et al. 2010). Additionally, HTA has shown to have a negative effect on complex decision-making tasks, such as the Iowa Gambling Task (Miu, Heilman, & Houser, 2008).

An individual's risky behavior has been linked to the frontal lobe and decision making (Spinella, 2005). The connection between risky behavior and anxiety is further highlighted in a study conducted by Hunter (2005), who found that a measure of anxiety was significantly correlated with risk perception and risk tolerance measures in pilots. The correlation between anxiety and risk perception has important implications in aviation. Involvement in dangerous aviation situations can be predicted by inaccurate risk perception (Hunter, 2006). State anxiety may indicate the degree of risky behavior a pilot may partake. If state anxiety does suggest a higher chance of aviation accidents than future training should incorporate instruction on preparing for state anxiety.

To examine these predictions we tested a total of 69 college students, 34 with extensive aviation experiment and 35 without such experience. We defined aviation experience by asking for total hours of flight time, total hours as a pilot in commend on cross country flights, total hours of instrument flight (actual and simulated) and the type of pilot certification and rating. We also asked about age, education, self-rated health, medications currently being taken, mood, vocabulary ability and anxiety. Table 1 lists these various measures. We also had subjects fill out the Executive Function Index (Spinella, 2007), which measures five components of executive function. Our main goal was to examine anxiety (state, trait) and executive function. Results indicated that Aviation students showed greater relationship of their state anxiety with two aspects of executive function (motivation/drive, organization) such that these aspects of executive function decreased as State anxiety increased (r's > -.34, ps < .05). No such relationships were observed for Trait anxiety (r's = -.18, ns). In the Non-Aviation students, an opposite pattern emerged such that no relationships were observed between State anxiety and motivation/drive, organization (r's = -.31, ns). However, for Trait anxiety, relationships existed such that as these components of executive function decline, Trait anxiety increased (r's = -.41, p's < .05).

These results highlight the importance of state and trait anxiety as it related to executive function performance in individuals with extensive (versus no) aviation experience. Since state anxiety relates to the current situation, and trait anxiety is more of an in-grained observation, difference between these types of anxiety and whether the subject was an aviation student or not suggests that factors related to situational awareness are critical. Situational awareness (Hunter, 2006) refers to how the pilot performs in real time as the aircraft is being flown. That is, how does the current situation impact performance? It makes sense that correlations with some components of executive function were reliable with state anxiety in aviation students and not in non-aviation students, since aviation students had more piloting experience. Likewise, non-aviation students, who have no aviation experience should not show any sort of relationship with executive function and state anxiety (which was the observation in the present study). Making aviation students aware of this context-related effect is important. While the anxiety levels were not in the clinical range, the results are nonetheless important for training purposes. Since all subjects were current university students, awareness of the relationship between anxiety and executive function could be included in current aviation training programs. If an aviation student realizes that their state anxiety level may impact their executive function, they could be taught specific strategies to aid in overcoming or at least dealing with these issues.

In summary, we have demonstrated reliable effects based on type of anxiety and aviation experience across various domains of executive function. Given the vast importance of adequate executive functioning to many everyday cognitive activities, and given the impact of human error on aviation accident rates, these results suggest training potential aviation pilots in the identification and control of their reaction to state and trait anxiety situations may be helpful.

Table 1. Mean Performance Measures for Subjects with (A+) and without (A-) Extensive Aviation Experience

Measure	A+	A-
Age (years)	21.35	22.43
Education (years)	15.00	15.56
Self- Rated Health(1 = excellent, 5 = poor)	2.18	2.14
Medications (number currently taking)	.17	.28
Mood	1.34	1.49
WAIS-R Vocab.	52.14	50.00
State Anxiety	31.17	31.85
Trait Anxiety	32.03	34.79
Flight Time (hours)	132.23	
Pilot in Command on	26.34	
Cross Country Flights(hours)		
Actual Instrument Flight(hours)	5.63	
Simulated Instrument Flight(hours)	14.80	

REFERENCES

Bensi, L., Giusberti, F., Nori, R., & Gambetti, E. (2010). Individual differences and reasoning: A study on personality traits. *British Journal of Psychology, 101*, 545-562.

Eyesenck, M. W., Derakshan, N., Santos, R., & Calvo, M. G.. (2007). Anxiety and cognitive performance: Attentional Control Theory. *Emotion, 7*(2), 336-353.

Hunter, D. R. (2005). Measurement of hazardous attitudes among pilots. *The International Journal of Aviation Psychology, 15*(1), 23-43.

Hunter, D. R. (2006). Risk perception among general aviation pilots. *The International Journal of Aviation Psychology, 16*(2), 135-144.

Lyvers, M., Thorberg, F. A., Ellul, A., Turner, J., & Bahr, M. (2010). Negative mood regulation expectancies, frontal lobe related behaviors and alcohol use. *Personality and Individual Differences, 43*(3), 332-337.

McFadden, K.L., Towell, E.R. (1999). Aviation human factors: a framework for the new millennium. *Journal of Air Transport Management* 5, 177–184.

Miu, A. C, Heilman, R. M., & Houser D. (2008). Anxiety impairs decision-making: Psychophysiological evidence from an Iowa Gambling Task. *Biological Psychology 77,* 353-358).

Mogg, K., Bradley, B.P., & Hallowell, N. (1994). Attentional bias to threat: roles of trait anxiety, stressful events, and awareness. *The Quarterly Journal of Experimental Psychology*, *47*(4), 841-864.

Paul, E. S., Cuthil, I., Kuroso, G., Norton, V., Woodgate, J., & Mendl, M. (2011). Mood and the speed of decisions about anticipated resources and hazards. *Evolution and Human Behavior, 32,* 21-28.

Phan, L. K., Fitzgerald, D. A., Nathan, P. J., Moore, G. J., Uhde, T. W., & Tancer, M. E. (2005). Neural substrates for voluntary suppression of negative affect: A functional magnetic resonance imaging study. *Biological Psychiatry, 57,* 210-219.

Spielberger, C.D. (1963). *Manual for the state-trait anxiety inventory.* Palo Alto, CA: Consulting Psychologists Press, Inc.

Spinella, M. (2007). Measuring the executive regulation of emotion with self-rating scales in a nonclinical population. *The Journal of General Psychology, 134* (1), 101-111.

Tvaryanas, A. P. & Thompson, W. T. (2008). Recurrent Error Pathways in HFACS data: Analysis of 95 mishaps with remotely piloted aircraft. *Aviation, Space, and Environmental Medicine, 79* (5), 525-532.

In: Trait Anxiety
Editor: Anna S. Morales

ISBN 978-1-61324-551-4

Chapter 8

TRAIT ANXIETY AND NEUROPHYSIOLOGY OF EXECUTIVE CONTROL IN THE STOP-SIGNAL PARADIGM

A. N. Savostyanov*[*1,2], *A. C. Tsai*[1], *A. Yu. Zhigalov*[1], *E. A. Levin*[2], *J. D. Lee*[1] and *M. Liou*[1]

[1]Institute of Statistical Science, Academia Sinica, Taiwan
[2]Institute of Physiology, Siberian Branch of Russian Academy of Medical Sciences, Russia

ABSTRACT

The stop-signal paradigm (SSP) is an experimental method that allows research into brain mechanisms of executive control. In the SSP, subjects either react to a target stimulus or withdraw a reaction when a stop-signal appears after target. In this chapter we investigate neurophysiologic mechanisms underlying regulation of motor responses in healthy subjects given different trait anxiety (TA) levels. SSP experiment with simultaneous EEG recording was performed on 21 subjects. Event-related spectral perturbations (ERSP, Makeig, 1993) were analyzed in order to study brain oscillatory activity in different frequency bands. The data were partitioned into four experimental conditions: successful reaction (Go), successful withdraw (Stop), missed reaction (unsuccessful Go), and failure to stop (unsuccessful Stop).

* Address for correspondence: Alexander.Savostyanov@gmail.com

In the Go condition, power increase in delta and theta bands (1-7 Hz) was observed between 150-1000 ms after the target onset. Beta (15-25 Hz) desynchronization (power decrease) appeared before button-press (200-700 ms), while posterior alpha and central mu (7-14 Hz) desynchronization were revealed in 200-1200 ms, i.e. both before and after button-press. Successful reaction invited beta "rebound" (power increase, 1000-1600 ms). In the Stop condition additional low-frequency (1-7 Hz) power increase appeared 200-800 ms after the stop-signal onset. The low-frequency synchronization had maximal amplitude in the occipital-parietal region in Go condition, while in the Stop condition, the two maxima were observed – early in the posterior and late in the frontal area, implying co-occurrence of two different processes – activation of sensory areas, and active inhibition of prepared motor activity. Both types of mistakes were associated with prolonged low-frequency power increase (200-1200 ms).

Several components of EEG reactions depended on the TA level. Post-movement desynchronization in alpha and beta bands was significantly stronger in subjects with higher TA, while beta "rebound" had higher amplitude and shorter latency in subjects with lower anxiety. The amplitude of delta (1-4 Hz) synchronization was positively related with TA level in all experimental conditions. We have interpreted these results basing on attentional control theory (Eysenck et al., 2007). We hypothesize that subjects with high TA exert more attention to experimental task, which is reflected by higher amplitudes of alpha and beta desynchronization. On the contrary, subjects with low TA are less predisposed to elevated attentional control, and instead, they are more inclined to relax after a successfully completed task. The latter feature is mirrored in shorter latency and higher amplitude of "beta rebound" after successful performance of the trial in subjects with lower TA.

Keywords: Trait anxiety, Stop-signal paradigm, Brain oscillatory systems, EEG

INTRODUCTION

Executive control or executive functions is a human ability to regulate personal behavior based on the information received from environment and internal motivations. The executive functions are regarded as a "top down" mechanism in contrast to stimulus-driven and more or less automated "bottom up" processes and are related with a choice between several possible behavioral reactions. Some of these reactions are adequate to situations and should be activated, but other ones are inadequate and should be suppressed.

In this reason, one of the important features of executive control is the ability to inhibit responses that are inappropriate in the current context (Ramautar et al., 2006; Verbruggen & Logan, 2008; Verbruggen & Logan, 2009).

The stop-signal paradigm (SSP) (Lappin & Erikson, 1966) is one of widely applicable experimental methods for studying activation and inhibition of responses as the components of executive functions both in clinical patients (Alderson et al., 2007) and healthy subjects (Dimoska et al., 2006; Johnstone et al., 2007; Xue et al., 2008; Congdon et al., 2010). The stop signal task involves two concurrent tasks: a "Go" task and a "Stop" task. The "Go" task is usually a two choice reaction time (CRT) task, when subjects have to react on a presented stimulus (one of two "Go" stimuli with different responses associated with each of them) as fast as possible. But in some randomly chosen trials (typically 20–30%) the "Go" stimulus is followed by presentation of the "Stop-signal", which signals participants to inhibit their response on that trial. The horse-race model (Logan, et al., 1984; Band et al., 2003) provides theoretical interpretation of results obtained using the SSP. According to this model, two alternative neural processes compete after the stop-signal onset – activation and inhibition of response. If activation processes "win the race", subject responds, and otherwise the reaction is successfully inhibited. Besides the studying of response activation and inhibition mechanisms, the SSP could be useful for exploring processes, associated with another important component of executive control – the error monitoring, as design of SSP usually presumes that number of errors made by participants would be relatively large. These erroneous responses include pressing the wrong button, missing button-press (unsuccessful activation or "missed Go" condition) or, in opposite, pressing the button after Stop-signal onset ("missed Stop" or unsuccessful inhibition).

Brain processes providing executive control are a topic of numerous studies, as their violations can be found in many cases of neurological and psychiatric pathology. The majority of studies relating brain mechanisms of activation and inhibition of reactions with personality traits in healthy persons and pathological conditions in patients utilize such constructs as impulsivity and aggressiveness, which are directly associated with this control and specific overt modes of behavior. Particularly, executive function deficits were identified in several neuropsychiatric conditions associated with impulsivity, namely attention deficit hyperactivity disorder (ADHD) (Alderson et al., 2007), Parkinson's disease (Beste et al., 2009), and alcohol dependency (Li et al., 2009). Aggressive, suicidal and violent behaviors have been also associated with impulsive personality and problems in inhibiting responses

(Horn et al., 2003). At the same time, anxiety, which could be defined as an inclination to perceive environment as potentially dangerous and develop corresponding emotional and behavioral reactions, being a more “internal” and “covert” trait, is also closely interrelated with executive functions, though in a more complex way. There are several theories of anxiety; among neurobiologically oriented ones the Gray’s BIS/BAS theory, M. Eysenck’s theory of attentional control and Davidson’s works concerning the “emotional side” of anxiety should be referred to here.

Neuropsychological theory of J. Gray postulates that three principal systems determine human personality: Behavioral Approach and Inhibition Systems (BAS and BIS) and Fight/Flight/Freeze System (FFFS). In the current version of this theory (Gray and McNaughton, 2000; McNaughton and Corr, 2004) anxiety as a state is proposed to be a result of conflict between BAS and FFFS in situations of uncertainty, then person could not predict whether the situation and/or his/her own activity would lead to positive or negative reinforcement. First is associated with expectation of reward or avoided punishment and activates BAS, while second – with expectation of punishment or non-reward and activates FFFS. The “collision” of these two systems activates BIS and its activity causes the state of anxiety. Furthermore, as the uncertainty is seen by most people as something negative, it would itself provoke anxiety, especially when it concerns the possibility of getting a reward or avoiding a punishment. The anxiety as a personality trait would be in this case the outcome of high excitability of BAS, FFFS and especially BIS (while, for example, high excitability of only BAS, with low excitability of BIS would lead to impulsive personality). The prefrontal cortex, amygdala and basal ganglia are proposed to be the neuroanatomical basis of BAS, while the orbital frontal cortex, septohippocampal system and Papez circuitry are described as such basis for BIS (Gray & McNaughton, 2000). Unfortunately, these descriptions are until now mostly speculative as there are yet no verified means to assess BIS or BAS activity/excitability to correlate it with activity of proposed structures. The popular BAS/BIS questionnaire of Carver and White (1994) is based on a previous version of Gray’s theory (Gray, 1982) and could give misleading results, especially concerning BIS, as conceptualization of this system was quite changed in the current version. Nevertheless, the BAS/BIS approach is, to our mind, one of the most promising attempts to model neurobiological grounds of state and trait anxiety and to link them with psychological mechanisms and behavioral manifestations of this trait.

Theory of attentional control proposed by M. Eysenck et al. (2007) focuses rather on cognitive aspects of anxiety. According to this theory, persons with high anxiety are inclined to suppress their behavior in threat-related and novel conditions in comparison with those with lower anxiety. However, behavioral suppression is compensated by increase of attention to external stimuli and to results of one's own reactions. Persons with a high anxiety level try to control situations as much as possible. It can be hypothesized that the differences in brain activity between higher and lower anxiety groups can be found in conditions in which they have to realize or stop an activity.

Finally, R.J. Davidson's approach to anxiety lies in line with other works of his group concerning affective styles and emotionality-related disorders and considers the neuroanatomical background of emotional processes associated with anxiety being based mainly on data on patients with anxiety disorders (Davidson et al., 1999). This approach links anxiety with the amygdala and prefrontal (especially its ventromedial and orbital zones) cortex (Davidson, 2002). Another important region in this circuitry is the anterior cingulate cortex (ACC), which is supposedly involved in control of anxious reactions depending on their relevance in the current situation (Nitschke et al., 2009). Correspondingly, if ACC activity indeed plays such an adaptive role, we could expect that in highly anxious but yet non-patient subjects reactivity in anxiety-provoking situations would be increased both in the amygdala and ACC. In their earlier works Davidson and coauthors (e.g. Wheeler et al., 1993, Sutton and Davidson, 1997, Davidson, 1998) observed pronounced cortical asymmetry in functional specialization of brain hemispheres with positive affect and approach being linked to activity of the left, while negative affect and withdrawal – of the right frontal cortex. However, though these affective dimensions are closely related with anxiety, links between brain asymmetry and this trait are not so clear, especially in non-patient samples. Another important approach of Davidson's group, apparently concerning the subject of this work, is so-called "affective chronometry". Using startle reflex potentiation as a measure of affective reactivity they (Larson et al., 2007) demonstrated that in anxious subjects the state of increased reactivity is much prolonged after offset of aversive (and, moreover, affectively charged with any valence) stimulus in anxious in comparison with normal control subjects. Although the task we used is scarcely provoking strong affects, we still could expect that EEG reactions of subjects with higher anxiety would be more prolonged especially in lower frequencies, which are associated with emotionality (Knyazev et al., 2008a; Knyazev et al., 2009), and particularly reactions related with errors (Knyazev et al., 2008b; Savostyanov et al., 2009).

In general, the three mentioned approaches are not contradicting but rather consider different aspects of anxiety. At the same time all these aspects are more or less directly associated with executive functions. Indeed, the activation/approach and inhibition/withdrawal are the core processes of executive control, which inevitably requires voluntary attention, and although theoretically it could be realized without emotions, in practice they usually accompany it. In the narrower context of this chapter these aspects are also present: the Stop-signal paradigm we used involves activation and inhibition of motor reactions, both requiring attentional control as well as does the error-monitoring, while the errors the participants made and their worry about general successfulness of task completion provide some level of emotionality. Summing up, we could expect that level of anxiety would exert influence on executive control processes, and that this influence would be mediated through neurophysiological systems and processes associated with both executive functions and anxiety.

Thus, the topic of this chapter is a research on the dependency between trait anxiety level and brain processes, which are related with such executive functions as activation and inhibition of motor responses and error monitoring. Studies of Spielberger (see e.g. Spielberger and Reheiser, 2004) demonstrated that trait anxiety is a stable psychological trait with low variability in long-term (several years) period. At the same time, being a stable trait, anxiety is far not always manifested as a state, at least in non-pathological conditions. Therefore, we propose that brain processes/systems associated with anxiety should have a "covert" nature of the same kind, manifesting only in certain situations. The most promising candidates for this role are, in our opinion, oscillatory systems of the brain. The concept of brain oscillatory systems (Stryker, 1989; Basar, 1998; von Stein and Samthein, 2000) is relatively recent in neuroscience. Being based mostly on electroencephalographic and systems electrophysiology findings (Basar et al., 2001; Eckhorn et al., 1988), it is also supported by converging evidences from fields of cellular electrophysiology, neuroanatomy and even functional genomics. Particularly, intrinsic oscillatory properties of neurons (see e.g. Silva et al., 1991) and abundance of small-scale neural circuits in the cerebral cortex (Steriade et al., 1996) provides the basis for "local" high-frequency oscillations, while long-distance cortico-cortical (Nunez, 1989) and cortico-subcortical (Miller, 1991, Steriade et al., 1993) loops are thought to be the substrate of lower-frequency oscillatory activity. And frequency-specific mechanism of some synaptic proteins' genes expression activation by oscillations of postsynaptic potential (Fields et al., 2005) could be the ground for development of such frequency-tuned neural nets in ontogenesis. As postsynaptic potentials determine excitability of neurons, the oscillations of these potentials, either endogenous or exogenous, provide a core mechanism for temporal binding of synchronously oscillating neurons into one functional system, and at the same time for "filtering out" any non-synchronized (irrelevant) activity from other neural circuits. During the recent three decades much work has been carried out not only for understanding neurophysiological basis of oscillatory systems (Lopes da Silva, 1991), but also to elucidate their roles in organization of behavior, in emotional reactions and cognitive processes (see Wang, 2010 for expansive review in this field). The most widely used tool for the later purposes is the electroencephalography (EEG), therefore, oscillatory systems are commonly named by EEG rhythms of corresponding frequency (e.g. alpha-system, theta-system etc.). According to evolutionary based interpretations of brain oscillatory activity (Basar, 1998; Knyazev & Slobodskaya, 2003; Knyazev, 2007), oscillations in delta band (1-4 Hz) are associated with reward-related motivational structures, theta (4-8 Hz) with emotions and contextual memory, and alpha (8-12 Hz) with semantic memory, perception and attention. We should note that alpha rhythm since pioneering works on EEG (Berger, 1929, Adrian & Matthews, 1934) was for a long time considered just as a sign of general "inhibition" or "idling". However, recent findings suggest that the situation is not that simple. Being indeed the correlate of behaviorally inhibited states, increased alpha oscillations are rather providing the readiness for possible future physical or mental actions (Klimesch, 1999) and/or active selective inhibition of irrelevant perceptions and activities (Klimesch et al., 2007, Knyazev et al., 2006). Delta, theta and alpha rhythms are considered to be "global", providing long-range inter-regional connectivity, while higher frequency bands (beta, 13-30 Hz, and gamma, >30 Hz) are usually characterized as more "local" (Nunez, 1989). Changes in beta band activity have been associated with various functions such as visual attention (Wrobel, 2000), movement and motor imagery related changes (Neuper & Pfurtscheller, 2001), face recognition (Ozgoren et al., 2005), cognitive tasks (Ray and Cole, 1985), etc. Functions of gamma oscillations include perceptual binding (Singer et al., 1997), top-down attentional control (Gonsales Andino et al., 2005), short-term memory (Tallon-Baudry et al., 1996) and other complex cognitive functions (Kaiser & Lutzenberger, 2003). As the oscillatory activity appears to be the one of constitutive principles of brain functioning, the number of corresponding studies grows very rapidly. For the scope of this chapter important data were obtained in works interrelating brain oscillatory activity with state and trait anxiety and with executive functions such as activation and inhibition of reactions and error monitoring.

EEG correlates of anxiety were found both for certain frequency bands of background EEG and event-related oscillatory reactions. Particularly, several studies demonstrated that anxiety level and BIS reactivity are correlated positively with alpha band spectral power, but negatively related with power of slow-wave (i.e. delta and theta) rhythms in background EEG records (Knyazev et al., 2002, 2003, 2004). Moreover, alpha power further increases (Knyazev et al., 2004, 2005) and theta power further decreases (Aftanas et al., 2003) in anxiogenic situations in highly anxious subjects. At the same time, reduction of anxiety level using anxiolythic drugs (Breimer et al., 1990; Hotz et al., 2000), autogenic training (Jacobs & Lubar, 1989) and other methods (Diego et al., 2004, Field et al., 1996) is accompanied by decrease of alpha power. Event-related oscillatory activity in their dependency from anxiety level corresponds with the notion about reciprocal relationships between background EEG power and phasic EEG reactions (Klimesch, 1999). Particularly, event-related desynchronization (ERD, *reduction* of spectral power) in alpha band was stronger in subjects with higher anxiety (Aftanas et al., 1996; Knyazev et al., 2006), while in slow-wave bands synchronization (*increase* of spectral power) was higher in individuals with high anxiety than in low-anxious persons (Knyazev et al., 2008a). We should note, however, that while findings for alpha-band are quite repeatable across studies, results for theta and delta bands are less consistent and seem to depend on other factors unrelated to anxiety. It has been shown that the emotion-related delta/theta synchronization, in particular, depends on a type of instruction presented to subjects before experiment (Knyazev et al., 2009). Also, this reaction differs among the people from different ethno-cultural groups (Wu et al., 2010).

Dependence between EEG parameters and anxiety was stronger expressed in the conditions of uncertainty, i.e. if individuals were not sure if there unpredictable events could not happen (Knyazev et al., 2005). It is possible to assume that anxiety should influence executive control especially strongly in those situations when the individuals make their decision with time or information lacking for event evaluation. EEG reactions related to activation or inhibition of behavior should show dependence on trait anxiety if individuals are compelled to make fast decisions in conditions of unguaranteed success.

Recently we have studied the brain oscillatory responses using analysis of EEG recorded in conditions of SSP (Levin et al., 2007; Knyazev, et al., 2008b; Savostyanov et al., 2009). We showed that "Go" response is accompanied by spectral power decrease (desynchronization) in alpha and beta frequency range, whereas during response inhibition ("Stop" trials) the additional increase of spectral power (synchronization) in slow (delta and theta) bands was found. Successful ending of reaction was accompanied by synchronization in beta band or "beta rebound" as Pfurtscheller et al. (1996) named it. Summing up, analysis of EEG oscillations showed that in conditions of SSP there are three kinds of oscillatory changes relating with different frequency ranges– activation of motor response (alpha and beta band desynchronization), inhibition of prepared response (delta and theta band synchronization), and inhibition after successfully ended response (beta band synchronization).

Besides, the dependence between successful activation/inhibition of motor response on anxiety level was obtained. Similarly to the results mentioned above, the amplitude of alpha/beta desynchronization was stronger for higher-anxious subjects in Go and Stop conditions of SSP (Savostyanov et al., 2009). Earlier we didn't find significant correlations between anxiety and low-frequency reaction in SSP, but negative dependence on anxiety was revealed for beta rebound. In that study we didn't explore the dependence between brain oscillatory reactions and anxiety in conditions of unsuccessful responses. Meanwhile, it is plausible to assume that the situation of making an error would, from one side, evoke negative emotional reactions, and from the other side, would force the participant to allocate more voluntary attention to the task completion. Both these factors could be supposed to increase the effects of anxiety. Therefore in this chapter we would like to compare the anxiety influence on successful and unsuccessful regulation of behavior in Go and Stop conditions.

Also, an important topic of this chapter is topological distribution of anxiety-related processes in the different conditions of SSP. The inhibitory control is typically associated with the prefrontal cortex (Ridderinkhof, et al., 2004; Forstmann et al., 2008). However, as soon as inhibitory control is based on analysis of external signals and participates in regulation of motor responses, this process cannot be limited by only the frontal cortex. Specific and nonspecific sensory areas, motor and associative cortices are also involved in response regulation. According to Fuster (2006), behavioral control is provided by long reciprocal cortico-cortical connections between posterior and frontal networks. These connections support the dynamics of the perception-action cycle in sequential behavior. It is possible to assume that dependence of various SSP components on anxiety will have a topological specificity, i.e. this dependence will be related either with anterior or with posterior areas. However, according to other hypothesis the anxiety level is modulated by activity of deep subcortical structures (Gray and McNaughton, 2000, McNaughton and Corr, 2004). In this reason, the effect of anxiety should not have topological specificity in EEG reactions. Here we would like to check up hypotheses about topological distinctions in reactions related with activation, inhibition or estimation of success of motor responses in the persons with different anxiety levels. Therefore we have made a detailed, multiple-factor analysis of EEG reactions in different time-frequency intervals in the SSP conditions.

Thus, in this chapter we have compared brain reactions in four (successful Go, successful Stop, unsuccessful Go and unsuccessful Stop) conditions of the SSP in the individuals with different levels of trait anxiety. The analysis of topological distribution of reaction on a scalp surface has been made for the time-frequency intervals reflecting different aspects of regulation of the motor responses.

METHODS

Subjects: EEG data were obtained in 21 healthy right-handed subjects (15 males), aged 25-33 years old (with average age 26±3.0 years). All participants gave informed consent before enrollment into the study. The study was approved by the ethics committee in accordance with the Declaration of Helsinki. The Chinese version of the State Trait Anxiety Inventory (Shek, 1993; Spielberger et al., 1970) (cSTAI) was used for measuring the trait anxiety level. A median split was applied to divide subjects into the relatively high- and low-anxiety groups. The cSTAI has been validated and its psychometric characteristics can be found in the study of Shek (1993). The face validity of cSTAI was doubly examined by a senior psychometrician, and we also interviewed several subjects who voluntarily took the cSTAI. The final cSTAI used in the experiment had minor corrections on the Chinese translations of the original STAI based on the interview results.

*Procedure:*_The experimental procedure was described in the paper of Savostyanov et al., (2009). During the experiment, each participant was seated comfortably in a chair with eyes open in a sound-insulated dimly lit chamber. Visual stimuli were presented via a 24.4 x 18.3 cm monitor located 60 cm in front of the subject. The procedure was designed in a form of EEG-interfaced interactive computer game, during which the subject was motivated to get the maximum score. After 15 minutes of background EEG recording, participants performed 30 training trials of a choice reaction task in which they had to press the left or right button after presentation of one of two pictures (a deer or a tank). The pictures (15 x 10 cm) were presented at the center of the computer monitor for 500 ms. Subjects should choose a weapon to strike a target (a rifle or an antitank rocket launcher) and shoot. Subsequently in 130 trials of the stop-signal task, they had to refrain from pressing any button if a stop-signal (red bar, 3 x 2 cm, 250 ms in duration) was presented after the picture. In the pre-task instruction, the participants were told to respond as fast and accurately as possible. The deer and tank alternated randomly and the inter-stimulus interval randomly varied between 3.5 and 5.5 seconds. The stop-signal was randomly presented in 30 (approximately 23%) trials. The interval between onset of the picture and stop-signal was 250 ms. If response was correct, the subject received additional points, and a deduction of points was applied to mistakes and to insufficient speed of reaction. Thus, four different conditions (successful Go and Stop; unsuccessful Go and Stop) were considered in the experimental procedure. EEGs were registered simultaneously with the game. The target and stop-signal presentations along with the subject's reactions were automatically labeled during EEG recording.

EEGs were recorded in 21 subjects using 132-channels (122 EEG, VEOG, HEOG, EKG, EMG, and 6 face muscle channels) via Ag/AgCl electrodes. The EEG electrodes were placed on 122 head sites according to the extended International 10-10 system (Oostenveld and Praamstra, 2001) and referred to Cz with ground at FzA. The monopolar reference scheme was applied for the montage of electrodes. The Quik-Cap128 NSL was used for electrode fixation. The electrode resistance was maintained below 5 κΩ. The signals were amplified using "Neuroscan (USA)" amplifiers, with 0.1-100 Hz analog bandpass and digitized at 1000 Hz.

Data processing: Event-related spectral perturbations (ERSP) were calculated using the *timef* function in the EEGLAB toolbox (http://sccn.ucsd.edu/eeglab/) (Delorme and Makeig, 2004). The ERSP shows mean log event-locked deviations from baseline-mean power at each frequency. For time-frequency representation of EEG data, the wavelet transformation using the *Morlet* waveform as a mother wavelet was chosen.

Ongoing EEG from 1.0 sec before to 2.5 sec after the target stimulus onset was selected for data analyses. EEG from 1.0 to 0.25 sec before the target stimulus onset was used for baseline-correction. In other words, the "baseline" interval did not contain any task-related activity. EEG was preliminarily band-pass filtered in 1-50 Hz using elliptic filters. Re-reference to average reference and baseline adjustment procedures were performed during data preprocessing using *pop_reref* and *pop_rmbase* EEGlab functions (Delorme and Makeig,

2004). In EEGlab re-reference to average reference is realized as follows: first, the activity in the original reference channels is estimated as minus (sum of all electrodes activity divided by number of electrodes) and, second, this activity is added to each channel. Baseline for each channel and each epoch was removed by subtracting the mean EEG value in the baseline time range from epoch EEG. Some trials (1-7 per person) with non-stereotyped artifacts were removed after visual inspection of EEG records. The presence of eye-blink or eye-movement artifacts was not a criterion for rejection of the episode.

The 80-99 (mean 91.6; SD 8.9) EEG trials were selected in successful Go condition, 17-30 (mean 25.4; SD 3.8) EEG trials in successful Stop condition, 0-33 (mean 4.2; SD 7.5) in unsuccessful Go and 0-10 (mean 2.3; SD 2.5) in unsuccessful Stop conditions. A particular EEG-channel (mean 2.9; SD 1.5) was reconstructed by means of the *EEG-interp* function, if there were irremovable artifacts.

Independent component analysis (ICA) was used for correcting eye blink and eye-movement artifacts (Makeig et al., 1996; Hyvärinen et al., 2010). ICA transforms EEG channels data into "EEG components" representation (with number of components equal to number of channels), which are supposed to reflect activity of sources independent from one another. The components' weights were computed individually for each subject. The components corresponding to eye artifacts were identified by visual inspection of component sets together with electrooculogram records. For each person, 5-15 components were identified as "artifactual". These components had the highest weights in the electrooculographic channels and contained spectral power changes in time intervals corresponding to eye activity in oculogram. After removal of artifactual components EEG for each subject was transformed back to standard representation, but now EEG channels were "cleaned" from electrooculographic artifacts. This approach allows avoiding rejection of trials contaminated by eye-movements and blinks, which is especially important in studies where activity associated with relatively rare events, such as missed stop trials, is to be explored. Then, we computed ERSP-indices separately for each EEG-channel and each subject.

The averaged ERSP patterns were firstly investigated separately for different subject groups without direct statistical comparison between groups and brain areas. Given a subject group, ERSPs were averaged across subjects and all channels. The random permutation method (bootstrap) with $p<0.01$ significance level was applied in the statistical analysis of ERSPs separately for each experimental condition. Here we used the bootstrap statistical method realized in EEGLAB toolbox (*statcond* function) and based on random data resampling. In this method, a surrogate data distribution is constructed by selecting spectral estimates from randomly selected samples and then averaging these. Applying this process 500 times produces a surrogate data distribution where the specified percentiles are then taken as significance thresholds (Delorme and Makeig, 2004). This method was used to visualize significant deviations from baseline random fluctuations that were observed after stimulus presentation, such that non-significant features of the output plots were zeroed out (i.e., plotted in green).

We partitioned 122 EEG scalp channels into 11 regions: the left (10 channels), midline (14 channels), and right frontal (10 channels); left (13 channels), and right temporal (13 channels); and the left (9 channels), midline (14 channels) and right central (9 channels), left (9 channels), midline (12 channels), and right occipital-parietal (9 channels). ERSPs were averaged across channels within each region for each individual subject. The Kolmogorov-Smirnov test did not show significant deviations from normal distribution in our data. Thus, conventional ANOVA was applied for testing between-condition and between-group differences. The Greenhouse–Geisser correction for the sphericity assumption violation was used whenever necessary. Repeated measures ANOVA was applied to testing the main effects of regions (11 levels) and groups (high vs. low-anxious), as well as the interaction effect between regions, groups and conditions.

RESULTS

Behavioral data: The average reaction time in the Go condition was 697.8 ms (SD 68) for the whole group. In high-anxious subjects the average reaction time was 672.7 ms (SD 87.2) and in low-anxious subjects – 716.6 ms (47.7). The inter-group differences in reaction time between high and low-anxious subjects were insignificant. The mean number of missed button-presses (unsuccessful Go reaction) was 4.2 (SD 7.5) for whole group, 5.2 (SD 10.5) in high-anxious subjects and 3.4 (SD 4.6) in low-anxious subjects. The mean number of incorrect button-presses after stop-signal onset (unsuccessful Stop reaction) was 2.3 (SD 2.5) for whole group, 2.2 (SD 3.1) in high-anxious subjects and 2.3 (SD 2.1) in low-anxious subjects. The inter-group differences in the number of behavioral errors were statistically insignificant for all experimental conditions. Thus, the significant differences between high and low-anxious subjects were obtained for no behavioral parameter.

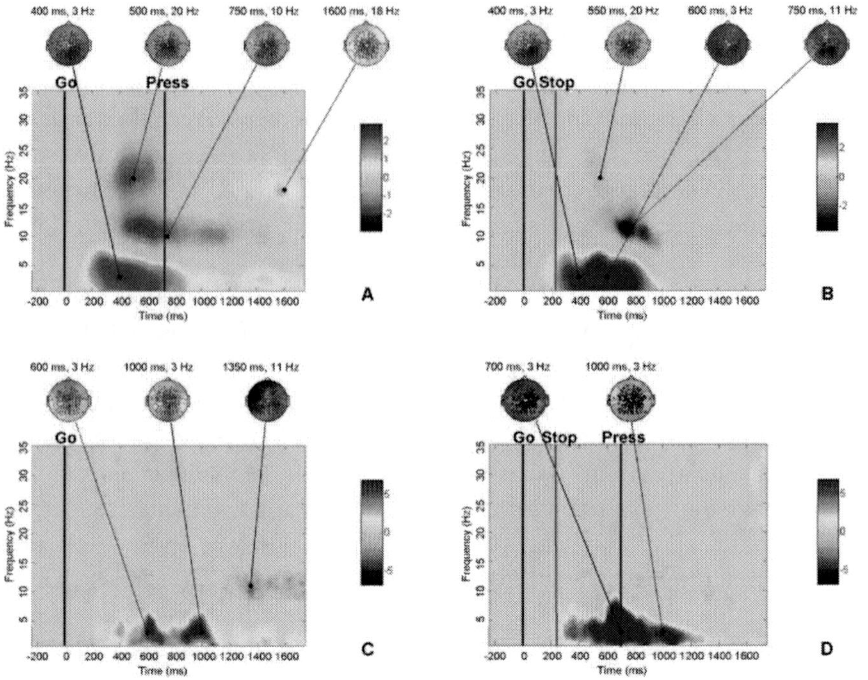

Figure 1. ERSP plots for successful Go (A), successful Stop (B), unsuccessful Go (C) and unseccessful Stop (D) conditions. ERSP values are averaged for whole group. Warm colors mean increase of power; cold colors – decrease. Black vertical line (zero time point) represents time of target stimulus onset. Blue vertical line corresponds to button-press and red vertical line – to Stop-signal onset. $P < 0.01$.

EEG patterns for successful and unsuccessful conditions: EEG patterns in different experimental conditions were firstly investigated without reference to the anxiety level. In the successful Go condition EEG spectral power was increased in 1-7 Hz band during 150-1000 ms after target stimulus onset (See Fig. 1a). A decrease of spectral power was found in EEG between approximately 250-1200 ms after the target stimulus onset. During movement preparation, this reaction covered a wide frequency range in 8-25 Hz corresponding to boundaries of alpha and beta rhythms. After the button press it was sustained at 7-14 Hz frequency range. Increases in spectral power were observed in a frequency range 12-25 Hz during 1000-1600 ms after target stimulus onset (i.e. about 300 – 900 ms after the button press). In the successful Stop condition, significant desynchronization was observed in the frequency range 7-25 Hz during approximately 300-1000 ms after the target stimulus onset (See Fig. 1b). Besides, significant synchronization in the frequency range of 1-7 Hz was found during 150-1000 ms after the target stimulus onset. The amplitude of alpha/beta power decrease in successful Stop condition was approximately the same as in Go condition, whereas the amplitude of slow-wave synchronization was essentially higher for Stop than that for Go condition. In both unsuccessful conditions only slow-wave synchronization was obtained in 1-7 Hz during 150-1400 ms after target stimulus onset (See Fig. 1c,d). No alpha/beta desynchronization or high-frequency synchronization was found in unsuccessful conditions.

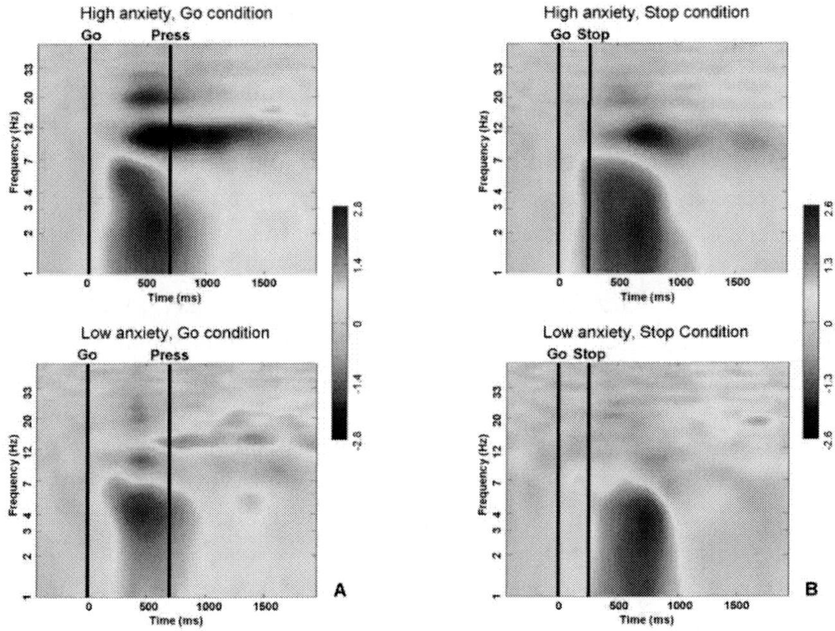

Figure 2. ERSP plots for successful Go (A) and successful Stop (B) conditions in high and low anxiety groups. Upper panels represent high anxiety group, and lower panels – low anxiety group. Warm colors mean increase of power; cold colors – decrease. P < 0.01.

For additional control of our results we compared ERSP plots, which had been prepared separately for relatively high and low anxious persons in the successful Go and Stop conditions. In both of these conditions, subjects with higher anxiety showed a higher level of alpha/beta desynchronization (See Fig. 2a,b). The amplitude of slow-wave synchronization was also higher in high-anxious subjects in comparison with low-anxious ones, but those differences were obtained only in delta (1-4 Hz) and not in theta (4-7 Hz) frequency band.

The amplitude of high-frequency synchronization (12-25 Hz) was stronger in low-anxious subjects in comparison with high-anxious ones in both successful conditions. Besides, the latency of this reaction in Go condition was shorter for low-anxious subjects than that in high-anxious subjects (about 600 ms vs about 1400 ms), whereas such differences were not seen in the latencies of Stop condition (See Fig. 2a). No differences between anxiety groups were found by comparison of ERSP plots in unsuccessful conditions.

The ANOVA results: Fourteen time-frequency intervals of interest (1-7 Hz in 200-400 ms; 1-4 Hz in 200-400 ms; 4-7 Hz in 200-400 ms; 1-7 Hz in 400-800 ms; 1-4 Hz in 400-800 Hz; 7-12 Hz in 400-700 ms; 12-16 Hz in 400-700 ms; 16-20 Hz in 400-700 ms; 20-25 Hz in 400-700 ms; 7-12 Hz in 700-1000 ms; 12-16 Hz in 700-1000 ms; 16-20 Hz in 700-1000 ms; 20-25 Hz in 700-1000 ms; 12-25 Hz in 1000-1500 ms) were chosen basing on analysis of ERSP plots described above and further analyzed for all four experimental conditions using repeated measures ANOVA. The significant main effects and interactions obtained in this analysis for different intervals are summarized in Table 1.

In 1-7 Hz and 200-400 ms time-frequency interval main effect of region, $F(10, 670) = 4.38$, $p < 0.00001$, and two-way interaction region × condition, $F(30, 670) = 2.61$, $p < 0.00001$, were highly significant. Planned comparisons showed that the amplitude of synchronization was the strongest in all occipital-parietal areas. These areas significantly ($p = 0.0032$) differed from all other cortical regions, whereas the differences between other regions were insignificant. The main effect of condition was insignificant. In the same time-frequency interval repeated measures ANOVA was made separately for two successful and two unsuccessful conditions. For successful conditions the effect of region, $F(10, 380) = 20.39$, $p < 0.00001$, was significant, but two-way interaction region × condition, $F(10, 380) = 1.14$, $p = 0.33$, was insignificant. Oppositely, for unsuccessful conditions the effect of region, $F(10, 290) = 0.88$, $p = 0.55$, was insignificant, but two-way interaction region × condition, $F(10, 290) = 3.20$, $p = 0.0006$, was significant. Thus, the amplitude of early low-frequency synchronization didn't differ between successful Go and Stop conditions. In these conditions the synchronization had a maximum in occipital-parietal regions. However, the between-region differences were not obtained for all unsuccessful conditions, but posterior synchronization in the unsuccessful Stop condition was stronger in comparison with unsuccessful Go condition. For whole 1-7 Hz frequency band the effect of anxiety was insignificant. However, the main effect of anxiety, $F(1, 67) = 6.86$, $p = 0.011$, was significant for synchronization in delta (1-4 Hz) band, but was insignificant, $F(1, 67) = 0.144$, $p = 0.71$, for theta (4-7 Hz) band. The amplitude of delta (not theta) synchronization was stronger for high- than that for low-anxious persons in all four conditions. At the same time, the effects of region and conditions for delta and theta bands were similar to the effect for 1-7 Hz band.

In 1-7 Hz and 400-800 ms time-frequency interval main effect of condition, $F(3, 67) = 5.52$, $p = 0.0019$ was significant. Post-hoc comparisons showed that both the Go conditions significantly differed from both the Stop conditions ($p < 0.05$). The differences between successful and unsuccessful Go conditions ($p > 0.7$), and also between successful and unsuccessful Stop conditions ($p > 0.22$) were insignificant. The main effect of region, $F(10, 670) = 4.46$, $p < 0.00001$, was highly significant. To further elucidate the effect of region, ANOVA were run separately in successful and unsuccessful conditions. In both successful conditions the effect of region, $F(10, 380) = 13{,}85$, $p < 0.00001$ was significant. Planned comparisons show that the amplitude of synchronization was minimal in all central areas. These areas significantly ($p = 0.0012$) differed from all other cortical regions, whereas the differences between other regions were insignificant. The cortical topology of later synchronization did not differ between successful Go and successful Stop conditions. In both unsuccessful conditions the effect of region, $F(10, 290) = 1.09$, $p = 0.37$, was insignificant. Similar to 200-400 ms interval, for later synchronization the main effect of anxiety was insignificant for 1-7 Hz and 4-7 Hz bands, but it was significant for delta (1-4 Hz) band, $F(1, 67) = 5.00$, $p = 0.029$. In this interval (1-4 Hz, 400-800 ms) the amplitude of delta synchronization was stronger for high- than for low-anxious persons in all four conditions.

Thus, for synchronization in 1-7 Hz the differences between conditions were significant only in later (400-800 ms), but not in earlier (200-400 ms) time intervals. The amplitude of later synchronization was stronger for both Stop conditions in comparison with both Go conditions. The successful and unsuccessful conditions didn't differ in amplitude of reaction, but differed in its cortical distribution. In earlier time intervals successful reactions are maximum in occipital-parietal areas, whereas in later intervals two regions with strong amplitude (anterior and posterior, but not central) were found. The between-region differences were insignificant in all unsuccessful conditions in both time intervals. Also, the differences between anxiety groups were significant for all conditions and all time intervals, but only in delta frequency band. The amplitude of delta synchronization always was stronger for high- than that for low-anxious subjects.

For pre-movement (250-700 ms) time interval in alpha (7-12 Hz), beta1 (12-16 Hz), and beta2 (16-20 Hz) frequency bands only main effect of region was significant (See Table 1). The amplitude of desynchronization was the strongest in central cortical areas for all bands. The effects of condition and anxiety in these time-frequency intervals were insignificant. The influence of anxiety was obtained by post-hoc comparisons only for beta1 desynchronization in successful (both Go and Stop) conditions and only in central cortical areas. In these areas the amplitude of reaction was significantly ($p < 0.01$) stronger for high- than that for low-anxious persons. For beta3 (20-25 Hz) band the effects of condition $F(3, 67) = 12.10$, $p < 0.00001$, and anxiety, $F(1, 67) = 4.10$, $p = 0.047$, were significant. The beta3 desynchroniza-tion was stronger for unsuccessful, than that for successful conditions. Also, the amplitude of beta3 desynchronization was stronger in high-anxious persons for all regions and conditions with between-group differences being stronger for successful, than for unsuccessful conditions.

In post-movement (700-1000 ms) time interval, similar to pre-movement desynchronization, only main effect of region was significant for alpha, beta1 and beta2 bands and the cortical distribution of reaction amplitude also was similar to that in pre-movement time interval. Then, ANOVA were run separately in successful and unsuccessful conditions. The significant effects of region, anxiety and condition were obtained only in successful conditions, whereas all effects and interactions in unsuccessful conditions were insignificant or marginal. In alpha band the effect of region, $F(10, 380) = 3.43$, $p < 0.00001$, was highly significant. In both successful conditions the maximal alpha desynchronization was obtained in central areas. Also, the effect of anxiety, $F(1, 38) = 8.28$, $p = 0.007$, was significant. Desynchronization was stronger in high- in comparison with low-anxious subjects. For beta1 and beta2 bands the effects of region, $F(10, 380) = 7.34$, $p < 0.00001$ (beta1), $F(10, 380) = 5.42$, $p < 0.00001$ (beta2), condition, $F(1, 38) = 5.63$, $p = 0.023$ (beta1), $F(1, 38) = 3.8$, $p = 0.058$ (beta2), and anxiety, $F(1, 38) = 7.66$, $p = 0.0087$ (beta1), $F(1, 38) = 3.80$, $p = 0.052$ (beta2) were significant in successful conditions. The amplitude of beta1 and beta2 desynchronization was stronger for Stop, than that for Go condition, and also stronger in high-anxious subjects in comparison with low-anxious ones. In beta3 (20-25 Hz) frequency band the main effects of region, $F(10, 670) = 4.26$, $p = 0.00001$, and anxiety, $F(1, 67) = 5.27$, $p = 0.025$, were significant in all four experimental conditions. The desynchronization in this band also was stronger in high-anxious group. Besides, the effect of condition, $F(3, 67) = 8.70$, $p = 00006$, was significant.

The desynchronization was stronger for unsuccessful, that that for successful conditions.

Table 1. The ANOVA results

Time-frequency interval	Effect	G-G Epsilon	Degrees of Freedom	MS	F	p
1-7 Hz, 200-400 ms	region	0.34	3.4	228.1	4.38	0.00001
	region* condition	0.34	10.2	228.1	2.61	0.00001
1-4 Hz, 200-400 ms	anxiety		1	67	6.86	0.011
1-7 Hz, 400-800 ms	condition		3	67	5.52	0.002
	region	0.43	4.3	289.7	4.46	0.00001
1-4 Hz, 400-800 ms	anxiety		1	67	5.00	0.029
7-12 Hz, 250-700 ms	region	0.49	5.0	331.5	2.63	0.004
12-16 Hz, 250-700 ms	region	0.49	5.0	325.1	2.19	0.017
16-20 Hz, 250-700 ms	region	0.52	5.2	350.4	1.86	0.048
20-25 Hz, 250-700 ms	anxiety		1	67	4.10	0.047
	condition		3	67	12.10	0.00001
7-12 Hz, 700-1000 ms, successful conditions	anxiety		1	38	8.28	0.007
	region	0.46	4.6	175.4	5.88	0.00001
12-16 Hz, 700-1000 ms, successful conditions	anxiety		1	38	7.66	0.009
	condition		1	38	5.63	0.023
	region	0.44	4.4	168.5	7.34	0.00001
16-20 Hz, 700-1000 ms, successful conditions	anxiety		1	38	3.8	0.052
	condition		1	38	3.8	0.058
	region	0.48	4.8	183.0	5.42	0.00001
20-25 Hz, 700-1000 ms	anxiety		1	67	5.27	0.025
	condition		3	67	8.70	0.00006
	region	0.44	4.4	297.8	4.26	0.00001
12-25 Hz, 1000-1500 ms	anxiety		1	67	9.68	0.0027
	condition		3	67	10.98	0.00001
	region	0.42	4.2	278.3	1.99	0.032
	region* condition	0.42	12.5	278.3	1.77	0.007

Thus, both pre- and post-movement desynchronization had maximal amplitude in central cortical areas. The effects of anxiety were significant in alpha, beta1 and beta2 bands only in post-movement interval and only in successful conditions (both Go and Stop). In beta3 band the effects of anxiety were significant in all conditions and intervals. The amplitude of desynchronization was in all these cases stronger for high-, than that for low-anxious subjects. The two-way interactions anxiety*region were insignificant or only marginal.

For 12-25 Hz and 1000-1500 ms time-frequency interval main effects of both anxiety, $F(1, 67) = 9.68$, $p = 0.003$, and condition, $F(3, 67) = 10.98$, $p < 0.00001$, were significant. In this interval the positive values of ERSPs (synchronization) were obtained for successful conditions (both successful Go and Stop), but negative values (desynchronization) were found for both unsuccessful conditions. Post-hoc comparisons (Fisher LSD) show that each of the successful conditions differed from each of the unsuccessful conditions ($p < 0.0001$), but the conditions with same success did not differ from each other ($p > 0.8$). The amplitude of synchronization was stronger for low- than that for high-anxious persons. Post-hoc comparisons show that the anxiety groups significantly differed only for successful conditions ($p < 0.01$), but for unsuccessful conditions the between-group differences were insignificant ($p > 0.1$). Besides, the main effect of region, $F(10, 670) = 1.99$, $p = 0.03$, and two-way interaction region × condition, $F(30, 670) = 1.77$, $p = 0.007$, were significant. Planned comparisons show that between-region differences were insignificant ($p > 0.8$) for all successful conditions. For all unsuccessful conditions desynchronization in this time-frequency interval was significantly stronger in central regions in comparison with frontal ($p = 0.003$) and occipital-parietal ($p = 0.040$) regions.

Discussion

This chapter was aimed at finding dependencies between brain processes underlying executive control and the level of trait anxiety in healthy subjects. According to the neuropsychological model of Gray and McNaughton (Gray & McNaughton, 2000, McNaughton & Corr, 2004) trait anxiety is associated with inclination to activation of Behavioral Inhibition System, which leads to inhibition of ongoing behavioral patterns if information about environment is insufficient and a person is unable to predict results of own behavior. In our experiment subjects had to choose appropriate reactions to presented stimuli of an unpredictable type, but in some cases (also unpredictable) Stop-signal forced them to stop a prepared or already started reaction. Based on Gray & McNaughton's model we proposed that these uncertain conditions would enhance activity of BIS and strengthen manifestations of neurophysiological differences between subjects with different levels of trait anxiety. Analysis of EEG recorded in these conditions could improve understanding of mechanisms underlying these differences.

Behavioral control is associated with execution of several interacting brain functions, including sensory, motor and cognitive components. We supposed that different brain processes coupled with behavioral control are differentially related with trait anxiety. Some of them could be enhanced in persons with high trait anxiety, while others are manifested more intensively in low-anxious persons. Testing of this hypothesis requires specific measures, sensitive to relatively short-term changes of activity of different functional systems of the brain. Such measures are provided by the concept of brain oscillatory systems (Basar, 1998; Knyazev, 2007). According to this concept different functional activities of the brain are mirrored in EEG oscillations of different frequencies and temporal changes of these oscillations' spectral power could be interpreted as signs of execution of corresponding functions. Besides, EEG is characterized by spatial distribution of reactions. Before considering differences in executive control mechanisms related to anxiety level we would interpret their common patterns observed in this chapter in terms of the above-mentioned characteristics and their functional meanings.

Slow-wave synchronization with maximal amplitude in occipital-parietal region in the Go condition could be interpreted as a sign of activation of the visual cortex after target stimulus appearance (Basar, 1998). Widespread desynchronization in alpha/beta band is presumably related to task non-specific attention concentration, typical to all situations when task-related stimuli are presented (Klimesh et al., 2007). Besides, in the Go condition this desynchronization is more pronounced in the central region (desynchronize-tion of mu-rhythm), mirroring activation of motor areas, associated with hand movement regulation (Neuper and Pfurtscheller, 1999). The power increase in upper beta band after successfully ended motor task was earlier interpreted as so-called "beta rebound" (Pfurtscheller et al., 1996), i.e. brain reaction induced by suppression of task-related activity and relaxation. Our results show that the alpha/beta desynchronization and "beta rebound" is also present in the Stop condition in the same time-frequency intervals and cortical areas as in the Go condition. The amplitude of these reactions was lower than in the Go condition, but statistical significance of this difference was weak. This result could partly be correlated with data of Neuper and Pfurtscheller (1999) on motor imagery, considering that reaction, being not completed due to Stop-signal appearance, was still "imagined". However, if higher frequency (alpha and beta) reactions allow such "imaginary" interpretation, the lower-frequency (delta and theta) Stop-related activity could not be explained this way.

In general, amplitude of low-frequency synchronization was significantly larger in the Stop than in the Go condition. Earlier (Savostyanov et al., 2009) we interpreted this larger synchronization only as a sign of inhibition of prepared movement after Stop-signal onset. However, analysis of its cortical distribution showed that the situation is more complex. Indeed, quite predictably, in 200 – 400 ms after target stimulus onset differences between conditions were insignificant and maximal synchronization was observed in occipital-parietal regions. But in later interval (400 – 800 ms after target stimulus) differences between the Go and Stop became significant with maximal Stop-related synchronization in parietal, frontal and temporal, but not in the central region. Accordingly, low-frequency synchronization in the Stop condition could be explained as a result of two processes, overlapping in time: sensory activation by "bottom-up" mechanisms and "top-down" inhibition. Though they utilize the same frequency band, spatial distribution and timing of these processes differ. Bottom-up sensory activation is observed in 200 – 1000 ms after target stimulus with maximum in occipital-parietal region. It is stronger in successful (both Go and Stop) trials than in trials with erroneous reaction/non-reaction, but do not differentiate between Go and Stop conditions. We suggest that it is initially generated in the visual cortex and then spreads to more anterior areas. Top-down inhibitory reaction is observed after Stop-signal onset (400 – 1000 ms after target stimulus) with maximum in frontal and temporal areas. It is stronger in Stop (both successful and erroneous) than in Go conditions and spreads from frontal to more posterior regions. Noteworthy, in the Stop condition these two reactions are observed simultaneously in the same frequency band, but in different cortical regions.

In unsuccessful trials only changes in slow-wave activity were revealed as significant compared with the baseline by bootstrap statistics. Having the same amplitude and topography as in successful trials, slow-save synchronization was significantly prolonged both in erroneously missed Go and in unsuccessful Stop. This prolonged reaction was described as error-related activity (Luu et al., 2004; Trujillo and Allen, 2007). However when we compared successful vs. unsuccessful trials, the most significant differences were found for "beta rebound". This reaction occurs only when a result (either button-press or its inhibition) is evaluated as "successful", but it is absent in case of any kind of mistakes. Therefore, "beta rebound" is related not only to motor relaxation as it was suggested earlier (Chen, 1998), but also with self-rating of personal behavior as successful or unsuccessful.

In general, ERSP patterns for all experimental conditions could be explained using the horse-race model proposed by Logan and coauthors (1984, 2003). This model suggests that in SSP a competition exists in the brain between processes regulating behavioral activation and inhibition, and motor response or its cancellation occurs depending on which of the processes "wins the race". Processes related to activation were mirrored in early posterior low-frequency synchronization and pre- and post-movement alpha and beta desynchronization, without significant differences between Go and Stop trials. Inhibition in Stop trials (both successful and unsuccessful) was associated with late low-frequency synchronization in the frontal region. In successful trials these reactions had clear spatial maximums in functionally relevant regions, while unsuccessful trials were characterized by weaker and more widespread early reactions, but prolonged late low-frequency synchronization. In addition to processes described in the horse-race model (Logan et al, 1984, Band et al., 2003), we observed brain activity, specifically associated with self-rating of own behavior as successful or unsuccessful. "Beta rebound" could not be associated either with activation, or inhibition of response, as it occurred post factum and depends on successfulness of reaction, but not on type of trial.

Significant main effect of trait anxiety was observed in delta (1 – 4 Hz), but not in theta (4 – 7 Hz) frequency band. Both early and late synchronizations were significantly stronger in high- than in low-anxious subjects for all four experimental conditions (Go and Stop, successful and unsuccessful). That is, anxiety-related differences in amplitude of low-frequency synchronization were not specifically associated with either activation or inhibition of motor reaction, or successful or erroneous responses. Also, in successful, but not in unsuccessful conditions (both Go and Stop) desynchronization in alpha and beta bands (7-25 Hz) was significantly stronger in subjects with high than with low trait anxiety level. On the contrary, amplitude of "beta rebound" in successful (and again, not in unsuccessful) conditions was significantly stronger in low-anxious subjects. Besides, as could be seen in ERSP plots (Fig. 2), differences between groups with high and low anxiety are related with not only amplitude, but also timing of reactions. Desynchronization in alpha and beta bands lasts 200 – 300 ms more in high- than in low-anxious subjects, while "beta rebound" occurs in later group about 800 ms earlier than in first. Almost all of the above-mentioned anxiety-related differences had not spatial specificity: interactions Anxiety * Region were insignificant for all reactions.

Therefore, anxiety-related differences could be observed in SSP in components of reaction, related to its activation, inhibition and evaluation. These differences could interact with successfulness of reaction, but not depend on type of trial (Go or Stop). Also, they have "global" properties, and are not specific for any local brain area. This result lies in line with the hypothesis of global brain oscillatory systems integrating separate structures into a united functional system and regulating all cortical regions (Basar, 1998; Knyazev, 2007). Although initial sources of these oscillations could be localized in some brain regions, they nonetheless spread to wide areas and could influence several brain functions.

The amplitude of slow-wave synchronization (related to both early sensory activation and late top-down inhibition) was positively correlated with trait anxiety in all experimental situations. We could interpret this fact based on the idea that slow-wave oscillations are modulated by (or even originate from) non-specific activity of the thalamus (Aron and Poldrack, 2006). This activity is associated with attention switching and choice between possible behavioral reactions (McFarland and Haber, 2002; Herrero et al., 2002; Li et al., 2008). Accordingly, although the thalamic activity was not directly measured, we could speculate that trait anxiety level could be correlated with non-specific activity of thalamus. This hypothesis could be considered in the future using neuroimaging techniques and/or additional EEG studies.

Background spectral power of alpha- and beta-band activity in most of studies was positively correlated with trait anxiety, as well as did amplitudes of event-related desynchronization in various experimental paradigms, such as face recognition, motor and linguistic tasks (Wu et al., 2010). Earlier (Savostyanov, 2009) we interpreted this dependency based on M. Eysenck's theory of attentional control (Eysenck et al., 2007). According to this theory subjects with high trait anxiety are inclined to enhance their control over a situation using additional allocation of attention to external stimuli. Oscillations in alpha and beta band could be interpreted as a sign of readiness/preparation to possible nearest future tasks (Klimesch, et al., 2007). In conditions of behavioral uncertainty activity in these bands is elevated in high-anxious subjects, as they try to be ready for following actions. During successful completion the SSP task both sensory and motor activation was stronger in subjects with higher anxiety, as mirrored in higher amplitudes of desynchronization in alpha and beta bands. At the same time, in unsuccessful trials there are no significant differences between subjects with high and low anxiety. We suggest that the main reason for errors was the (temporarily) dropped level of attention in some trials. In this case, the attentional control-related differences in brain activity should be leveled for these trials as it happened.

Functions of "beta rebound" are not completely clear yet. Initially it was associated with inhibition of cortical motor activity after task completion (Chen, 1998; Jurkiewicz et al., 2006). Our results demonstrated that this reaction also reflects self-rating of personal behavior. Stronger and faster "beta rebound" in subjects with lower anxiety correlates well with both of these interpretations. Indeed, subjects with a low anxiety level are more inclined to evaluate a situation (including, as in our case, results of personal behavior) positively and this positive appraisal could allow them to be more relaxed. On the contrary, according to the theory of attentional control, high-anxious subjects are inclined to keep control longer and stay arduous for some time after completion of task.

CONCLUSION

This chapter revealed dependencies between trait anxiety level and brain reactions related to execution of different behavioral control functions. Amplitude of slow-wave synchronization is positively related to anxiety suggesting that subcortical structures, particularly the thalamus, are involved in mechanisms of anxiety. Trait anxiety level is correlated positively with amplitude of alpha and beta desynchronization confirming the idea of anxiety influence on control of specific attention. High-frequency "beta rebound", reflecting self-rating of own behavior and relaxation, associated with evaluating it as successful, is, on the contrary, negatively related to anxiety level suggesting that low-anxious people are more inclined to evaluate the situation positively. Finally, analysis of cortical topology of EEG changes demonstrates that anxiety is linked to "global" parameters of brain activity, being personality trait modulating execution of several behavioral functions.

ACKNOWLEDGMENT

This research was supported by grants NSC96-2413-H-001-001-MY3, NSC-98-2410-H-001-012-MY3 and NSC-099-2811-H-001-002 from the National Science Council (Taiwan). The authors are grateful to Professor Gennady G. Knyazev for valuable comments on the original version of the manuscript, and to Mr. Grigory Dorin for helpful English editing.

References

Adrian, E.D., Matthews, B.H. (1934) The Berger rhythm: potential changes from the occipital lobes in man. *Brain, 57*, 355-385.

Aftanas, L.I., Koshkarov, V.I., Pokrovskaya, V.L., Lotova, N.V., Mordvintsev, Y.N. (1996) Pre- and post-stimulus processes in affective task and event-related desynchronization: do they discriminate anxiety coping styles? *Int J Psychophysiol., 24,* 197-212.

Aftanas, L.I., Pavlov, S.V., Reva, N.V., Varlamov, A.A. (2003) Trait anxiety impact on the EEG theta band power changes during appraisal of threatening and pleasant visual stimuli. *Int J Psychophysiol., 50*, 205–212.

Alderson, R.M., Rapport, M.D., Kofler, M.J. (2007) Attention-deficit/hyperactivity disorder and behavioral inhibition: a meta-analytic review of the stop-signal paradigm. *J Abnorm Child Psychol, 35*, 745-758.

Aron, A.R., & Poldrack, R.A. (2006). Cortical and Subcortical Contributions to Stop Signal Response Inhibition: Role of the Subthalamic Nucleus. *J. Neurosci., 26(9),* 2424-2433.

Band, G.P.H., van der Molen, M.W., Logan, G.D. (2003). Horse-race model simulations of the stop-signal procedure. *Acta Psychologica, 112,* 105-142.

Basar, E. (1998) *Brain Function and Oscillations. I. Brain Oscillations: Principles and Approaches.* Springer, Berlin, Heidelberg.

Basar, E., Basar-Eroglu, C., Karakas, S., Schurmann, M. (2001) Gamma, alpha, delta, and theta oscillations govern cognitive processes. *Int J. Psychophysiol., 39*, 241-248.

Berger, H. (1929) Uber das Elektroenkephalogramm des Menschen. *Archiv fur Psychiatrie und Nervenkrankheiten, 87,* 527-570.

Beste, C., Dziobek, I., Hielscher, H., Willemssen, R., Falkenstein, M. (2009) Effects of stimulus–response compatibility on inhibitory processes in Parkinson's disease. *Eur J Neuroscience, 29(4),* 855-860.

Breimer, L.T.M., Hennis, P.J., Burn, A.G.L. (1990) Quantification of the EEG effect of midazolam by aperiodic analysis in volunteers. *Clinical Pharmacokinetics, 18,* 245-253.

Carver, C.S., White, T.L. (1994) Behavioural inhibition, behavioural activation and affective responses to impending reward and punishment: The BIS/BAS scales. *Journal of Personality and Social Psychology, 67,* 319-333.

Chen, R, Yassen, Z, Cohen, LG, Hallett, M. (1998) The time course of corticospinal excitability in reaction time and self-paced movements. *Ann Neurol, 44,* 317-325.

Congdon, E., Mumford, J.A., Cohen, J.R., Galvan, A., Aron, A.R., Xue, G., Miller, E., Poldrack, R.A. (2010) Engagement of large-scale networks is related to individual differences in inhibitory control. *Neuroimage, 53(2),* 653-63.

Davidson, R.J. (1998) Anterior electrophysiological asymmetries, emotion and depression: Conceptual and methodological conundrums. *Psychophysiology, 35,* 607-614.

Davidson, R.J., Abercrombie, H., Nitschke, J.B., Putnam, K. (1999) Regional brain function emotion and disorders of emotion. *Current Opinion in Neurobiology, 9,* 228-234.

Davidson, R.J. (2002) Anxiety and affective style: role of prefrontal cortex and amygdala. *Biological Psychiatry, 51,* 68-80.

Delorme, A., Makeig, S. (2004) EEGLAB: an open source toolbox for analysis of single-trial EEG dynamics including independent component analysis. *J Neurosci Methods, 134(1),* 9-21.

Diego, M.A., Field, T., Sanders, C., Hernandez-Reif, M. (2004) Massage therapy of moderate and light pressure and vibrator effects on EEG and heart rate. *Int J Neurosciences, 114,* 31-44.

Dimoska, A., Johnstone, S.J., & Barry, R.J. (2006) The auditory-evoked N2 and P3 components in the stop-signal task: indices of inhibition, response-conflict or error-detection? *Brain and Cognition, 62(2),* 98-112.

Eckhorn, R., Bauer, R., Jordan, W. et al. (1988) Coherent oscillations: a mechanism of feature linking in the visual cortex? *Biol. Cybern., 60,* 121-130.

Eysenck, M.W., Derakshan, N., Santos, R., Calvo, M.G. (2007) Anxiety and cognitive performance: attentional control theory. *Emotion, 7(2),* 336-356.

Fields, R.D., Lee, P.R., Cohen, J.E. (2005) Temporal integration of intracellular Ca2+ signaling networks in regulating gene expression by action potentials. *Cell Calcium, 37,* 433-442.

Field, T., Ironson, G., Scafidi, F., Nawrocki, T., Goncalves, A., Burman, I., Pickens, J., Fox, N., Schanberg, S., Kuhn, C. (1996) Massage therapy reduces anxiety and enhances EEG pattern of alertness and math computations. *Int J Neurosciences, 86,* 197-205.

Forstmann, B.U., Jahfari, S., Scholte, H.S., Wolfensteller, U., Wildenberg van der, W., Ridderinkhof, K.R. (2008). Function and structure of the right inferior frontal cortex predict individual differences in response inhibition: a model-based approach. *Journal of Neuroscience, 28,* 9790-9796.

Fuster, J.M. (2006) The cognit: a network model of cortical representation. *Int J Psychophysiol., 60*, 125-132.

Gonzalez Andino, S.L., Michel, C.V., Thut, G., Landis, T., Grave de Peralta, R. (2005) Prediction of Response Speed by Anticipatory High-Frequency (Gamma Band) Oscillations in the Human Brain. *Human Brain Mapping, 24*, 50 –58.

Gray, J.A. (1982) *Neuropsychology of anxiety: an enquiry into the functions of the septo-hippocampal system.* UK, Oxford: Oxford University Press.

Gray J.A., McNaughton N. (2000) The Neuropsychology of anxiety: an enquiry into the functions of the septo-hippocampal system (2nd edition). UK, Oxford: Oxford University Press.

Herrero, M.T., Barcia, C., Narro, J.M. (2002) Functional anatomy of thalamus and basal ganglia. *Childs Nerv Syst., 18(8),* 386-404.

Horn, N.R., Dolan, M., Elliott, R., Deakin, J.F.W., Woodruff, P.W.R. (2003) Response inhibition and impulsivity: an fMRI study. *Neuropsychologia, 41*, 1959-1966.

Hotz, M.A., Ritz, R., Linder, L., Scollo-Lavizzari, G., Haefell, W.E. (2000) Auditory and electroencephalographic effects of midazolam and a-hydroxy-midazolam in healthy subjects. *British Journal of Clinical Pharmacology, 49,* 72-79.

Hyvärinen, A., Ramkumar, P., Parkkonen, L., Hari, R. (2010) Independent component analysis of short-time Fourier transforms for spontaneous EEG/MEG analysis. *Neuroimage, 49(1)*, 257-71.

Jacobs, G.D., Lubar, J.F. (1989) Spectral analysis of the central nervous system effects of the relaxation response elicited by autogenic training. *Behavioral Medicine, 15,* 125-132.

Johnstone, S.J., Dimoska, A., Smith, J.L., Barry, R.J., Pleffer, C.B., Chiswick, D. et al. (2007). The development of stop-signal and Go/Nogo response inhibition in children aged 7–12 years: Performance and event-related potential indices. *Int J Psychophysiol., 63,* 25-38.

Jurkiewicz, M., Gaetz, W., Bostan, A., Cheyne, D. (2006) Post-movement beta rebound is generated in motor cortex: evidence from neuromagnetic recordings. *NeuroImage, 32(3),* 1281-1289.

Kaiser J., Lutzenberger, W. (2003) Induced gamma-band activity and human brain function. *Neuroscientist, 9,* 475-484.

Klimesch, W. (1999) EEG alpha and theta oscillations reflect cognitive and memory performance: a review and analysis. *Brain Research Reviews, 29*, 169-195.

Klimesch, W., Sauseng, P., Hanslmayr, S. (2007) EEG alpha oscillations: The inhibition–timing hypothesis. *Brain Research Reviews, 53*, 63-88.

Knyazev, G.G. (2007) Motivation, emotion, and their inhibitory control mirrored in brain oscillations. *Neuroscience and Biobehavioral Reviews, 31*, 377-395.

Knyazev, G.G., Slobodskaya, H.R. (2003) Personality trait of behavioral inhibition is associated with oscillatory systems reciprocal relationships. *Int J Psychophysiol., 48*, 247-261.

Knyazev, G.G., Slobodskaya, H.R., Wilson, G.D. (2002) Psychophysiological correlates of behavioural inhibition and activation. *Pers. Individ. Differ., 33(4),* 647–660.

Knyazev, G.G., Savostyanov, A.N., Levin, E.A. (2004) Alpha oscillations as a correlate of trait anxiety. *Int J Psychophysiol., 53*, 147-160.

Knyazev, G.G., Savostyanov, A.N., Levin, E.A. (2005) Uncertainty, anxiety and brain oscillations. *Neuroscience Letters, 387*, 121-125.

Knyazev, G.G., Savostyanov, A.N., Levin, E.A. (2006) Alpha synchronization and anxiety: implications for inhibition vs. alertness hypotheses. *Int J Psychophysiol., 59(2),* 151-8.

Knyazev, G.G., Bocharov, A.V., Levin, E.A., Savostyanov, A.N., Slobodskoj-Plusnin, JY. (2008) Anxiety and oscillatory responses to emotional facial expressions. *Brain Res., 1227*, 174-88.

Knyazev, G.G., Levin, E.A., Savostyanov, A.N. (2008) Impulsivity, anxiety, and differences in evoked and induced brain oscillations. *Int J Psychophysiol., 68(3)*, 242-254.

Knyazev, G.G., Slobodskoj-Plusnin, J.Y., Bocharov, A.V. (2009) Event-related delta and theta synchronization during explicit and implicit emotion processing. *Neuroscience, 164(4)*, 1588-600.

Lappin, J.S., Erikson, C.W. (1966) Use of a delayed signal to stop a visual reaction-time response. *Journal of Experimental Psychology, 72(6),* 805-811.

Larson, C.L., Nitschke, J.B. & Davidson R.J. (2007) Common and Distinct Patterns of Affective Response in Dimensions of Anxiety and Depression. *Emotion, 7(1),* 182–191.

Levin, E.A., Savostyanov, A.N., Lazarenko, D.O., Knyazev, G.G. (2007) Human Brain Oscillatory Activity in activation and inhibition of motor reactions. *Rev. of SB RAMS, 2,* 64-72.

Li, C.S., Luo, X., Yan, P., Bergquist, K., Sinha, R. (2009) Altered impulse control in alcohol dependence: neural measures of stop signal performance. *Alcoholism: Clinical and Experimental Research, 33,* 1-11.

Li, C.S., Yan, P., Sinha, R., Lee, T.W. (2008) Subcortical processes of motor response inhibition during a stop signal task. *Neuroimage, 41(4),* 1352-63.

Logan, G.D., Cowan, W.B., Davis, K.A. (1984) On the ability to inhibit simple and choice reaction time responses: a model and a method. *J.Exp.Psychol.Hum.Percept.Perform., 10,* 276-291.

Lopes da Silva, F. (1991) Neural mechanisms underlying brain waves: from neural membranes to networks. *Electroencephalogr. Clin. Neurophysiol., 79,* 81-93.

Luu, P., Tucker, D.M., Makeig, S. (2004) Frontal midline theta and the error-related negativity: neurophysiological mechanisms of action regulation. *Clin. Neurophysiol., 115(8),* 1821-35.

Makeig, S. (1993) Auditory event-related dynamics of the EEG spectrum and effects of exposure to tones. *Clin.Neurophysiol., 86,* 283-293.

Makeig, S., Bell, A.J., Jung, T.P., Sejnowski, T.J. (1996) Independent component analysis of electroencephalografic data. *Adv. Neural Inf. Process. Syst. 8,* 145-151.

McFarland, N.R., Haber, S.N. (2002) Thalamic relay nuclei of the basal ganglia form both reciprocal and nonreciprocal cortical connections, linking multiple frontal cortical areas. *J. Neurosci., 22(18),* 8117-32.

McNaughton, N., Corr, P.J. (2004) A two-dimensional neuropsychology of defense: fear/anxiety and defensive distance. *Neuroscience and Biobehavioral Reviews, 28,* 285-305.

Miller, R. (1991) *Cortico-Hippocampal Interplay and the Representation of Contexts in the Brain.* Berlin-Heidelberg-New York, Springer.

Neuper, C., Pfurtscheller, G. (1999) Motor imagery and ERD. Event-related desynchronization and related oscillatory phenomena of the brain. In: G. Pfurtscheller, F.H. Lopes da Silva, editors. *Handbook of electroencephalography and clinical neurophysiology, vol. 6, revised edition,* 303-326. Amsterdam: Elsevier.

Neuper, C., Pfurtscheller, G. (2001) Event-related dynamics of cortical rhythms: frequency-specific features and functional correlates. *Int J Psychophysiol., 43(1)*, 41-58.

Nitschke, J.B., Sarinopoulos, I., Oathes, D.J., Johnstone, T., Whalen, P.J., Davidson, R.J., Kalin, N.H. (2009) Anticipatory activation in the amygdala and anterior cingulate in generalized anxiety disorder and prediction of treatment response. *Am J. Psychiatry, 166(3),* 302-10.

Nunez, P.L. (1989) Generation of human EEG by a combination of long and short range neocortical interactions. *Brain Topography, 1*, 199-215.

Oostenveld, R., Praamstra, P. (2001) The five percent electrode system for high-resolution EEG and ERP measurements. *Clinical Neurophysiology, 112*, 713-719.

Ozgoren, M., Basar-Eroglu, C., Basar, E. (2005) Beta oscillations in face recognition. *Int J Psychophysiol., 55,* 51-59.

Pfurtscheller, G., Stancak, A., Neuper, C. (1996) Post-movement beta synchronization. A correlate of an idling motor area? *Electroencephalography and Clinical Neurophysiology, 98,* 281-293.

Ramautar, J.R., Slagter, H.A., Kok, A., & Ridderinkhof, K.R. (2006) Probability effects in the stopsignal paradigm: the insula and the significance of failed inhibition. *Brain Research, 1105,* 143-154.

Ray, W.J., Cole, H.W. (1985) EEG alpha activity reflects attentional demands, and beta activity reflects emotional and cognitive processes. *Science, 228,* 750-752.

Ridderinkhof, K.R., Ullsperger, M., Crone, E.A., Nieuwenhuis, S. (2004). The role of the medial frontal cortex in cognitive control. *Science, 306,* 443-447.

Savostyanov, A.N., Tsai, A.C., Liou, M., Levin, E.A., Lee, J.D., Yurganov, A.V. & Knyazev, G.G. (2009) EEG correlates of trait anxiety in the stop-signal paradigm. *Neuroscience Letters, 449,* 112-116.

Shek, D.T. (1993) The Chinese version of the State-Trait Anxiety Inventory: its relationship to different measures of psychological well-being. *J Clin Psychol. 49(3),* 349-58.

Silva, L.R., Amitai, Y., Connors, B.G. (1991) Intrinsic oscillations of neocortex generated by layer 5 pyramidal neurons. *Science, 251*, 432-435.

Singer, W., Engel, A.K., Kreiter, A., Munk, M.H.J., Neuenschwander, S., Roelfsema, P.R. (1997) Neuronal assemblies: necessity, signature and detectability. *Trends Cogn Sci, 1,* 252–261.

Spielberger, C.D. & Reheiser, E.C. (2004) Anxiety: Its meaning and measurement. In N.B. Anderson (Ed.), *Encyclopedia of Health and Behavior,* 59-62. Thousand Oaks, CA. Sage Publications Inc.

Spielberger, C.D., Gorsuch, R.L., Lushene, R.E. (1970) Manual for the State–Trait Anxiety Inventory. Consulting Psychologists Press, Palo Alto, CA.

von Stein, A., Sarnthein, J. (2000) Different frequencies for different scales of cortical integration: from local gamma to long range alpha/theta synchronization. *Int J Psychophysiol, 38,* 301–313.

Steriade, M., McCormick, D.A., Sejnowski, T.J. (1993) Thalamocortical oscillations in the sleeping and aroused brain. *Science, 262,* 679-685.

Steriade, M., Amzica, F., Contreras, D. (1996) Synchronization of fast (30–40 Hz) spontaneous cortical rhythms during brain activation. *J Neurosci, 16,* 392–417.

Stryker, M.P. (1989) Is grandmother an oscillation? Nature, 338, 297-298.

Sutton, S.K., Davidson, R.J. (1997) Prefrontal brain asymmetry: A biological substrate of the behavioral approach and inhibition systems. Psychological Science, 8, 204 –210.

Tallon-Baudry, C., Bertrand, O., Peronnet, F., Pernier, J. (1998) Induced gamma-band activity during the delay of a visual short-term memory task in humans. *The Journal of Neuroscience, 18(11)*, 4244–4254.

Trujillo, L.T., Allen, J.J. (2007) Theta EEG dynamics of the error-related negativity. *Clin. Neurophysiol., 118(3),* 645-68.

Verbruggen, F., Logan, G.D. (2008) Response inhibition in the stop-signal paradigm. *Trends in Cognitive Sciences, 12,* 418-424.

Verbruggen, F., Logan, GD. (2009) Automaticity of cognitive control: goal priming in responseinhibition paradigms. *J Exp Psychol Learn Mem Cogn., 35,* 1381-1388.

Wang, X.-J. (2010) Neurophysiological and computational principles of cortical rhythms in cognition. *Physiol. Rev., 90(3),* 1195–1268.

Wheeler, R.E., Davidson, R.J., Tomarken, A.J. (1993) Frontal brain asymmetry and emotional reactivity: A biological substrate of affective style. *Psychophysiology, 30,* 82 –89.

Wrobel, A. (2000) Beta activity: a carrier for visual attention. *Acta Neurobiol. Exp. (Wars.), 60,* 247-260.

Wu, A., Wu, M.Y., Savostyanov, A.N., Tsai, A.C, Liou M. (2010) Brain oscillation in emotional faces recognition and syntactic errors detection: task-free activity. *16th Annual Meeting of the Organization for Human Brain Mapping, Barcelona, Spain.* 1173 MT-AM.

Xue, G., Aron, A.R., Poldrack, R.A. (2008) Common neural substrates for inhibition of spoken and manual responses. *Cereb. Cortex., 18(8),* 1923-32.

INDEX

A

B

C

D

E

H

I

J

K

L

M

N

O

P

Q

R

T

U

V

W

Y